Mike Meyers' Certification
Passport ★

CompTIA®
Linux+™
Certification

MICHAEL JANG

D1275710

New York • Chicago • San Francisco
Lisbon • London • Madrid • Mexico City
Milan • New Delhi • San Juan
Seoul • Singapore • Sydney • Toronto

The *McGraw-Hill* Companies

Cataloging-in-Publication Data is on file with the Library of Congress

McGraw-Hill books are available at special quantity discounts to use as premiums and sales promotions, or for use in corporate training programs. To contact a special sales representative, please visit the Contact Us page at www.mhprofessional.com.

Mike Meyers' CompTIA® Linux+™ Certification Passport

Copyright © 2008 by The McGraw-Hill Companies. All rights reserved. Printed in the United States of America. Except as permitted under the Copyright Act of 1976, no part of this publication may be reproduced or distributed in any form or by any means, or stored in a database or retrieval system, without the prior written permission of publisher, with the exception that the program listings may be entered, stored, and executed in a computer system, but they may not be reproduced for publication.

1234567890 FGR FGR 0198

ISBN: Book p/n 978-0-07-154673-7 and CD p/n 978-0-07-154674-4
of set 978-0-07-154671-3

MHID: Book p/n 0-07-154673-1 and CD p/n 0-07-154674-X
of set 0-07-154671-5

Sponsoring Editor Timothy Green	**Proofreader** Paul Tyler
Editorial Supervisor Patty Mon	**Indexer** Ted Laux
Project Editor Laura Stone	**Production Supervisor** Jean Bodeaux
Acquisitions Coordinator Jennifer Housh	**Composition** Apollo Publishing Services
Technical Editors Elizabeth Zinkann	**Illustration** Apollo Publishing Services
Copy Editor Bill McManus	**Art Director, Cover** Jeff Weeks

My wonderful wife, Donna, is also widowed. I dedicate this book to her late husband, Randy. May his spirit and dedication to life be remembered by all who knew him. I thank him, and my dearly departed Nancy, for bringing us together from the hereafter. I know that he's happily fishing now with Bub.

Contents

II Managing Linux Users, Files, Packages, Processes, and Services 49

3 Managing Files and Directories 51

7 Basic Server Configuration 181

IV Securing Accounts and Services 215

8 Security and Users 217

9 System Security 247

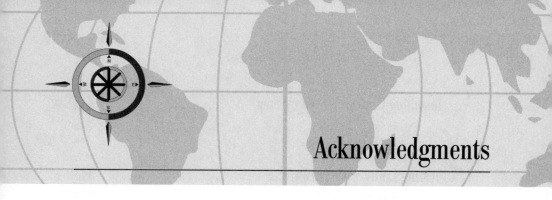

Acknowledgments

As with every book, a lot of work from a lot of people went into making this happen. Thank you, Tim Green, for supporting this book and working to get the LearnKey software working as well as it does with Linux. Jenni Housh did wonders keeping the book on track. Thank you once again to the technical editor, Elizabeth Zinkann. Your knowledge and friendship are important to me.

Thanks also go to Laura Stone, Bill McManus, Apollo Publishing Services, and Paul Tyler for their tireless work to get this book into production and print.

Finally, thank you Donna. The best years of our lives are yet to come!

Check-In

May I See Your Passport?

What do you mean, you don't have a passport? Why, it's sitting right in your hands, even as you read! This book is your passport to a very special place. You're about to begin a journey, my friend, a journey toward that magical place called *certification*! You don't need a ticket, you don't need a suitcase—just snuggle up and read this passport, because it's all you need to get there. Are you ready? Let's go!

Your Travel Agent: Mike Meyers

Hello! I'm Mike Meyers, president of Total Seminars and author of a number of popular certification books. On any given day, you'll find me replacing a hard drive, setting up a website, or writing code. I love every aspect of this book you hold in your hands. It's part of a powerful book series called the *Mike Meyers' Certification Passports*. Every book in this series combines easy readability with a condensed format—in other words, it's the kind of book I always wanted when I went for my certifications. Putting a huge amount of information in an accessible format is an enormous challenge, but I think we have achieved our goal, and I am confident you'll agree.

I designed this series to do one thing and only one thing: to get you the information you need to achieve your certification. You won't find any fluff in here. Michael Jang and I packed every page with nothing but the real nitty-gritty of the CompTIA Linux+ Certification exam. Every page has 100 percent pure concentrate of certification knowledge! But we didn't forget to make the book readable, so I hope you enjoy the casual, friendly style.

Your Destination: CompTIA Linux+ Certification

This book is your passport to CompTIA Linux+ Certification, the vendor-neutral industry-standard certification for newer Linux administrators, the folks who are spearheading the new Linux revolution. To get CompTIA Linux+ certified, you need to pass the CompTIA XK0-002 exam.

The Linux+ exam tests your ability to provide "basic installation, operation, security, troubleshooting, and basic Linux hardware services for the Linux operating system on workstations and servers." It's designed for the Linux professional with 6 to 12 months of experience. This book assumes that you already have basic Linux experience, and does not go beyond the topics directly associated with the exam.

The Linux+ exam is focused on four selected Linux distributions: Red Hat, SUSE, Mandrake (now Mandriva), and Turbolinux. They are all built on packages developed to the Red Hat Package Manager (RPM) format. There are a number of ways to download and install these distributions.

Red Hat distributions are available as Fedora Linux and Red Hat Enterprise Linux. Fedora Linux (www.fedoraproject.org) is Red Hat's release with community-based support. Red Hat Enterprise Linux (www.redhat.com) includes enterprise-hardened software with paid-support options for the server and desktop. While Red Hat Enterprise Linux includes Red Hat trademarks, third parties have effectively created their own version of Red Hat Enterprise Linux without the trademarks.

Linux distributions are built from source code; because third parties such as Community Enterprise Operating System (CentOS) use the same source code, their releases are known as "rebuilds." Functionally, their releases are identical to the Red Hat operating systems, and are also excellent tools to use to study for the Linux+ exam. We describe the installation process for CentOS-5 Linux (www.centos.org) in Appendix C.

Similarly, SUSE, now owned by Novell, is available as a commercial SUSE Linux Enterprise distribution and as a community-based openSUSE distribution. If you use either distribution, you may prefer to use it to study for the Linux+ exam.

There is no longer a current version of Mandrake Linux (of France), as they have merged with Conectiva of Brazil. Their combined distribution is known as Mandriva, and those of you in Europe or Latin America may prefer to use this distribution to study for the Linux+ exam.

The Turbolinux distribution may still be the most popular option in the Far East, and can also be used to study for the Linux+ exam. Even though there is no free version of this distribution available, the "Trial Version" is sufficient, as it is fully functional, except for updates, which are not tested.

While there are a number of other Linux distributions available, such as Ubuntu and Debian Linux, they are based on different package systems, use different runlevels, and more. Questions are based on what you might see on the selected distributions, which do not include Ubuntu or Debian Linux.

To write this book, the author (Michael Jang) installed Red Hat Enterprise Linux 5, openSUSE Linux 10.2, Mandriva Free 2007, and Turbolinux Celica on separate virtual machines. As CentOS 5 (and related "rebuilds") is built on the same source code as Red Hat Enterprise Linux 5, it is also an excellent way to study for the Linux+ exams.

The Linux+ exam concentrates on your knowledge of installation methods, management of clients and servers, and basic understanding of system settings, services, and access rights. It also focuses on knowledge of common security terms and practices, as well as documentation practices, and even A+-style hardware knowledge. The current Linux+ exam is the CompTIA XK0-002 exam, which includes 98 questions to be completed in 90 minutes. Passing requires a score of 675 on a scale of 100–900.

The Linux+ exam tests knowledge of Linux principles and commands in depth. Some of the required knowledge goes beyond what the author needed to know when he first passed the RHCE exam back in 2002. Some questions are also comparable in difficulty to the questions encountered by the author when he passed the LPIC Level 1 and 2 exams in 2007. When you take the Linux+ exam, all 98 questions are multiple choice. The following is an example of the type of question you will see on the exams:

Which of the following commands lists pending print jobs in all available printer queues?

A. lpr

B. lprm

C. lpq

D. lpq -a

The correct answer is D, **lpq -a**. Answering this question requires detailed knowledge of Linux commands and associated switches.

As an operating system, Linux is primarily configured from the command-line interface. While there are excellent graphical tools available, the Linux+ exam tests your knowledge of command-line tools and a variety of switches.

While it's a risky practice in service, you may choose to study for certification exams by logging into the root user account. When logged into that account, you'll be presented with a prompt similar to this:

```
[root@LinuxCert root]#
```

Because a prompt of this length would create far too many wrapped code lines in this text, the root account prompt in this book is abbreviated as follows:

```
#
```

Be careful. The hash mark (#) is also used as a comment character in Linux scripts and programs; for example, here is an excerpt from the SUSE version of /etc/inittab:

```
# The default runlevel is defined here:
```

When logged in as a regular user, the prompt is slightly different; for user michael, it would typically look like the following:

```
[michael@LinuxCert michael]$
```

Again, because a prompt of this length would create too many wrapped code lines in this text, it is abbreviated as follows:

```
$
```

CompTIA Linux+ Certification can be your ticket to a career in IT or simply an excellent step in your pathway to more advanced certifications such as those available from LPI, Novell, and Red Hat. This book is your passport to success on the CompTIA Linux+ Certification exam.

Your Guides: Mike Meyers and Michael Jang

You get a pair of tour guides for this book, both me and Michael Jang. I've written numerous computer certification books—including the best-selling *All-in-One A+ Certification Exam Guide*—and significant parts of others, such as the first edition of the *All-in-One Network+ Certification Exam Guide*. More to the point, I've been working on PCs and teaching others how to make and fix them for a *very* long time, and I love it! When I'm not lecturing or writing about PCs, I'm working on PCs, naturally!

Michael Jang (Linux+, RHCE, LPIC-2, UCP, LCP, MCP) is currently a full-time writer, specializing in operating systems and networks. His experience with computers goes back to the days of jumbled punch cards. He has written other books on Linux certification, including *RHCE Red Hat Certified Engineer Linux Study Guide*, *Linux+ Exam Cram*, and *Sair Linux/GNU Installation and Configuration Exam Cram*. His other Linux books include *Linux Annoyances for Geeks*, *Linux Patch Management*, and *Mastering Fedora Core 5*. He has also written or contributed to books on Microsoft operating systems, including *MCSE Guide to Microsoft Windows 98* and *Mastering Windows XP Professional, Second Edition*. Look for his upcoming *Ubuntu Certified Professional Study Guide*.

Why the Travel Theme?

The steps to gaining a certification parallel closely the steps to planning and taking a trip. All of the elements are the same: preparation, an itinerary, a route, even mishaps along the way. Let me show you how it all works.

This book is divided into 11 chapters. Each chapter begins with an *Itinerary* that lists the objectives covered in that chapter, and an *ETA* to give you an idea of the time involved in learning the skills in that chapter. Each chapter is broken down by the objectives, which are either those officially stated by the certifying body or our expert take on the best way to approach the topics. The chapters also correspond to the Domains listed in the CompTIA Linux+ objectives, as shown in the following table.

Domain	Chapter(s)
Installation	Basic Installation (1); Configuring During and After Installation (2)
Management	Managing Files and Directories (3); Media, Process, and Package Management (4); User and Service Management (5)
Configuration	Basic Client Configuration (6); Basic Server Configuration (7)
Security	Security and Users (8); System Security (9)
Documentation	Documentation and Configuration (10)
Hardware	Hardware on Linux (11)

Each chapter contains a number of helpful items to call out points of interest:

Exam Tip

Points out critical topics you're likely to see on the actual exam.

Local Lingo

Describes special terms, in detail and in a way you can easily understand.

Travel Advisory

Warns you of common pitfalls, misconceptions, and downright physical peril!

The end of the chapter gives you two handy tools. The *Checkpoint* reviews each objective covered in the chapter with a handy synopsis—a great way to review quickly. The end-of-chapter *Review Questions* test your newly acquired skills.

CHECKPOINT

But the fun doesn't stop there! After you've read the book, pull out the CD-ROM and take advantage of the free practice exam! Use the full practice exam to hone your skills, and keep the book handy to check answers. Appendix A explains how to use the CD-ROM. For additional practice questions, you can register for a second, bonus MasterExam online.

When you reach the point that you're acing the practice questions, you're ready to take the exam. Go get certified!

The End of the Trail

The IT industry changes and grows constantly, *and so should you*. Finishing one certification is just a step in an ongoing process of gaining more and more certifications to match your constantly changing and growing skills. Read Appendix B, "Career Flight Path," to determine where this certification fits into your personal certification goals. Remember, in the IT business, if you're not moving forward, you're way behind!

Good luck on your certification! Stay in touch.

Mike Meyers
Series Editor
Mike Meyers' Certification Passport

Installing and Configuring Linux

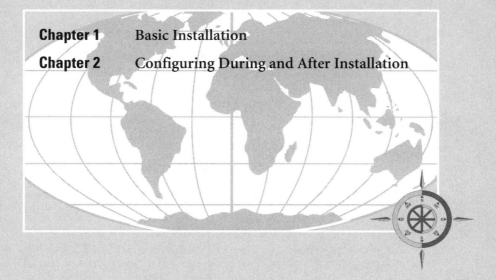

Basic Installation

	NEWBIE	SOME EXPERIENCE	VETERAN
ETA	4+ hours	2 hours	1 hour

3

The Linux distributions listed in the CompTIA Linux+ objectives Installation domain (Domain 1.0) are all RPM-based distributions. In other words, the exam is focused more on the Red Hat Package Manager (RPM) than on the distributions associated with DEB packages, such as Debian, Linspire, and Ubuntu.

Even within these limits, the installation routines are as diverse as the number of distributions. That's why the Linux+ objectives state in Domain 1.0 that "The candidate is not expected to know how to install a specific distribution…." As you read through the chapter, focus on the information required to make decisions on what to install on a system—and where.

Remember, these objectives were released in 2005, so some of these tools may no longer be available in the latest distributions. But in my experience, CompTIA does an excellent job introducing new questions, keeping the exam as current as possible.

Exam Tip

By the end of this book, you'll recognize general prerequisites for installing Linux in regard to hardware, partitions, services, and packages.

Objective 1.01   Determine Customer Needs

Linux is freely available. Linux is reliable. Linux is customizable. Linux is supported by a world of developers. No other operating system has all of these advantages, which is why CIOs and CTOs around the world are making the move to Linux.

Linux also has a number of disadvantages, however. Some of these disadvantages are real; others are a matter of perception. As a Linux administrator, you may at some point recommend Linux to your managers and customers. When you do so, you need to be able to explain four things: the history of Linux, what applications Linux can include for clients, what you can install on Linux servers, and how to select a distribution. The following sections provide some pointers for your explanation.

The History of Linux

Linux was developed as a clone of the Unix operating system. To understand the strengths associated with Linux (and to be able to explain them to your customers), you need to understand a bit of the history of Unix.

Unix was developed in 1969 by Bell Labs, which was then the research arm of the American Telephone and Telegraph Company (AT&T). Bell Labs worked closely with a number of universities. AT&T, as a regulated monopoly, was prohibited from selling software. AT&T chose to keep the license for Unix and gain the goodwill of universities by distributing Unix for a nominal fee, without a warranty, with the source code. This release technique has evolved into what is now known as *open source*.

When the U.S. government settled its antitrust suit against AT&T in 1982, one condition allowed AT&T to get into the computer business. AT&T was soon selling Unix for profit, without the source code, with all of the standard protections associated with a copyright.

In 1985, Richard Stallman started the nonprofit Free Software Foundation (FSF) to develop an alternative operating system with all of the functionality of Unix. To get around AT&T's copyrights, the FSF needed to develop commands and programs that did not use Unix's source code. This type of development creates software known as a *clone*.

Stallman dubbed this Unix clone GNU, short for "GNU's Not Unix." By 1991, the FSF had cloned all the major components of Unix except the kernel.

Local Lingo

GNU, FSF, RPM...at this point, some of you may feel as if you have actually used a real passport, and ended up somewhere where acronyms are the official language. Actually, that isn't far off. If you are already familiar with GNU, FSF, RPM, and the many other acronyms you'll encounter in this book, that's great. If not, these technologies will be spelled out, and explained, over the course of the book. Look for this Local Lingo icon for explanations of important terms. Some of the acronyms may appear strange; GNU really does stand for "GNU's Not Unix." Recursive acronyms like GNU are sort of Linux's jab at the normal way of doing things.

In 1991, Linus Torvalds wanted a free operating system that would work with his 386 CPU-based personal computer. He developed what became known as the Linux kernel and incorporated much of the work of the FSF to create a relatively complete operating system that is now known as Linux. Because it's a combined work, the FSF believes that the Linux operating system is more properly known as GNU/Linux.

What Applications Linux Can Include for Clients

Linux is a serious option for regular PCs and workstations. It provides a variety of desktop environments such as GNOME and KDE. Most distributions are packaged with a substantial number of client applications. As you review your favorite distribution, examine the package groups associated with clients. For a bit more detail, see the "Identify Machine Requirements" section later in this chapter.

Local Lingo

GNOME stands for the GNU Network Object Model Environment, but it's really just one of the major Linux GUI desktops. The other most prominent Linux GUI desktop is known as KDE, short for the KDE Desktop Environment (or K Desktop Environment).

Linux developers have gone to great lengths to make applications compatible with their Microsoft counterparts, and for the most part have succeeded. For example, while the editors of this book are using Microsoft Word, I'm writing it using OpenOffice.org Writer and saving files in Microsoft Word format.

What Server Services Can Be Installed

To understand much of what Linux can do on the server requires another history lesson. In the 1970s, the U.S. Department of Defense (DoD) developed a communications network that could survive a nuclear war. This required a network with multiple routes and a set of network protocols that can automatically bypass broken or congested routes. This redundant network evolved into the Internet.

Much of this work was done at the same universities where Unix was popular. The network protocols they developed with the DoD became known as the TCP/IP protocol suite. TCP/IP was developed on Unix, so Linux, as a Unix clone, carries its advantages as an operating system for the Internet.

To support Internet communication, Linux servers can include a wide variety of services, as detailed in the "Identify Machine Requirements" section later in this chapter.

Selecting a Distribution

As noted in Domain 1.0 of the Linux+ objectives, "The scope of the exam is limited to software and settings common to Linux software from Red Hat, SUSE, Mandrake, and Turbolinux." This list is slightly out of date, as MandrakeSoft of France, the company behind Mandrake Linux, merged its distribution with Conectiva of Brazil in 2005 and changed its corporate name to Mandriva to reflect the merged distribution, now known as Mandriva Linux. Furthermore, SUSE has been acquired by Novell, which now offers a supported SUSE Linux Enterprise distribution as well as a community openSUSE distribution. Red Hat now releases two major distributions; Fedora Linux is the test bed for Red Hat Enterprise Linux (RHEL). There are probably a few hundred other Linux distributions available, including the popular distributions Ubuntu and Debian Linux.

Travel Advisory

When I cite the "selected Linux distributions" throughout the book, I'm referring to the distributions specified in the Linux+ objectives, Red Hat, SUSE, Mandriva (successor to Mandrake), and Turbolinux.

Providing the details of each distribution is beyond the scope of the Linux+ objectives. Fortunately, you only need to know one of these distributions to prepare for the Linux+ exam. In general, when selecting a distribution, consider the following factors:

- **Software**   While every Linux distribution includes the kernel and basic packages, not all distributions include applications such as the Apache Web server or the OpenOffice.org suite.
- **Support**   Some Linux distributions, such as Red Hat Enterprise and SUSE Linux Enterprise, offer some level of corporate support with a subscription; others, such as Fedora and openSUSE, are supported by a community of users and developers.

Of course, as discussed throughout the book, you need to consider a substantial number of other factors, including hardware, package management, documentation, suitability as a client or server, and more.

Objective 1.02 Identify Required Hardware

Three elements are associated with this objective. They include identifying whether the basic hardware is compatible with your selected Linux distribution, whether you have enough space, and whether the overall system is scalable.

As the amount of RAM and hard drive space varies by distribution and release, there's no need to memorize minimum requirements. As quoted in the previous section, per Domain 1.0 of the Linux+ objectives, the scope of the exam is limited to software and settings common to the selected distributions.

Basic Hardware

The vast majority of PC hardware is compatible with Linux. A few problem areas remain. Not all manufacturers include Linux drivers when releasing new hardware. Fortunately, Linux developers are often able to create drivers for such hardware just a few weeks after release.

HCL

If you have any doubts about your own hardware, review applicable Hardware Compatibility Lists (HCLs). They should be available on the websites associated with your preferred distribution. There's also the general Linux HCL, available online at http://tldp.org/HOWTO/Hardware-HOWTO/.

As suggested in the objectives, the basic system hardware is the CPU, RAM, and hard drive. Linux distributions are built for different types of CPUs; for example, I downloaded different CPU-specific repositories for installing Fedora 7 on my 64-bit desktop and 32-bit laptop systems. Every distribution requires some minimum amount of RAM, and it varies based on distribution, release date, and other requirements. For example, less RAM is required for a dedicated server that does not require graphics support.

Exam Tip

Know where to find appropriate Hardware Compatibility Lists.

Required Space

If someone asks how much space is required for a Linux system, there's no single answer. It varies widely. There are even Linux distributions that can be loaded from 1.44MB floppy disks.

Based on the selected distributions, several hundred megabytes of hard drive space are required. Depending on what's installed, several gigabytes of space can be used.

But that's just the space required for the operating system and applications. It does not include the space required by logs, shared files, and users in their home directories. It does not include the space required for applications that may be installed at a later date. It does not include the space required for temporary files, such as those required to start an X Window. And it does not include required swap space, which is normally configured in Linux as a dedicated partition. The most common standard for a swap partition is twice the amount of RAM. For example, if there's 1GB of RAM on a local system, the standard is to configure a swap partition with 2GB of space.

> **Exam Tip**
>
> It's most common to configure swap partitions with twice the amount of installed RAM.

> **Travel Advisory**
>
> There is no hard and fast rule for the size of a swap partition. Systems with more RAM can often work with a swap partition of a size equal to the amount of RAM. For example, my laptop with 2GB of RAM is configured with a 2GB swap partition.

Scalability

Scalability is the ability of a system to handle greater amounts of work. In part, scalability is based on the capacity of the hardware, namely the hard drives. With logical volume management (LVM), it is now easier to add needed hard drive space to partitions and more.

Understand That Linux Is Just the Kernel

Stallman's FSF developed most of what we know as the Linux operating system. Torvalds developed the kernel. So strictly speaking, Linux is just the kernel. But what is a kernel?

A *kernel* is the part of an operating system that translates commands from programs or utilities to hardware instructions. The Linux kernel communicates with hardware through dedicated device drivers. For example, when a computer communicates with a CD/DVD drive, a specific kernel driver transmits messages to and from that drive.

Numbering Schemes

The Linux kernel on your system is based on a label such as 2.6.22.1. This is a version number in a specific three- or four-digit format, A.B.C.D:

- The first number (A) is the kernel version, and was last changed in 1996.
- The second number (B) specifies the major revision of the kernel. Until kernel version 2.6, second numbers that were even were associated with stable kernel releases, and odd numbers, through 2.5, were developmental releases. This is changing. Kernel version 2.7 will also be a stable release.

- The third number (C) is associated with <u>minor revisions</u>. Until kernel version 2.6.11, it was changed for new features, drivers, bug fixes, and security patches. Starting with 2.6.11.1, changes to the third number are made only for new features and drivers.
- The fourth number (D) is changed with <u>bug fixes and security patches</u>.

Some distributions may not follow this policy with respect to the third and fourth numbers. For example, the current kernel version on my RHEL 5 system is 2.6.18-8.el5, where -8 refers to the eighth Red Hat build of kernel version 2.6.18.

Local Lingo

A driver is a part of the kernel that allows Linux to communicate with hardware and more. Some drivers are integrated directly into the kernel; others are loaded as modules after the main kernel is loaded.

Exam Tip

Learn the numbering system associated with the Linux kernel.

Upgrades

Sometimes, you just need to upgrade (or update) or recompile a kernel. You do not need to know the actual process for the exam. You may want to upgrade a kernel for any of the following reasons:

- A new driver, such as for new hardware or an additional file system.
- A "bug fix" for a flaw in the kernel.
- A security issue; distributions often provide updated kernels that address security issues.

For a bit more information on recompiling a kernel, see Chapter 6. For detailed information on rebuilding a kernel, see Chapter 8 of this author's *RHCE Red Hat Certified Engineer Linux Study Guide*, Fifth Edition (McGraw-Hill, 2007).

Custom Kernels

Custom kernels come in two forms: a recompiled kernel and settings in the /proc directory. You do not need to know how to recompile a kernel for the exam; kernel settings are available and listed in the config-*versionnum* file in the /boot directory, where *versionnum* is the version number of the kernel, similar to what's shown in Figure 1.1.

```
[michael@enterprise5fc6d ~]$ \ls /boot
config-2.6.20-2925.9.fc7xen      System.map-2.6.20-2925.9.fc7xen
config-2.6.21-1.3194.fc7         System.map-2.6.21-1.3194.fc7
grub                             vmlinuz-2.6.20-2925.9.fc7xen
initrd-2.6.20-2925.9.fc7xen.img  vmlinuz-2.6.21-1.3194.fc7
initrd-2.6.21-1.3194.fc7.img     xen.gz-2.6.20-2925.9.fc7
lost+found                       xen-syms-2.6.20-2925.9.fc7
[michael@enterprise5fc6d ~]$
```

FIGURE 1.1   Kernel-related files in /boot

Kernel settings can be modified in the /proc directory, using the /etc/sysctl.conf configuration file. For an example of how this works, see the discussion on IP forwarding in Chapter 6.

Objective 1.04   Determine the Appropriate Installation Method

Home users often install Linux from a local source, namely from a CD or DVD, inserted in a local drive. Business users often have to install Linux on numerous computers, and administrators frequently find it more convenient to install Linux from a network source, which eliminates the need to go from system to system with one or more CDs or DVDs. But all installations require some sort of boot method.

Boot Method

The methods available to boot into a Linux installation program are as diverse as those for booting a computer. If your system can boot from a CD, the major Linux distributions support booting their installation programs from such media. Some distributions also support booting from a 1.44MB floppy disc, a USB key, or even the Preboot eXecution Environment (PXE) associated with a network boot card. To review the boot methods available on your system, navigate to the BIOS or boot menu, available on most systems just after the Power-On Self-Test (POST). One example is shown in Figure 1.2.

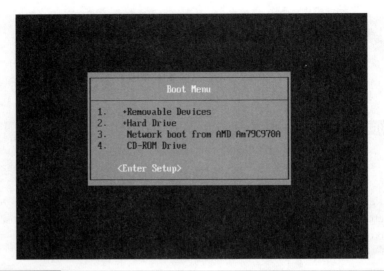

FIGURE 1.2 Example of a boot menu

Exam Tip

Remember, the Linux+ exam objectives were developed in 2004; one common method for creating boot disks uses the DOS-based **rawwrite.exe** utility.

Once a system is booted, it can point to local or network sources for installation. The four distributions associated with the Linux+ exam can all be installed in an automated fashion using appropriate scripts. To create those scripts, SUSE uses the AutoYaST system. In contrast, Red Hat, Mandriva, and Turbolinux all use Kickstart to create automated installation scripts. Kickstart and AutoYaST installations can both specify local and network sources.

Local Source

When installing locally, there are two basic options: CD/DVD media, or installation files on a local hard drive partition. Installation from CD/DVD media is pretty basic; in most cases, you can boot directly from CD/DVD installation media downloaded for the preferred distribution, and the installation program starts automatically. Installation from a local hard drive partition requires copying the installation files (or the associated ISO files) to a partition, as well as an installation program that allows you to specify the right partition.

The Mandriva installation program allows you to copy from the CD/DVD to the local hard drive during the installation process. Red Hat supports installation from the ISO files, which represent downloaded CD/DVDs.

Local Lingo

ISO file   When downloading the data for a Linux installation CD/DVD, it's most commonly done through an ISO file, with an .iso extension. (What ISO stands for is not relevant.) ISO files are a standard format for CD/DVDs that can be used to "burn" CD/DVD media using common Linux and Microsoft tools.

Network Source

When administering a network, having a central repository for the installation files can be valuable. When installing Linux on a new system, all you need is an appropriate boot disk or installation CD/DVD, which can then connect to that repository to install Linux on that system. You can use the same repository to install Linux on as many systems as you need, without having to change CDs.

There are four network installation services listed in the Linux+ objectives: HTTP, FTP, NFS, and SMB. Installations from SMB shares, also known as Samba, are obsolete in current versions of the selected Linux distributions. The other three network servers are briefly described in Table 1.1.

Network installation servers, by their nature, are configured on different computers (local or remote). If you have only one system, you could create a network installation server on the local system, and install the Linux distribution of your choice on a virtual machine such as VMware Server, Xen, or Kernel-based Virtual Machine (KVM).

To create a network installation server, copy the installation files from the CD/DVDs or Internet repository to a dedicated directory. Share the directory using the appropriate network server protocol. Make sure the applicable TCP/IP port is not blocked by a firewall, or by another layer of security such as Red Hat's Security-Enhanced Linux (SELinux) or SUSE's AppArmor.

TABLE 1.1   Servers That Can Be Used for Network Installations

Network Server	Description
NFS (Network File System)	The standard file sharing system for Linux and Unix operating systems
FTP (File Transfer Protocol)	An older fast file sharing system
HTTP (Hypertext Transfer Protocol)	The same file sharing system used for the World Wide Web

You can then install the selected Linux distribution over a network, using the IP address and shared directory of the network server.

Define Multimedia Options

There are multimedia options associated with installation, as listed in the Linux+ objectives: video, sound, and codecs. Naturally, some multimedia requires installation of some software from all three categories. For example, the MPEG (Motion Picture Experts Group) standards provide audio and video compression for network multimedia communication.

These options require Linux to detect available video and sound hardware. When installing Linux, the selected distributions allow installation of video and audio applications that incorporate appropriate codecs. There are many books (including other Linux+ exam prep books) that include an extended discussion of video and audio hardware. I believe that is beyond the scope of the Linux+ objectives.

Travel Advisory

DreamWorks and Disney have demonstrated their confidence in Linux multimedia—both create special effects for their movies on Linux workstations.

Video

Linux does an excellent job with most video cards. It supports installation on most video cards at least in text mode. But support is less than perfect. For example, I was not able to install RHEL 5 on my widescreen laptop system in graphical mode. I had to configure the video card from a remote system before the GUI would work.

While most Linux distributions have converted from the XFree86 video server to that released by X.Org, the principles remain the same. Configuration files are still stored in the /etc/X11 directory. The major configuration directives are the same. And it's still possible to create a configuration file from the command line. When the XFree86 server is installed, the following command creates an X Window configuration file from installed hardware:

```
# XFree86 -configure
```

If the X.Org server is installed, the command is similar:

```
# Xorg -configure
```

For more information on configuring the X Window Server, see Chapter 6.
The resolution available on a video card depends on the available RAM. Remember, RAM is specified in bytes. There are 8 bits in a byte. So let's calculate how much RAM is needed to support 24-bit color for a 1280×800 system:

1. Calculate the number of pixels on the screen: 1280×800 = 1,024,000.

2. For 24 bits of color in each pixel, multiply the result by 24:
   1,024,000×24 = 24,576,000 bits.

3. To convert this number to bytes, divide by 8: 24,576,000 ÷ 8 = 3,072,000 bytes. This requires a video card with 4MB of RAM, a trivial amount by current standards.

Any leftover video memory may be used to store information on different GUI desktops. Try this out with the maximum resolution available for your monitor.

Sound

When the Linux+ objectives were released, sound cards often had to be selected manually, using configuration tools such as **sndconfig** or YaST. The latest Linux distributions configure sound cards automatically, and you only need to tune them, using tools such as **alsactl** and **alsamixer**. The **alsamixer** tool, shown in Figure 1.3, can be run from the command line.

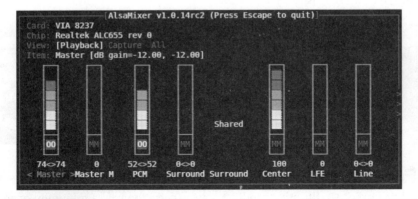

FIGURE 1.3   The **alsamixer** tool

Codecs

Codecs (short for coder/decoder) translate multimedia into (usually) compressed audio and video signals. They are associated with many formats, including the open source Vorbis, various MPEGs, RealAudio/RealVideo, and more. Codecs are incorporated into various sound and video applications. While I could cite the formats associated with typical Linux multimedia applications such as MPlayer, Kaffeine, and Totem, most Linux multimedia players can handle most popular nonproprietary formats.

Exam Tip

One popular MPEG option is MPEG-2, which is a standard for the coding of moving pictures and associated audio information. In other words, it requires video and sound hardware.

Objective 1.06

Identify Machine Requirements

The Linux+ objectives suggest that you need to identify the purpose of a Linux system "based on predetermined customer requirements." Dedicated systems are sometimes known as appliances. Linux systems, of course, can be configured as functional servers or desktop/workstations. If a customer gives you a list of requirements, you need to know what you're going to install—before you start the installation process.

Travel Advisory

Capitalization matters in Linux. Commands are case sensitive; for example, while **mount** can connect to network directories, there is no Mount command in Linux. Package names are often in lowercase; the Red Hat DHCP server package is dhcp. The open source sendmail server is different from the commercial Sendmail server.

Packages and Package Groups

While Linux+ Certification candidates are expected to have a minimum of six months of experience, the exam does not require a thorough understanding of server configuration. However, you need to know the names of more important services, and what they can do. I've listed the packages associated with major Linux network services in Table 1.2. In some cases, package names vary, and may not be included in the table. More information on these packages is available primarily in Chapters 5 and 7.

TABLE 1.2	Services, Packages, and Functionality	
Service	**Package**	**Functionality**
CUPS	cups	Print server; successor to LPD.
DNS	bind	Name server.
DHCP	dhcp, dhcp-server	Dynamic Host Configuration Protocol server.
FTP	vsftpd, proftpd	FTP *File* server (there are commonalities between the vsFTP and ProFTP servers).
HTTP	httpd, apache, apache2	The Apache Web server is the most popular Web server on the Internet.
IMAP/POP	dovecot, imap	Incoming e-mail server; the dovecot package is new (the imap package was in common use when the Linux+ objectives were released).
LPD	lpd, lprng	The Line Printer Daemon was still in common use when the current Linux+ objectives were released.
NFS	nfs-utils, many others	NFS *File* server; many NFS files come from standard Linux packages.
NTP	ntp, xntp	Network Time Protocol server.
Proxy	squid	The Squid Web Proxy caches web content and logs where users navigate online.
SMB/CIFS	samba	The Samba server shares configured directories on Microsoft SMB and successor CIFS networks; a File server.
SMTP	postfix, sendmail	The Postfix and sendmail servers process outgoing e-mail.
SQL	mysql, postgresql	The MySQL and PostgreSQL servers can help manage databases using their own structured query languages.
SSH	openssh, openssh-server	The Secure Shell (SSH) encrypts network connections at the command line.
Telnet	telnet-server	Telnet is an older but still popular and insecure method for remote connections to the command line.

Exam Tip

If you've been using Linux for 6 to 12 months (as suggested by the Linux+ objectives), you should have no problem recognizing the more popular applications included with most Linux distributions. For example, you need to know that MySQL and PostgreSQL packages are associated with a database server; Samba and NFS are associated with a File server; and so on.

Appliance

There are two categories of computer appliances. The standard computer appliance, such as a cell phone, router, or GPS, isn't even a PC. When Linux is configured as a single-function system, such as a DNS server on a PC, it's known as a software appliance. Software appliances have the following characteristics:

- Other network services are not installed (except possibly the Secure Shell to allow remote administration).
- A firewall or other security tools prevent access to all ports other than that required for the dedicated appliance (or administration).

With the popularity of virtual machine systems such as VMware, Xen, and KVM (available on systems with Linux kernel 2.6.19 and above), more Linux systems are being configured as appliances.

Any system configured with just one of the services described in Table 1.2 can be defined as an appliance.

Functional Server

Some Linux systems with more than one service have a single function. For example, a system configured with Samba, NFS, and FTP is a File server. A system configured with CUPS and LPD is a print server. Table 1.3 correlates the functionality of a server with appropriate packages.

TABLE 1.3   Server Functionality and Services

Server Functionality	Packages
Print server	cups, lpd, lprng
DNS name server	bind
File server	nfs-utils, samba, vsftpd, proftpd
Database server	mysql, postgresql
Mail server	sendmail, postfix, dovecot, imap

TABLE 1.4	Desktop Functionality and Applications
Desktop Functionality	**Typical Applications**
Office suites	OpenOffice.org, KOffice, GNOME Office
Graphics	The GIMP, digiKam, ImageMagick, SANE
Graphical Internet	Firefox, Evolution, Thunderbird
Multimedia	Kaffeine, Totem, MPlayer, RealPlayer

Most Linux systems have multiple functions. The default RHEL 5 installation includes NFS and CUPS for file and print sharing. My multifunctional Fedora 7 system is also configured as an e-mail, NTP, Samba, and DNS server.

Desktop

Linux developers have worked hard to create fully functional desktop environments. Although not all popular applications work on Linux, I believe that the Linux desktop is more fully functional than any Microsoft operating system. Desktop applications are available in a number of categories, including those described in Table 1.4. This table includes only some of the more popular packages; many more packages are available.

This just scratches the surface of available applications, as there is a variety of educational, gaming, authoring, finance, and other applications available for the Linux desktop.

CHECKPOINT

✔**Objective 1.01: Determine Customer Needs**   Even a junior Linux administrator needs to know something about selling Linux. Client applications are diverse, and are usually compatible with files created by Microsoft applications. Linux services work well on networks such as the Internet. The distribution that you should select depends on the software and support needs of your customer.

✔**Objective 1.02: Identify Required Hardware**   All but the latest hardware works with Linux, and is often documented in HCLs. The installation space required can vary from several hundred megabytes to several gigabytes—and that doesn't include space required for logs and home directories.

✔**Objective 1.03: Understand That Linux Is Just the Kernel**   Linux kernels used a three-number format when the current Linux+ objectives were released. They now have a four-number format, with variations by distribution.

✔**Objective 1.04: Determine the Appropriate Installation Method** While many home users install Linux from a local CD/DVD, network administrators need a central repository from which to install Linux on multiple systems. Some distributions use the **rawwrite** utility to create a boot disk in DOS.

✔**Objective 1.05: Define Multimedia Options** Linux works well with most video cards, and may even be configured from the command line. Sound configuration tools such as **sndconfig** or YaST used to be required. Codecs are available as part of many Linux multimedia applications.

✔**Objective 1.06: Identify Machine Requirements** Before installing Linux, know your needs. Linux configured with a single service is an appliance. Linux can also be configured with multiple functions such as file, print, and database services. With packages such as the OpenOffice.org suite, Linux also makes an excellent desktop.

REVIEW QUESTIONS

Before leaving for the next chapter, take a few minutes to go through these questions. While doing so, take in both the content and the question format. Understanding what to expect on the exam can increase your chances for success.

1. If the MySQL and Secure Shell software is installed on a local system, what kind of server is it?

    A. File server
    B. Database server
    C. Print server
    D. Secure Shell server

2. Which of the following service packages would you install on a File server?

    A. httpd
    B. ssh
    C. filed
    D. samba

3. If you need more information on hardware compatibility with your selected Linux distribution, which of the following sources would *not* help?

    A. The Hardware Compatibility List at http://tldp.org
    B. The Linux.org website
    C. The website associated with the selected Linux distribution
    D. Information from hardware manufacturers' websites

4. If you're installing a Linux desktop and don't want it used as a server (possibly except for sharing files and directories), which of the following packages or applications are not appropriate?

   A. cups

   B. openoffice.org

   C. Multimedia applications

   D. FTP clients

5. Which of the following do you *not* need to know prior to installation?

   A. Packages to install

   B. Hardware information

   C. Usernames in remote databases

   D. Partition configuration

6. You're working with a system with Linux kernel version number 2.7.1.2. Which of the following statements is true about the kernel?

   A. It's a production kernel.

   B. It's a developmental kernel.

   C. It's only supposed to have three numbers.

   D. It wasn't installed on Red Hat Enterprise Linux.

7. To install Linux over a network connection, which of the following network services won't work to host the installation files?

   A. HTTP

   B. FTP

   C. Telnet

   D. NFS

8. Which of the following hardware components do you *not* need to know before acquiring Linux distribution files?

   A. Hard disk capacity

   B. Mouse hardware

   C. CPU

   D. RAM

9. If your customer tells you that she wants a secure DNS server, which of the following best describes the type of Linux machine you should create?

   A. Web server

   B. File server

   C. Appliance

   D. Database

10. Which of the following commands can be used to create a boot disk in DOS to install some distributions?

   A. rawwrite.exe

   B. boot.iso

   C. diskboot.img

   D. dd

REVIEW ANSWERS

1. **B** MySQL is a database service. Secure Shell is just one method to connect to a server.

2. **D** Samba is the only file sharing service on the list. The httpd package is associated with the Apache Web server. The ssh package is associated with the Secure Shell. There is no filed package, at least in the distributions associated with the Linux+ exam.

3. **B** While the Linux.org website does have some valuable information on hardware, it is not one of the standard sources for hardware compatibility information.

4. **A** The cups package is associated with the CUPS print server.

5. **C** Even if you're configuring a database server for usernames, you don't need to know those usernames, certainly not prior to installation.

6. **A** Prior to kernel version 2.6, Linux kernels with an odd second number were developmental kernels. Starting with version 2.7, that's no longer true. Standard kernels only had three numbers through version 2.6.11.

7. **C** It's possible to create a Linux installation server on an HTTP, FTP, or NFS server. No current Linux installation server can be created on a Telnet server.

8. **B** While a mouse can be a terrific convenience, it's not required for Linux, especially if you're not installing a GUI.

9. **C** A single-function Linux system defines a computer appliance. While a DNS server does define a database, it's not a standard database service, such as that associated with MySQL or PostgreSQL.

10. **A** The **rawwrite.exe** command can be used from the DOS command line to create boot disks. While installation boot disks can be created from boot.iso and diskboot.img files, they are not commands, and while the **dd** command can be used to create boot disks, it's not a DOS command.

Configuring During and After Installation

CHAPTER 2

	NEWBIE	SOME EXPERIENCE	VETERAN
ETA	8+ hours	4 hours	2 hours

23

A good part of the installation process helps to configure Linux. While this chapter does not specify what's done per distribution, it does address common elements. Linux installations typically configure an installation language, keyboard, mouse or pointing device, and a time zone. They set up and format partitions. They install a bootloader and set up a network configuration.

After the basic installation is complete, you still need to configure essential peripherals. You also need to know how to install and update RPM packages, or RPMs for short, as well as install new software from compressed packages known as *tarballs*.

Select Appropriate Parameters for Installation

Objective 2.01

There are four basic parameters common to all installations: language, keyboard, pointing device, and time zone. Some of the latest distributions automatically configure pointing devices such as a mouse. But all of these components need to be detected and/or configured during the installation process. Sometimes an installation program does its best to detect your hardware, and you'll have the opportunity to customize that hardware in a screen like that shown in Figure 2.1.

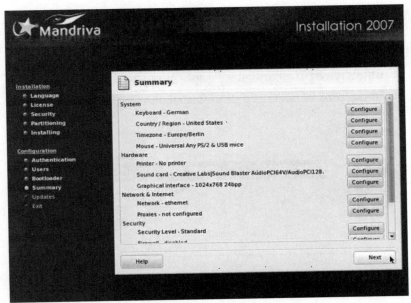

FIGURE 2.1 Sometimes, you can customize hardware from a summary screen.

Exam Tip

The best way to learn how to customize Linux during installation is by installing Linux. Use a spare computer or a virtual machine such as Xen or VMware. Practice with the selected Linux distributions.

In this chapter I'm describing common elements of four different installation programs, so the steps are necessarily vague.

Language

There are two steps associated with language during the installation process. First, there's the language that is used during the installation process, typically the first step after booting the installation program. Then there's the language to be installed, which can be different from the language used for installation.

In many cases, you're able to select between different language dialects, such as U.S. and Canadian English. Figure 2.2 shows one example of a language selection menu . Once configured, the setting is stored in the *i18n* or *language* files in the /etc/sysconfig directory.

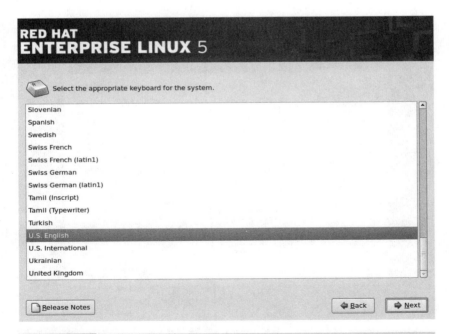

FIGURE 2.2   Language selection during installation

Keyboard

Linux can accommodate a wide variety of keyboards; for example, Fedora 7 supports five different kinds of French keyboards during the installation process. The keyboard menu may be customized depending on the language just selected.

As shown in Figure 2.3, some keyboards configured during the installation process can accommodate so-called "dead keys," commonly used to generate special characters, such as letters with accents (for example, ö, ñ, and é). Once configured, keyboard settings are stored in /etc/sysconfig/keyboard.

Pointing Device

The pointing device for most users is the mouse, touchpad, or trackball. These devices are often automatically detected and configured by the installation program.

Linux is optimized for mice with three buttons. Many mice have only two buttons. If there's a scroll wheel on your mouse, press it. If it clicks, some distributions may detect and configure it as a middle mouse button. Otherwise, installation programs may (but do not always) present an option such as "Emulate Three Buttons." If selected, you can simulate the middle mouse button by pressing both left and right mouse buttons simultaneously.

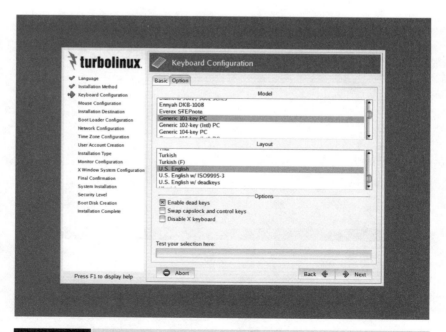

FIGURE 2.3   Keyboard selection during installation

While some of the selected distributions (not Red Hat) store this information in /etc/sysconfig/mouse, the configuration is also stored in the X Window configuration file, *XF86Config* or *xorg.conf*.

Time Zone

Linux accommodates a wide variety of time zones, and has been kept up to date with the recent changes in daylight saving time (DST) in the United States and Western Australia, without the difficulties encountered by Microsoft Windows. ✴But Linux can work with DST only if the local system is set to UTC, in the BIOS. And that won't work if the local computer is in a dual boot configuration with an operating system such as Microsoft Windows.

> **Local Lingo**
>
> **UTC** is an acronym based on a political compromise. What matters is that it's the atomic realization of Greenwich Mean Time.

In some cases, the installation program allows you to configure whether to keep the time updated with a local or remote network time server. Once configured, the time zone configuration is stored in binary format in /etc/localtime.

Objective 2.02 Partition with fdisk and More

There are several ways to partition Linux during the installation process. The basic utilities are **fdisk** and **parted**. The tools seen during the installation process, such as Disk Druid, **cfdisk**, and GParted, are front-ends to **fdisk** and **parted**.

But before doing any partitioning, you need a plan. You need to make choices on appropriate directories and mount points for dedicated partitions. And that means you need to know the basics of RAID (Redundant Array of Independent Disks) and LVM (Logical Volume Management).

For more information on **fdisk**, see "Configuring with fdisk" in Chapter 4.

Appropriate Directories for Dedicated Partitions

When partitioning a system for Linux, you could mount all directories on a single partition. That would be like creating just a C: drive for a Microsoft Windows installation. Available Linux directories are based on the Filesystem Hierarchy Standard (FHS), described in more detail in the Chapter 4 section "Manage Storage Devices and Filesystems."

Many Linux distributions automatically configure three different partitions during the installation process:

- **A partition for the top-level root directory** (/)   All other Linux directories are subdirectories of /. Unless otherwise configured on separate partitions, they share the same partition as /.
- **A dedicated /boot directory partition**   Older PCs required that the /boot directory be configured on a bootable hard drive, below the 1024th cylinder. Several major Linux distributions retain that standard, as critical boot files are stored in that directory.
- **A swap partition**   While it's possible to configure a swap file in Linux, swap partitions provide dedicated space for virtual memory.

SUSE is a notable exception, as its installation program does not automatically configure the /boot directory on a separate partition. It's a common practice to configure directories such as /home, /usr, and /var on separate partitions.

Local Lingo

root   There are three major uses for the word "root" in Linux. The root user is the default Linux administrative user. The top-level root directory, signified by the forward slash (/), is the highest-level directory on a Linux system. And the /root directory, which is the home directory of the root user, is a subdirectory of the top-level root directory (/). Linux commands, files, directories, and usernames are case sensitive, so the word is root; "Root," in contrast, is meaningless.

RAID Configuration

RAID includes the promise of redundancy. At most levels of RAID, if there's a failure in one hard drive, no data is lost.

There are two categories of RAID on Linux: hardware and software. Hardware RAID is configured from separate physical hard drives, with dedicated controllers. Software RAID, which can be configured during the Linux installation process, can be configured from separate partitions. These partitions should also be on different physical hard drives.

RAID is short for Redundant Array of Independent Disks. In other words, RAID arrays are normally configured on independent hard drives. So if you configure software RAID and expect redundancy, make sure each component partition is on a different physical hard drive.

There are five different levels of RAID commonly used on Linux. You may be able to combine several levels of RAID; for example, RAID 10 is a disk mirror of two RAID 0 arrays. Yes, there are other levels of RAID available, such as RAID 2, RAID 3, RAID 7, and so on, but software versions of these RAID levels are not supported by the Linux kernel.

RAID can generally be configured during the graphical installation process. It can also be configured on most distributions from the console with commands such as **mdadm**. Be aware that the **raidtools** command was used more commonly when the Linux+ exam objectives were released.

Exam Tip

Know the basics associated with different levels of RAID on Linux, including the associated commands.

RAID 0   *SPEED*

RAID 0 makes it faster to read and write, but provides no data redundancy, unlike other levels of RAID. It requires at least two partitions or hard disks. RAID 0 is also known as *striping without parity*.

Reads and writes are done in parallel to the different disks or partitions. All disks or partitions in a RAID 0 array are filled equally. A failure of any one of the disks or partitions will result in total data loss.

RAID 1   *MIRROR*

RAID 1 mirrors information between two disks or partitions. In other words, identical copies of every file are written to each disk or partition. If one disk or partition is damaged, all data is still safe on the second disk or partition. RAID 1 is also known as *disk mirroring*.

There are two disadvantages to RAID 1. First, data has to be written twice, which can reduce performance. Second, RAID 1 requires twice the number of hard disks or partitions compared to regular storage.

RAID 4

While RAID 4 is supported by the Linux kernel, it is not supported by all Linux distributions. RAID 4 requires three or more disks or partitions. One of the disks maintains parity information, which can be used to reconstruct lost data.

RAID 5

Like RAID 4, RAID 5 requires three or more disks or partitions. Unlike RAID 4, RAID 5 distributes, or *stripes*, parity information evenly across all disks. If any disk in the array fails, data can be reconstructed from the parity information available on the remaining disks. RAID 5 is also known as *disk striping with parity*.

RAID 6

RAID 6 is similar to RAID 5. While it requires four or more disks or partitions, it has two levels of parity and can therefore survive the failure of two members of the array.

Logical Volume Management Configuration

Logical volume management (LVM) (also known as the Logical Volume Manager) can help you manage active partitions, especially the size allocated to specific filesystems. Without LVM, increasing the size available to any directory required a laborious series of backups, partition changes, and more. With LVM, all that you need to do is create and allocate more space to the filesystem of your choice.

Understanding LVM requires an understanding of the following:

- Physical volumes (PVs) are hard disk partitions, initialized for LVM use.
- Volume groups (VGs) are PVs collected together, in a logical format.
- Logical volumes (LVs) are created from a VG; once created, you can mount a directory on an LV just as you can mount a directory on a regular physical partition.

While you're not expected to create an LV during the multiple-choice Linux+ exam, you do need to know the basic commands and what they do. First, a partition must be created in a tool such as **fdisk**, with the appropriate partition type, 8e. Some of the basic commands are listed in Table 2.1.

Red Hat distributions (including Fedora) can configure LVs during installation. The default Red Hat installation configures the top-level root directory (/) as an LV.

TABLE 2.1	Key LVM Commands
LVM Command	**Description**
pvcreate	Creates a PV
pvremove	Removes a configured PV from availability for LVM
vgcreate	Creates a VG from two or more available PVs
vgextend	Extends an existing VG with a newly available PV
vgreduce	Removes a PV from an existing VG
lvcreate	Creates a new LV from the space of an existing VG
lvextend	Extends the space available to an LV
lvreduce	Reduces the size of an LV

Other Partition Management Tools

There are several options to **fdisk**, especially during the installation process. For example, Red Hat distributions use Disk Druid. The GNU **parted** tool is becoming increasingly popular, as it supports partition resizing. There are front-ends to both tools, such as **sfdisk** and **cfdisk**, as well as GParted and QTparted.

Objective 2.03 Configure a Filesystem

Filesystems are one method for storing and organizing computer files. Filesystems can be local, such as Linux's ext2, ext3, ReiserFS, XFS, and Microsoft's VFAT and NTFS. Filesystems can be configured over the network; directories mounted from remote computers can be mounted with protocols such as NFS and Samba.

Local Lingo

Filesystem (or **file system**)   A Linux directory mounted on a partition, logical volume, or RAID array.

Local Lingo

Filesystem format (or **Filesystem type**)   Examples include ext, ext2, ext3, NTFS, VFAT, ReiserFS, and XFS. When displayed in Linux, either in /etc/fstab or as a filesystem module, they are *all* displayed in lowercase.

Standard Linux Filesystems

There are several filesystems commonly used on Linux. "Journaling" filesystems are becoming more popular, because they enable faster checking during the boot process and they resist data loss from power failures due to a log (aka *journal*) that can be used to restore metadata for files on the relevant partition. Some of the more popular standard Linux filesystems are listed in Table 2.2.

For a fuller list of filesystem formats, review Figure 2.4, which illustrates what's available in **fdisk**.

TABLE 2.2 Standard Linux Filesystems

Filesystem Type	Description
ext	The first extended filesystem, used on early Linux distributions.
ext2	The second extended filesystem, commonly used on many versions of Linux (including Red Hat Linux 7.2) through 2001.
ext3	The third extended filesystem, which is the default for the selected distributions. With journaling, it takes too much space for smaller media such as floppies.
swap	Specialized filesystem type for swap partitions in Linux.
iso9660	The standard filesystem format for CD/DVD media.
JFS	IBM's journaled filesystem, commonly used on enterprise servers.
ReiserFS	Until recently, the default for SUSE Linux.
XFS	The journaling filesystem developed by Silicon Graphics, which supports very large files; as of this writing, limited to 9×10^{18} bytes.

```
Hex code (type L to list codes): l

 0  Empty            1e  Hidden W95 FAT1 80  Old Minix        be  Solaris boot
 1  FAT12            24  NEC DOS         81  Minix / old Lin  bf  Solaris
 2  XENIX root       39  Plan 9          82  Linux swap / So  c1  DRDOS/sec (FAT-
 3  XENIX usr        3c  PartitionMagic  83  Linux            c4  DRDOS/sec (FAT-
 4  FAT16 <32M       40  Venix 80286     84  OS/2 hidden C:   c6  DRDOS/sec (FAT-
 5  Extended         41  PPC PReP Boot   85  Linux extended   c7  Syrinx
 6  FAT16            42  SFS             86  NTFS volume set  da  Non-FS data
 7  HPFS/NTFS        4d  QNX4.x          87  NTFS volume set  db  CP/M / CTOS / .
 8  AIX              4e  QNX4.x 2nd part 88  Linux plaintext  de  Dell Utility
 9  AIX bootable     4f  QNX4.x 3rd part 8e  Linux LVM        df  BootIt
 a  OS/2 Boot Manag  50  OnTrack DM      93  Amoeba           e1  DOS access
 b  W95 FAT32        51  OnTrack DM6 Aux 94  Amoeba BBT       e3  DOS R/O
 c  W95 FAT32 (LBA)  52  CP/M            9f  BSD/OS           e4  SpeedStor
 e  W95 FAT16 (LBA)  53  OnTrack DM6 Aux a0  IBM Thinkpad hi  eb  BeOS fs
 f  W95 Ext'd (LBA)  54  OnTrackDM6      a5  FreeBSD          ee  EFI GPT
10  OPUS             55  EZ-Drive        a6  OpenBSD          ef  EFI (FAT-12/16/
11  Hidden FAT12     56  Golden Bow      a7  NeXTSTEP         f0  Linux/PA-RISC b
12  Compaq diagnost  5c  Priam Edisk     a8  Darwin UFS       f1  SpeedStor
14  Hidden FAT16 <3  61  SpeedStor       a9  NetBSD           f4  SpeedStor
16  Hidden FAT16     63  GNU HURD or Sys ab  Darwin boot      f2  DOS secondary
17  Hidden HPFS/NTF  64  Novell Netware  b7  BSDI fs          fd  Linux raid auto
18  AST SmartSleep   65  Novell Netware  b8  BSDI swap        fe  LANstep
1b  Hidden W95 FAT3  70  DiskSecure Mult bb  Boot Wizard hid  ff  BBT
1c  Hidden W95 FAT3  75  PC/IX
Hex code (type L to list codes):
```

FIGURE 2.4 Available filesystem types

Local Lingo

Don't confuse the XFS filesystem with the X Font Server, which uses the same acronym. As before, when shown in Linux, it is lowercase, but it may be shown in uppercase in documentation. Incidentally, this is also true for the X Font Server.

Exam Tip

Learn the typical filesystem formats, and where they might be useful. Recognize filesystems such as VFAT, which can be easily read from both Linux and Microsoft operating systems. Understand that ext3 isn't always useful, especially for smaller filesystems such as a floppy disk.

Other Filesystems

As shown in Figure 2.4, there are a number of other filesystems available, many of which can be read from within a Linux system, including the various MS-DOS–based filesystems, such as FAT16 and FAT32, which are often read from Linux systems as the VFAT filesystem.

While available filesystems now include the Microsoft NTFS filesystems, that was not the case when the Linux+ objectives were released, at least for filesystems mounted in anything more than read-only format. The ability to write to an NTFS filesystem from Linux is a recent development.

 **Objective 2.04**

Understand and Reinstall a Boot Manager

When the Linux+ objectives were developed, there were two standard Linux boot managers: the Linux Loader (LILO) and the Grand Unified Bootloader (GRUB). There's now also the Extended Firmware Interface LILO (ELILO) bootloader for Itanium 64-bit systems. While LILO was a popular option among the selected distributions when the Linux+ objectives were released, LILO is largely unused now on systems with regular Intel/AMD 32-bit CPUs. CompTIA has done an excellent job keeping the exam up to date, so I'm guessing that CompTIA no longer includes LILO questions in its exam pool, but that's just a guess.

Travel Advisory

Developers constantly adapt different packages; for example, ELILO is now used for Linux distributions installed on Intel-based Macintosh hardware.

Domain 1.0 of the Linux+ objectives does list ELILO; however, it also suggests that questions are limited to "32-bit and 64-bit x86-based PCs and servers, as of October, 2004." You'll have to make your own decision on whether to study LILO or ELILO. If you want to study ELILO, navigate to http://elilo.sourceforge.net.

The Linux Loader (LILO)

LILO is largely obsolete, and isn't even available in the latest Red Hat repositories. If you want to download and install LILO, navigate to http://lilo.go.dyndns.org. Because LILO was relatively popular when the Linux+ objectives were developed, it's still fair game for the exam. So I'll explain an excerpt of an older LILO configuration file from Red Hat Linux 9.

As LILO is loaded in the master boot record (MBR), the **boot** directive tells the MBR to look at the first IDE/PATA hard drive, with a default map file. The /boot/boot.b file is installed as the new boot sector. The **prompt** waits a **timeout** of 50 tenths of a second (5 seconds), with a message listed in /boot/message. The **lba32** directive supports logical block addressing. If no operating system is selected by the **timeout**, the **default** stanza is booted.

```
boot=/dev/hda
map=/boot/map
install=/boot/boot.b
prompt
timeout=50
message=/boot/message
lba32
default=linux
```

Travel Advisory

The terms associated with hard drives have changed. Standard PC hard drives, once known as IDE (Integrated Drive Electronics) drives, are now known as PATA (Parallel Advanced Technology Attachment) drives, due to the development of SATA (Serial Advanced Technology Attachment) drives. But this happened after the Linux+ objectives were released.

The following stanza specifies an **image** of the Linux kernel to be booted, in this case, vmlinuz-2.4.0. The **label** is used by the **default** directive described earlier. The loaded initial RAM disk is specified by the **initrd** directive. Finally, the top-level root directory is on the /dev/hda2 partition.

```
image=/boot/vmlinuz-2.4.0
    label=linux
    initrd=/boot/initrd-2.4.0.img
    read-only
    root=/dev/hda2
```

If there is more than one operating system or available kernel, there will be additional similar stanzas in the LILO configuration file. Once configured, the **/sbin/lilo** command writes that configuration file to the MBR of the boot hard drive.

The Grand Unified Bootloader (GRUB)

Unlike LILO, GRUB configuration files aren't written to the BIOS. All that's written is a pointer, which reads the grub.conf configuration file in the /boot/grub directory. Depending on distribution, it may be grub.conf or menu.1st. While the names may change, the information remains the same. Generally, there's a hard link from /etc/grub.conf to this file.

Like LILO, GRUB starts with basic directives, and then specifies stanzas for each kernel or operating system option. The first directives from my desktop GRUB configuration file are as follows:

```
default=0
timeout=5
splashimage=(hd0,4)/grub/splash.xpm.gz
hiddenmenu
password --md5 %(*jl%ygt$#U84feuoijlLLSDA%&#
```

These directives point to the first stanza as the **default**, set a **timeout** of 5 seconds before the default stanza is automatically booted, and use a **splashimage** in the first logical partition of the first hard drive. The menu is hidden, courtesy of the **hiddenmenu** directive, which isn't revealed unless the user presses a key before the **timeout**. The final directive in this area, **password**, specifies an encrypted password, in MD5 format. You can create this password with the **grub-md5-crypt** command.

Exam Tip

The use of **root** in the GRUB configuration can be confusing. While the **root (hd0,1)** directive points to a /boot directory partition on the first hard drive on the *second* partition, the **root=/dev/hda5** directive points to the top-level root directory on the first logical partition on the first IDE/PATA hard drive.

Now examine a typical stanza, in this case for a Fedora 7 kernel:

```
title Fedora (2.6.21-1.3194.fc7)
    root (hd0,4)
    kernel /vmlinuz-2.6.21-1.3194.fc7 ro root=/dev/sdb2 rhgb quiet
    initrd /initrd-2.6.21-1.3194.fc7.img
```

The *title* is what's seen as an option in the GRUB menu. The **root (hd0,4)** directive points to the *fifth* partition on the first hard drive—as the /boot directory. The **kernel** and **initrd** directives point to the **vmlinuz-*** kernel and initial RAM disk (**initrd-***) files in the /boot directory.

Finally, examine an alternative stanza, which points to a Microsoft Windows partition:

```
title  Windows XP Media Center Edition
    rootnoverify  (hd0,1)
    chainloader   +1
```

The title is straightforward, and can be customized. The **rootnoverify (hd0,1)** directive points to the second partition on the first hard drive, and does *not* attempt to mount it with a Linux format. The **chainloader +1** directive points to the file in the first sector of the partition; for a Microsoft Windows XP system, that's NTLDR.

If you haven't used GRUB as a bootloader before, and have just configured a GRUB configuration file, run the **/sbin/grub-install** command. It installs the pointer to the GRUB configuration file on the hard drive MBR. The boot manager should look something like Figure 2.5.

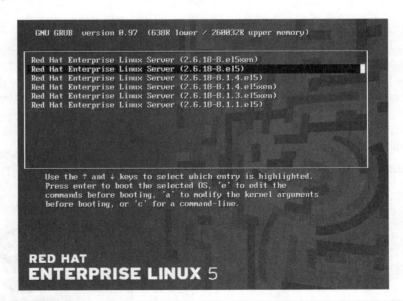

| **FIGURE 2.5** | A sample GRUB boot menu |

Exam Tip

Once a pointer to the GRUB configuration file is installed on the MBR, you don't have to repeat the process. Any subsequent changes to the GRUB configuration file are automatically reflected in the GRUB menu.

Other Bootloaders

There are several other bootloaders that can be used to start a Linux system; some are listed and described in Table 2.3.

Identify Network Configuration Issues

For those of you who have already taken the CompTIA Network+ exam, this section should be just a review. In fact, some of the information here may seem "oversimplified," which is a necessary evil in a book of this size. This section reviews some of the basics of TCP/IP, IP addressing, how to connect a Linux system to a LAN, and the issues associated with Linux and telephone modems. It also covers the basic structure of network services associated with the Internet Super Server, governed in Linux by the **inetd** daemon or **xinetd** daemon.

Network Fundamentals

A network consists of two or more computers connected together for the purpose of sharing information. A series of protocols is required to translate files and e-mails to the 1s and 0s of computer communication. The standard is TCP/IP. It's known as a protocol suite, as it is a series of protocols, organized in layers. It was developed for Unix and eventually adapted as the standard for communication on the Internet. With IP addresses, it can help you organize your network.

TABLE 2.3	Servers That Can Be Used for Network Installations
Bootloader	**Description**
NTLDR	The standard Microsoft bootloader; a different bootloader was used for Windows 95/98/Me. It does not work for Vista, but it can boot Linux.
Bootmgr	The Microsoft Windows Vista bootloader; can also boot Linux.
Boot Magic	A third-party bootloader (from Partition Magic) that can recognize standard Linux file formats.

IP Addresses

Every computer that communicates on a TCP/IP network needs its own IP address. If an IP address is assigned permanently, it's known as a *static* address. If it's leased from a DHCP (Dynamic Host Configuration Protocol) server, it's known as a *dynamic* address.

Travel Advisory

If you feel the need for more detailed information on IP addressing, see Chapter 6 of *Mike Meyers' Network+ Certification Passport,* Second Edition, by Schwarz, Clarke, and Meyers (McGraw-Hill, 2004).

There are two standards for IP addressing in use today: IP version 4 (IPv4) and IP version 6 (IPv6). IPv4 addresses have 32 bits and are set up in octets, generally written in dotted-decimal notation. IPv4 addresses can range from 0.0.0.0 to 255.255.255.255. While this range includes more than 4 billion IP addresses, this is not nearly enough for the current Internet.

In contrast, IPv6 addresses have 128 bits and are generally shown in hexadecimal (base 16) notation. An IPv6 address is normally organized in eight groups of four hexadecimal numbers, and may look like fe80:0000:0000:0000:0218:deff:fe38:4471. With 128 bits, that's a range of over 3.4×10^{38} addresses.

To ease the transition, a range of IPv6 addresses has been assigned for every one of the 4 billion IPv4 addresses. While actual routing on the Internet now commonly uses IPv6, network configuration in Linux (and other operating systems) is still normally based on IPv4.

IPv4 addresses are organized into five different classes, as shown in Table 2.4. Sharper readers may note that the information in this table is different from the IPv4 classes specified in RFC 1518, as specified by the Internet Engineering Task Force (IETF). The *assignable* address range includes those IP addresses that can be allocated to a specific computer on a network.

In addition, there are several private IP address ranges available for networks that are not directly connected to the Internet. The comments in Table 2.4 assume standard network masks; for example, a Class A network supports over 16 million systems if you use a standard Class A network mask of 255.0.0.0.

Local Lingo

Network mask and subnet mask are synonyms.

TABLE 2.4	IP Address Classes	
Class	**Assignable Address Range**	**Comments**
A	1.1.1.1–126.255.255.254	Supports networks of more than 16 million systems
B	128.0.0.1–191.255.255.254	Allows networks of over 65,000 systems
C	192.0.0.1–223.255.255.254	Allows networks of up to 254 systems
D	224.0.0.1–239.255.255.254	Reserved for multicasts
E	240.0.0.1–255.255.255.254	Reserved for experimental use

On my home network, I use a 192.168.0.0 network address with a 255.255.255.0 network mask. This allows me to assign IP addresses between 192.168.0.1 and 192.168.0.254. The 192.168.255.255 address is the broadcast address.

If I wanted two networks in this range, I'd set up a 255.255.255.128 network mask. That would support network addresses of 192.168.0.0 and 192.168.0.128. The first network would have available IP addresses of 192.168.0.1 through 192.168.0.126, with a broadcast address of 192.168.0.127. The second network would have available IP addresses of 192.168.0.129 through 192.168.0.254, with a broadcast address of 192.168.0.255.

IPv4 broadcast masks are often classified by the number of bits. For example, 255.255.255.0 is associated with 24 active bits; 255.255.255.128 is associated with 25 active bits. From a 32-bit address, that leaves 8 and 7 bits, respectively, assignable to computers and other networkable devices.

The number of assignable addresses, where n is the number of assignable bits, is $2^n - 2$. If the network has 8 assignable bits, that leaves 254 assignable addresses. If the network has 7 assignable bits, that leaves 126 assignable addresses.

> **Exam Tip**
>
> IPv6 was not in common use when the Linux+ objectives were released; so focus on IPv4 addressing. Know the range of assignable IP addresses associated with a certain network address and subnet mask.

Connecting to a LAN

To connect to a LAN, you need to configure an IP address within the assignable range for the LAN, as well as a route that sends messages to that LAN. Installation programs support configuration with the settings described in Table 2.5. The settings apply whether you're configuring a connection to an IPv4 or IPv6 network.

TABLE 2.5	Network Installation Settings
Network Setting	**Description**
IP address	Choices may be static or dynamic; static IP addresses require a network mask.
Hostname	The hostname may be assigned by a DHCP server.
Gateway IP address	Local IP address of the gateway to other networks such as the Internet; may be assigned by a DHCP server.
DNS server	Required only if you're using hostnames during the installation process, such as to find a network installation server; may be assigned by a DHCP server.

You also need to know how to configure a connection to a LAN using command-line tools; for more information, see the Chapter 6 section "Work Network Settings."

Connecting via Telephone Modem

Surprisingly, even in late 2007, telephone modems are still used by nearly half of U.S. home Internet users. Unfortunately for these users, so-called "software" telephone modems, designed to use Microsoft Windows driver libraries, have been a troublesome area for Linux. Such modems are known as "Winmodems."

The easiest solution is a "hardware modem," which does not depend on any operating system software. To my knowledge, Linux has no problems with hardware modems.

Because Microsoft does not share its source code under any open source license, Linux developers have had to create their own code to make a Winmodem work with Linux. So, a substantial number of Winmodems *now* work with Linux just as well as hardware modems. Some of the remaining Winmodems can be configured with a bit of help; for the latest information, see www.linmodems.org. An alternative clone (available for a price) for Conexant Winmodems is www.linuxant.com.

But, as Linux is primarily used on servers, connections during the installation process are normally made via standard higher-speed network connections, primarily Ethernet, so fewer Linux developers have been working on this issue.

Travel Advisory
As high-speed networking has progressed, Linux developers have focused on creating drivers for wireless cards. However, as most of this work has come after the Linux+ objectives were released, wireless networks are not addressed on the Linux+ exam.

It's also possible to configure Linux as a modem server, with the RADIUS service. Controlled by the **radiusd** daemon, it supports remote logins via modem. If modem connections are made but logins aren't working, the **radiusd** daemon may not be working.

The Internet Super Server

The Internet Super Server provides one service that governs different services. Common Super Server services include Telnet and the Remote Shell. There are two basic configurations associated with the Internet Super Server. Some Linux systems are configured with the /etc/inetd.conf file; most Linux systems today (including the selected distributions) are configured with /etc/xinetd.conf.

The xinetd.conf file commonly has at least five directives. The first, **instances**, limits to 60 the number of logged-in users to various Super Server services. Standard limits on the selected distributions may be as low as 30.

```
instances = 60
```

The next two lines describe what is sent to a log file when a user tries to connect. Naturally, they're associated with success and failure.

```
log_on_success = HOST
log_on_failure = HOST
```

Finally, the following directive supports service-specific configuration files in the /etc/xinetd.d directory:

```
includedir /etc/xinetd.d
```

For more information on securing services within the Internet Super Server, see the Chapter 9 section "Decipher Basic Firewall Configurations."

Objective 2.06   # Configure Peripherals as Needed

While not strictly part of the Linux operating system installation process, there are some peripherals that are essential for most users. As described in the Linux+ objectives, these peripherals include printers, scanners, and modems. Telephone modem configuration issues were described in the previous section.

Printers

When the Linux+ objectives were released, there were two print services in common use: the Line Printer Daemon (LPD) and the Common Unix Printing System (CUPS). Some distributions used a modified version of LPD, known as Line Printer, next generation (LPRng).

While CUPS is in common use today, LPD/LPRng is still popular among many users, especially those with Unix experience. As CUPS complies with the Internet Print Protocol (IPP), which makes it compatible with a heterogeneous variety of print services, I believe it's the future of Linux printing. But out of respect for LPD/LPRng users, related commands such as **lpr** (to print a file), **lprm** (to remove a print job), **lpc** (to administer printers), and **lpq** (to query the current print queue) work in most CUPS systems.

CUPS also uses some configuration files also used by LPD/LPRng. Shared printers are listed in /etc/printconf; LPD/LPRng versions of this file can be complex. The /etc/printconf file is cited in both cases by the Samba configuration file for sharing over Microsoft-based networks.

CUPS services automatically detect many attached printers, and can use the Simple Network Management Protocol (SNMP) to detect shared network printers. The associated printer database is known as Foomatic.

For more information, see the Chapter 5 section "Configure Printer Systems" and the Chapter 7 section "Set Up Linux Print Services."

Scanners

Linux scanners require drivers. The open source group responsible for developing most of these drivers is SANE, short for Scanner Access Now Easy. Depending on distribution, the Linux software that communicates with scanners are sane or libsane drivers.

Other Devices

Linux developers are creating and maintaining drivers for all popular peripherals. I no longer have problems with my digital cameras. Linux works well with most of the latest USB and IEEE 1394 (FireWire/iLink) peripherals.

Objective 2.07

Perform Post-Installation Package Management

Linux software is organized in packages. For the selected distributions, they're RPM packages. But you need to know how to install and update RPM packages, as well as install those packages available only in the so-called *tarball* format. Installing new software, upgrading existing components, and testing experimental software from tarballs are essential skills for even the newer Linux administrator, and are therefore also part of the Linux+ exam objectives.

A bit more information on the **rpm** command is available in the Chapter 9 section "Identify File Corruption" and the Chapter 10 section "Document Installed Configuration." But remember, because this book supports the Linux+ exam, you should rely on other books such as *Fedora 7 and Red Hat Enterprise Linux: The Complete Reference*, by Richard Peterson (McGraw-Hill, 2007) for rcal-world information on the **rpm** command.

Installing New RPM Packages

Run the **man rpm** command. This is the manual associated with the **rpm** command. Since this section deals with installation, we're working with the **rpm -i** or **rpm --install** command in this section. (The **-i** is a synonym for **--install**.) Many RPM packages can't be installed without their dependencies. For example, Red Hat won't let you install the system-config-samba administrative package unless you've already installed samba, or are installing it at the same time.

Some of the more important installation options are described briefly in Table 2.6.

One command I use frequently when installing packages is

```
# rpm -ivh packagename
```

This command installs (**-i**) in verbose mode (**-v**) with hash marks (**-h**). Verbose mode often provides error messages if there are problems, and hash marks indicate the progress of the installation. If an installation stops in the middle, there may be a problem with the package, the connection to the network, or possibly the local CD/DVD media.

Upgrading RPM Packages

If you've already installed an RPM package, you can't use the same installation commands to install a later version. Actually you could, if you erased them first, but if there are dependencies, that could cause all sorts of trouble.

The best option when updating RPM packages is the upgrade switch, **--upgrade** or **-U**. If you upgrade with a properly built RPM package, old configu-

TABLE 2.6 Options for the **rpm** command

rpm --install Option	Description
--aid	Automatically adds dependent packages, if you're already in the directory with those packages
--force	Forces installation even if the package is older
-h, --hash	Adds hash marks to indicate installation progress
--nodeps	Avoids checking for dependencies; may be dangerous
-v	Verbose mode; generic option usable for other **rpm** commands

ration files are saved with an .rpmsave extension. If there are no changes in dependencies, you won't have to install those other packages again.

If you're upgrading a kernel using the **rpm** command, you should use the installation switch. With an installation, a new kernel is installed side by side in the same directories as an existing kernel. If the new kernel doesn't work, you still have the existing working kernel. With an upgrade, the new kernel overwrites the files associated with an existing kernel, so if the new kernel has problems, there will be trouble.

Similar to an installation of an RPM package, the command I prefer is

```
# rpm -Uvh packagename
```

Exam Tip

To practice upgrading an RPM package, I recommend downloading a later version first. Every distribution now has some sort of update manager such as yum, YaST, and urpmi—which should be ignored for this book, as they are not listed in the Linux+ objectives. Download an RPM from an "updates" repository for your distribution.

Installing from a Compressed Tarball

A tarball is the common Linux name for a compressed archive, based on the **tar** command. It's commonly used by developers and others to share experimental and beta packages, which may not have been tested for specific Linux distributions.

Tarballs are generally distributed in Gzip and Bzip2 compressed formats. By convention, Gzip compressed tarballs have either a .tar.gz or a .tgz extension. Bzip2 compressed tarballs have either a tar.bz2, .tbz2, or .tb2 extension.

To extract the information from a tarball, you could first uncompress the tarball with the **gunzip** or **bunzip2** command. It's more common to uncompress and unarchive the tarball with a single command; for example, the following commands work on the Gzip and Bzip2 compressed archives of kernel source code version 2.6.21.5 downloaded from ftp.kernel.org:

```
# tar xzvf linux-2.6.21.5.tar.gz
# tar xjvf linux-2.6.21.5.tar.bz2
```

Both **tar** commands extract (**x**) the archive, in verbose mode (**v**), from the file that follows (**f**). The **z** option extracts from a Gzip compressed file; the **j** option extracts from a Bzip2 compressed file.

Once the archive is extracted, the next steps depend on what's available. Often, there are instructions in a file like INSTALL or README. In my experience, what you do falls into three categories:

- The files are installed directly in appropriate directories. For example, the latest LILO tarball installs commands such as **lilo** in directories such as /sbin.

- The extracted files are source code that must be compiled. If there's a *Makefile* file in the extracted directory, look for instructions. The next step may be as simple as running the **make** command.

- There's a script with a name like *configure* in the extracted directory. You may need to run it from the local directory with a command like the following, which runs *configure*, if it's executable, in the local directory:

```
# ./configure
```

For more information on the **tar** command, see the Chapter 4 section "Back Up and Restore Data."

CHECKPOINT

✔**Objective 2.01: Select Appropriate Parameters for Installation**   Some basic parameters associated with every installation are language, keyboard, pointing device, and time zone—unless otherwise detected and automatically configured, such as the mouse as a pointing device on the latest Red Hat distributions.

✔**Objective 2.02: Partition with fdisk and More**   The **fdisk** utility is the standard way to create partitions; other tools and front-ends such as **parted**, **cfdisk**, **sfdisk**, GParted, and Disk Druid are also available. Standard partitions are often dedicated, at least for the top-level root directory (/), the /boot directory, and swap space. Several levels of RAID are available. While it's not possible to demonstrate how to create an LVM system during the multiple-choice Linux+ exam, you do need to know the associated commands.

✔**Objective 2.03: Configure a Filesystem**   There are a large number of filesystem formats. Some associated with Linux include ext2, ext3, ReiserFS, and XFS. Some are appropriate for other operating systems, such as FAT16 and FAT32, both of which may be seen in Linux as VFAT. Just remember, in Linux configuration files, these formats are in lowercase.

✔**Objective 2.04: Understand and Reinstall a Boot Manager**   There are two standard boot managers associated with Linux: LILO and GRUB. The **lilo** command installs bootloader information in the MBR. The **grub-install** command installs a pointer to the GRUB configuration file in the MBR.

✔**Objective 2.05: Identify Network Configuration Issues**   The standard for network and Internet communication is the TCP/IP protocol suite. There are five classes of IP addresses. Private IP address ranges are appropriate for private networks. Different subnet masks support various ranges of IP addresses. Other network configuration issues relate to Winmodems and the Internet Super Server.

✔**Objective 2.06: Configure Peripherals as Needed**   Other peripherals include printers and scanners. Printing is associated with the CUPS or LPD/LPRng services. Scanners require the sane drivers.

✔**Objective 2.07: Perform Post-Installation Package Management**   Even a beginning Linux administrator needs to install and update RPMs, as well as understand how to install from a tarball.

REVIEW QUESTIONS

Before leaving for the next chapter, take a few minutes to go through these questions. While doing so, take in both the content and the question format. Understanding what to expect on the exam can increase your chances for success.

1. If you wanted to configure a keyboard with accents based on special control keys, which of the following would you configure?

   A. Macros

   B. Dead keys

   C. Special buttons

   D. Bluetooth

2. Which of the following filesystems is most appropriate for a boot floppy?

   A. ext3

   B. reiserfs

   C. ext2

   D. xfs

3. Which of the following filesystems can be mounted in read-write mode by default by both Linux and Microsoft Windows operating systems?

   A. ext3

   B. reiserfs

   C. xfs

   D. fat32

4. If you've already installed GRUB and just edited the configuration file, what do you need to write to the MBR?

   A. The configuration file

   B. A pointer to the configuration file

   C. Nothing

   D. The Linux Loader

5. Which of the following levels of RAID is a disk mirror?

   A. RAID 0

   B. RAID 1

   C. RAID 5

   D. RAID 6

6. There are two hard drives on the computer, and you see **root (hd0,1)** in the GRUB configuration file. Where is the /boot directory partition?

   A. Not enough information

   B. The first partition of the first hard drive

   C. The second partition of the first hard drive

   D. The first partition of the second hard drive

7. Which of the following commands would you use to add to the available space on a logical volume?

   A. pvextend

   B. lvextend

   C. vgextend

   D. lvcreate

8. If the network address is 192.168.0.0 and the subnet mask is 255.255.254.0, what is the last available IP address that can be assigned to a computer?

   A. 192.168.0.254

   B. 192.168.1.254

   C. 192.168.0.255

   D. 192.168.1.255

9. What is the directory associated with configuration files for the Internet Super Server?

   A. /etc/inetd.d/

   B. /etc/xinetd.d/

   C. /etc/inetd.conf

   D. /etc/xinetd.conf

10. Which of the following commands unpacks a Gzipped tar archive?

    A. tar czvf kernel.tar.gz

    B. tar cjvf kernel.tar.gz

    C. tar xzf kernel.tar.gz

    D. tar xjf kernel.tar.gz

REVIEW ANSWERS

1. **B**   Dead keys work with control keys to create special characters such as those with accents.

2. **C**   Journaling can overload media the size of a regular floppy disk. The ext3, ReiserFS, and XFS filesystems all support journaling.

3. **D**   Linux reads the fat32 Microsoft formatted filesystem by default; it may be labeled as vfat. Microsoft operating systems need special software to read Linux filesystems such as ext3, ReiserFS, and XFS.

4. **C**   If you've already installed GRUB, there should already be a pointer to the configuration file, so no changes to the MBR are required.

5. **B**   RAID 1 is a disk mirror.

6. **C**   Break down the **root (hd0,1)** directive. The 0 is associated with the first hard drive. The 1 which follows is associated with the second partition. Alternatively, if it were the first partition of the first hard drive, the directive would be **root (hd0,0)**.

7. **B**   The **lvextend** command can be used to add to the space allocated to a logical volume. See Table 2.1 (and the man pages) for an explanation of the other commands.

8. **B**   A subnet mask of 255.255.254.0 has 23 bits, leaving 9 bits or, more precisely, $2^9 - 2 = 510$ available IP addresses. The last available IP address in the 192.168.0.0 network based on this range is 192.168.1.254. Answer A would be correct if the subnet mask were 255.255.255.0. Answer C would be a broadcast address if the subnet mask were 255.255.255.0. Answer D is a subnet mask for the given network.

9. **B**   The directory associated with Internet Super Server configuration files is /etc/xinetd.d/. The /etc/xinetd.conf and /etc/inetd.conf files are regular configuration files associated with the Internet Super Server.

10. **C**   The **tar xzf** command unzips a Gzipped tar archive. In the chapter, there was reference to a **v** switch, and while that provides more information about what happens during the command, it's not required.

P A R T

II

Managing Linux Users, Files, Packages, Processes, and Services

Managing Files
and Directories

	NEWBIE	SOME EXPERIENCE	VETERAN
ETA	60+ hours	16 hours	4 hours

This chapter is focused on basic command-line skills. Most basic is the ability to create files and directories. You also need to know how to manage and edit text files, search for and through files and directories, create links, manage ownership and permissions, redirect command input and output, and configure basic scripts.

The commands are based on the default Linux shell, bash. It's an acronym for the Bourne Again SHell, which tells us that it's a derivative of the Bourne shell. While there are several other command-line shells available for Linux, this book focuses on bash. And the Linux+ objectives don't suggest any shell other than bash.

Local Lingo

Shell   A command-line user interface designed to control the operating system. The commands associated with Linux shells can be combined into executable files, which makes a shell also a scripting language of sorts. Available Linux shells include bash, ksh, zsh, ash, and dash.

Given the space constraints of this series, I can't cover the command line in sufficient detail for a user who is new to Linux. There are many excellent books dedicated to helping administrators manage Linux from the command line.

Travel Advisory

If you feel the need for more information on the command line, read *Fedora 7 and Red Hat Enterprise Linux: The Complete Reference*, by Richard Peterson (McGraw-Hill, 2007).

Objective 3.01

Work with Files and Directories

Before working with files and directories, you need a grounding in basic navigation at the command-line interface. This requires an understanding of basic concepts such as the tilde symbol (~) for the home directory and the **PATH**, as well as commands such as **pwd**, **cd**, and **ls**. The **find** and **locate** commands can help you keep track. The **grep** command can help search for text inside files. The **diff** command can help find differences between files.

Basic Navigation

To navigate around Linux files and directories, you need to know a few basic commands to tell you where you are, what files are there with you, and how to get around the directory hierarchy. You also need knowledge of basic concepts such as the dot, relative and absolute paths, and hidden files.

The Tilde (~)

First, every Linux user has a home directory. You can use the tilde (~) to represent the home directory of any currently active user. For example, if your username is gordonb, your home directory is /home/gordonb. If you've logged in as the root user, the home directory is /root. Thus, the effect of the **cd ~** command depends on your username. For example, if you've logged in as user mj, the **cd ~** command brings you to the /home/mj directory. If you've logged in as the root user, this command brings you to the /root directory. Similarly, you can list the contents of your home directory from anywhere in the directory tree with the **ls ~** command.

Directories as a Dot (.) and a Double Dot (..)

In the bash shell, you can represent the current directory as a dot. Try the **ls .** command; it should show all files in the current directory. If there's a script in the current directory, you can run it by itself only if it's in your **PATH**, as defined in the next section. Otherwise, you could run a script named *program* in the current directory only with the dot, as follows:

```
./program
```

But there's more. If you want to work with files in the parent directory, you can use the double dot. For example, when I'm working in my home directory and run the **ls ..** command, I get the following output, which is the same as running **ls /home**:

```
aquota.group  donna       johnbull    michael test1
aquota.user   lost+found  PublicShare test2
```

You can go further; when I run **ls ../..** from my home directory, I get the contents of the top-level root (/) directory:

```
bin   dos   inst        media net   root     srv usr xen
boot  etc   lib         misc  opt   sbin     sys var
dev   home  lost+found  mnt   proc  selinux  tmp www      .
```

Hidden Files

Hidden files in any Linux directory start with a dot. If you run the **ls -a** command in any home directory, you'll see files like .bashrc and .bash_history. Incidentally, the dot can also be used to represent the current directory; for example, if you run a command like **cp -r . /destdir**, the command copies all hidden and regular files and directories recursively to the destination directory named /destdir.

Wildcards

Two special characters in the bash shell are variations on the generic concept of wildcards. These characters are the asterisk (*) and the question mark (?). The asterisk represents zero or more letters and/or numbers. One question mark represents one alphanumeric character. For example, the following command would return a list of all files in the local directory that end with the letter *h*:

```
# ls *h
```

If you have a file named *h*, it would also be part of the list. Alternatively, the following command returns a list of all files with three alphanumeric characters that end with *h*:

```
# ls ??h
```

Unlike the previous command, files with names like *h* or *oh* would not be part of the list. But files with names like *Doh* would be. More complex file searches are possible. For example, the command

```
# ls ?on?
```

would return files with names such as tone, bone, zonk, mona, and so on. It would not list filenames such as crayons, Anthony, or bon.

It's also possible to specify a range of characters in a wildcard. Square brackets ([]) can define a range of characters associated with different files. For example, the following command uses a wildcard to define TIF images for this chapter:

```
# ls f030[1234].tif
```

This is another command that results in the same wildcard:

```
# ls f030[1-4].tif
```

The square brackets work just as well for upper- and lowercase characters. The following commands search for f0301a.tif through f0301d.tif, and f0301E.tif through f0301H.tif. Remember, Linux is case sensitive, so f0301.tif is a completely different file from f0301.TIF.

```
# ls f0301[a-d].tif
# ls f0301[E-H].tif
```

The PATH

One critical variable is the **PATH**, which can be checked at the command line with the **echo $PATH** command. The directories listed in the **PATH** are automatically searched when you try to run a command. For example, if you want to run the **fdisk** command from the /sbin directory, you could do it with the following command:

```
$ /sbin/fdisk
```

However, if the /sbin directory is in your **PATH**, you don't need the leading /**sbin** to call out the command; the following will work:

```
$ fdisk
```

You can easily change the **PATH** variable. For example, if you want to add the /sbin directory to your **PATH**, just run the following commands:

```
# PATH=$PATH:/sbin
# export PATH
```

To make sure the new **PATH** is in effect the next time you log in, add the previous commands to hidden files such as .bash_profile and .profile in your home directory. To change the **PATH** for all users, add these commands to the /etc/profile or /etc/bashrc configuration files.

Exam Tip

If you run the **echo $PATH** command and see a dot, it's a security risk. Crackers who break into the system can load and run their scripts from the local directory. Similar risks are associated with a dot in front of a directory name in the **$PATH**, as files in those directories are hidden.

Paths

Besides the **PATH** variable, there are two other path concepts associated with Linux directories: absolute paths and relative paths. An *absolute path* describes the complete directory structure based on the top-level directory, root (/). A *relative path* is based on the current directory, and does not include the leading slash.

The difference between an absolute path and a relative path is important. Absolute paths are essential, especially when you're creating a script. Otherwise, scripts executed from other directories may lead to unintended consequences.

pwd

In many configurations, you may not know where you are relative to the root (/) directory. The **pwd** command, which is short for print working directory, can specify where you are in the directory tree. Once you know where you are, you can determine whether you need to move to a different directory.

cd

It's easy to change directories in Linux. Just use **cd** and cite the absolute path of the desired directory. If you use the relative path, just remember that your final destination depends on the current directory. If you run **cd** by itself, it navigates to the home directory of the active account.

ls

The most basic of commands, **ls** lists the files in the current directory. But the Linux **ls** command, with the right switches, can be quite powerful. It can tell you everything about a file, such as creation date, last access date, and size. It can help you organize the listing of files in just about any desired order. Important variations on this command include **ls -a** to reveal hidden files (which start with a dot), **ls -l** for long listings, **ls -t** for a time-based list, and **ls -i** for inode numbers. You can combine switches; I often use the **ls -ltr** command to display the most recently changed files last.

Exam Tip

Try out the different **ls** command switches. See what it does on your system, what files it reveals, and what information is included.

Learn as much as you can about the **ls** command. For example, per the man page, the **ls -l** command returns output such as the following:

```
-rw-------  2 root root   1158 Jun  6 15:23 grub.conf
-rw-r--r--  1 root root   6720 Mar 15 08:22 iso9660_stage1_5
-rw-r--r--  1 root root   8192 Mar 15 08:22 jfs_stage1_5
lrwxrwxrwx  1 root root     11 Mar 15 08:22 menu.lst -> ./grub.conf
```

The columns are as defined in Table 3.1, with references to sections later in this chapter where applicable.

Finding More with whereis

As suggested by the Linux+ objectives, you should have 6 to 12 months of experience with Linux, so much of this chapter should just be a review. But there are helpful tips and tricks, such as the **whereis** command, which can identify the full path to a command, as well as the location of the man page. The importance of documentation and different types of man pages is discussed in the Chapter 10 section "Access System Documentation."

TABLE 3.1	**ls -l** Output Columns
Column	**Description**
1	File type and permissions; discussed later in "Modify Ownership and Permissions"
2	Number of links to the file; discussed later in "Create Linked Files"
3	User owner; discussed later in "Modify Ownership and Permissions"
4	Group owner; discussed later in "Modify Ownership and Permissions"
5	Size, in bytes
6	Date and time of last modification; time is omitted if the date is more than six months old
7	Filename; an arrow (->) pointing to another filename indicates a soft link

Using the find and locate Commands

There are two basic commands used for file searches: **find** and **locate**. Once you know these commands, you'll know what to do to locate that missing file, or those files (or possibly worms) that may have been stored in obscure locations by that now departed employee.

> **Travel Advisory**
>
> If you run the **find** command from a regular account, you may get a number of "Permission denied" messages if your search includes directories limited to users with administrative permissions.

find

The **find** command searches through directories and subdirectories for a desired file. For example, if you wanted to find the directory with the xorg.conf GUI configuration file, you could use the following command, which would start the search in the top-level root (/) directory:

```
# find / -name xorg.conf
```

But this search on my old laptop computer (on an older version of Linux) with a 200 MHz CPU took several minutes. You may get similar results when multiple virtual machines load a modern system. Alternatively, if you already know that this file is located in the /etc subdirectory tree, you could start in that directory with the following command:

```
# find /etc -name xorg.conf
```

The **find** command is flexible; with the **-uid** and **-gid** switches, it can identify all files associated with a specific user ID. (For more information on user and group IDs, see the Chapter 5 section "Manage User Accounts.") For example, if user johnbull (with a user ID of 600) has just left the company and has been identified as a cracker, you can see if any of his files are still on the system with the following command:

```
# find / -uid 600
```

Yes, you can cite the user or group directly; the following command would work for user johnbull:

```
# find / -user johnbull
```

> ### Local Lingo
>
> **Cracker** and **Hacker**   A *cracker* is someone who creates viruses and more for malicious purposes. In the Linux community, some think of crackers as people who create viruses and send spam, in comparison to *hackers*, who just want to improve software.

There are several other important switches. For example, **-xdev** can help avoid searches through mounted network and virtual partitions. Several **find** switches are described in Table 3.2.

TABLE 3.2   Command Switches for **find**

Switch for find	Description
-atime +*n*	Where the last access time was more than *n* days ago
-gid *n*	Associated with GID number *n*
-group *name*	Associated with the group named *name*
-name *pattern*	Searches for a filename with *pattern*; can use globbing
-nogroup	Finds files owned by no current group or GID
-nouser	Finds files owned by no current user or UID; like -nogroup, possible sign of cracked files
-perm *octal*	Identifies files with *octal* permissions
-type *t*	Finds files where *t* is the file type, such as *d* for directories and *l* for soft links
-uid *n*	Associated with UID number *n*
-user *name*	Associated with the user named *name*
-xdev	Does not search through directories mounted on other partitions

Local Lingo

Globbing The Linux term for wildcards such as * and ?.

locate

If the **find** command takes too much time, Linux includes a default database of all files and directories. Searches with the **locate** command are almost instantaneous, and don't even require the full filename. The drawback is that the **locate** command database is normally updated only once each day.

Exam Tip

While **locate** is faster than **find**, it's less accurate, because it's updated maybe once per day. Also, the **locate** command is available in only two of the four selected Linux distributions (Red Hat and Turbolinux).

Searching with grep

The **grep** command uses a search term to look through a file. It returns the full line that contains the search term. For example, **grep 'Michael Jang' /etc/passwd** looks for my name in the /etc/passwd file.

One specialized version of the **grep** command is **egrep**. This command is more forgiving; it allows you to use some unusual characters in your search, including +, ?, |, (, and). While it's possible to set up **grep** to search for these characters with the help of the backslash, the command can be awkward to use.

Comparing with diff

The **diff** command is relatively straightforward. It compares the contents of two different files. It's a relatively easy way to compare the contents of a current text file with a backup. Assuming /etc/passwd.bak is an older password file, the following command should reveal relatively new users:

```
# diff /etc/passwd /etc/passwd.bak
```

The following output shows that user test3 is listed only in /etc/passwd.bak; in other words, test3 is no longer a valid user on the local system. And there's a new user, named johnbull.

```
38a39
> test3:x:504:504::/home/test3:/bin/bash
45d45
< johnbull:x:507:507::/home/johnbull:/bin/bash
```

If there's no output, there's no difference between the two files.

Create Files and Directories

Objective 3.02

Just about everything in Linux is associated with a file. Directories are special kinds of files. Hardware device drivers are files. The nodes associated with active USB connections are files. Specialized files are linked to others, and more. This section focuses on typical commands used to create and modify files and directories.

Exam Tip

The best way to learn a command is to run it. Try each of these commands on your system. To learn more, read the man page associated with a command, and try at least a few of the command switches.

Before reading more of this section, run the **alias** command. It reviews the aliases associated with your account. You'll see output similar to

```
alias cp='cp -i'
```

which means that when you run the **cp** command, the shell thinks you want to run the **cp** command with the -i switch.

Creating Files with touch

The simplest way to create a new file is with the **touch** command, with the desired filename. For example, the command

```
# touch abc
```

creates the file named abc. While it's an empty file (0 bytes), it occupies an inode. If you run the **touch** command on an existing file, it applies the current date to the file, as if you've just edited it.

Creating Files with cp

The command used to copy files is **cp**. The simplest version of this command is cp *file1 file2*, where the contents of *file1* are copied and placed in destination *file2*. If *file2* doesn't already exist, it's created. Unless you see cp='**cp -i**' in the output to the **alias** command, it overwrites existing destination files without prompting. With the right switches, it copies all files in a directory, including subdirectories. For several examples of how the **cp** command works, review Table 3.3.

TABLE 3.3	cp Commands
Command	**Result**
cp *file1 file2*	Copies the contents of source *file1* to destination *file2*.
cp -p *file1 file2*	Copies the contents of source *file1* to destination *file2*, including the date stamp on *file1*.
cp -d *file1 file2*	Copies source *file1* to destination *file2*, including any links from *file1*.
cp *file* dir1*	Copies all files with names that start with *file* to destination directory *dir1*.
cp -i *file1 file2*	If you already have a file named *file2*, this command prompts for confirmation before overwriting *file2*.
cp -f *file1 file2*	If you already have a file named *file2*, this forces overwriting of *file2*.
cp -r *dir1 dir2*	Copies the contents of the directory named *dir1*, including subdirectories, to directory *dir2*.
cp -a *dir1 dir2*	Equivalent to **cp -dpr**; copies the contents of the directory named *dir1*, including subdirectories, to directory *dir2*, while preserving file times and links.

Modifying Filenames with mv

There is no rename command in Linux. To rename a file, the bash shell supports the **mv** command, which changes the name and possibly the directory where a file is located. Unless you move a file to a directory mounted on a different partition, everything else about the file stays the same. Several examples of how the **mv** command works are shown in Table 3.4.

Deleting Files with rm

The Linux command associated with deleting a file is **rm**. With the correct switches, this command can be used to delete files and directories. Several examples of the **rm** command are shown in Table 3.5.

TABLE 3.4	mv Commands
Command	**Result**
mv *file1 file2*	Changes the name of *file1* to destination *file2*, preserving the date stamp.
mv *file* dir1*	Moves all files with names that start with *file* to directory *dir1*.
mv -i *file1 file2*	If you already have a file named *file2*, this command prompts for confirmation before overwriting *file2*.
mv -f *file1 file2*	If you already have a file named *file2*, this command forces overwriting of *file2*.

TABLE 3.5	**rm** Commands

Command	Result
rm *file1*	Deletes *file1*.
rm -i *dir1*	Deletes *dir1* after prompting for confirmation.
rm -f *file1*	Deletes *file1* without prompting for confirmation.
rm -r *	Deletes files recursively; subdirectories (and files within) are also deleted.

Do not run the **rm** command as the root or superuser unless absolutely necessary. The consequences can be awful. For example, if user johndoe has left your company, you may want to delete all files in his home directory. The most direct way to do this is with the **rm -rf /home/johndoe** command. But if you make a mistake and enter a space between the first slash and **home**, the command would first delete all the files and directories under the root (/) directory. That is every file and directory on your Linux system. Then it would try to delete all the files in the home/johndoe subdirectory. You would have to reload all of your files from a backup (you have backed up your system, haven't you?).

Creating and Removing Directories with mkdir and rmdir

Although a directory is just a special file, there are special commands to create and delete directories. The **mkdir** command can create directories. With the right switches, as shown in Table 3.6, you can do a bit more.

Here's a little trick—try creating a hidden directory with a command like this:

```
# mkdir .trick
```

This command creates a hidden directory that isn't shown with a regular **ls** command. It's a common way crackers try to hide what they do on Linux systems. While we don't endorse cracking, you need to know what a cracker might do.

TABLE 3.6	**mkdir** Commands

Command	Result
mkdir -p *dir1/dir2*	Creates directory *dir1/dir2*. If *dir1* doesn't already exist, the -p switch creates it as well. Both *dir1* and *dir2* are subdirectories of the current directory.
mkdir -m 755 *dir3*	Creates a local *dir3* directory, with rwx permissions for the owner and r-x for other users. Permissions are described in more detail later in this chapter in "Modify Ownership and Permissions."

Exam Tip
Know the ins and outs of the **mkdir** command.

In contrast, the **rmdir** command deletes directories…if they're empty. You can delete several levels of directories if the first directory deleted empties the next directory. For example, assume there are no files in the dir1/dir2/dir3 subdirectory, and there's no other file in the dir2 directory. You can then delete all three levels of directories with the following command:

```
# rmdir -p dir1/dir2/dir3
```

Remember that the **rm** command, with appropriate switches, can also delete directories.

 **Objective 3.03 Manage Text Files**

There are a number of different commands available for reading and managing files in the bash shell. They include several file reading commands. They can help manage text streams and manipulate files with utilities such as **sed** and **awk**. Most important are the command-line file editors, because the GUI is not always available or even installed. The editor explicitly listed in the Linux+ objectives is **vi**.

File Reading Commands

Commands such as **file**, **cat**, **more**, **less**, **head**, and **tail** can help verify file types, read files from top to bottom, and more. They're suited to Linux/Unix, with the focus on text files for configuration.

file

There are no standard file extensions in Linux. Commands don't end in .com, and applications don't end in .exe. While there are a few configuration files that end in .conf, most text files don't bother with an extension. The **file** command can help differentiate between file types in a directory. Take a look at the sample output shown in Figure 3.1.

```
[root@enterprise5fc6d ~]# file *
0201.avi:                          RIFF (little-endian) data, AVI, 800 x 600, 10.00 f
ps, video:, audio: uncompressed PCM (mono, 44100 Hz)
anaconda-ks.cfg:                   ASCII English text
celica-2006112901-disk2.iso:       ISO 9660 CD-ROM filesystem data UDF filesystem dat
a (unknown version, id 'NSR01') 'Turbolinux2               ' (bootable)
CentOS-5.0-i386-bin-DVD:           directory
CentOS-5.0-i386-bin-DVD.iso:       ISO 9660 CD-ROM filesystem data UDF filesystem dat
a (unknown version, id 'NSR01') 'CentOS_5.0_Final          ' (bootable)
CentOS-5.0-i386-bin-DVD.torrent:   BitTorrent file
CentOS-5.0-i386-bin-of6.iso:       HTML document text
cupsd.conf:                        ASCII English text, with very long lines
ddrive:                            directory
Desktop:                           directory
install.log:                       ASCII text
install.log.syslog:                ASCII text
kernel-devel-2.6.19-1.2911.6.5.fc6.x86_64.rpm: RPM v3 bin i386 kernel-devel-2.6.19-1.2911.6.5.
mbox:                              ASCII mail text
scsrun.log:                        ASCII text
sda9:                              directory
test:                              directory
upgrade.log:                       ASCII text
upgrade.log.syslog:                ASCII text
vmware-any-any-update110:          setgid directory
vmware-any-any-update110.tar.gz:   gzip compressed data, from Unix, last modified: Su
n May 13 23:09:40 2007
[root@enterprise5fc6d ~]#
```

FIGURE 3.1   Output from the **file** command

cat
The **cat** command scrolls the contents of a file across the screen. You can use **cat** on any file for which you have the appropriate permissions. For example, if you want to see the contents of the file named cradle in the current directory, type the following command:

```
# cat cradle
```

head and tail
Although **head** and **tail** are two separate commands, they are like two sides of the same coin. By default, **head** returns the first ten lines of a file, and **tail** returns the last ten lines of a file. If you're not already familiar with this command, try it out on some log files:

```
# head /var/log/messages
# tail /var/log/messages
```

If you need just a bit more information from the front or end of a file, you can change the number of lines read. For example, to see the last 20 lines of /etc/passwd, use the following command:

```
# tail -n20 /etc/passwd
```

more and less
Although **more** and **less** are two separate but related commands, they are not exact opposites. Each command delivers text files as standard output, one screen at

a time. Ironically, **less** is more versatile; unlike **more**, it allows scrolling up and down with the PAGE UP and PAGE DOWN keys.

Because they don't need to read in the whole file, these commands can open a file more quickly than can a text editor such as **vi**. The **less** command also supports the use of some **vi** commands to search through the file.

The Stream Editor, sed

The **sed** command, which controls the stream editor, allows you to search for and change specified words or even text streams in a file. For example, the following command changes the first instance of the word Windows to the word Linux in each line of the file opsys, and writes the result to the file betteropsys:

```
# sed 's/Windows/Linux/' opsys > betteropsys
```

But you may want to do more. If a line contains more than one instance of Windows, the preceding **sed** command does not change the second instance of that word. To make a change to every appearance of Windows, add a "global" suffix to the command:

```
# sed 's/Windows/Linux/g' opsys > betteropsys
```

Note that the result is written to a second file, betteropsys; otherwise, the changes are not saved.

Exam Tip
Know how to change individual words globally from a file with the **sed** command.

The awk Text Manipulation Tool

The **awk** command, named for its developers (Aho, Weinberger, and Kernighan), is more of a database manipulation tool—its authors call it a programming language. It can identify lines with a keyword and read out the text from a specified column in that line. Try it out with the /etc/passwd file. To make it read out the name of every user with "Mike" in the comment column, use the following command:

```
# awk '/Mike/ {print $1}' /etc/passwd
```

The Visual Editor

While emacs may be the most popular and flexible text editor in the world of Linux, I believe every administrator needs at least a basic knowledge of **vi**, which may help you save a broken system. If you ever have to restore a critical configuration file using an emergency boot CD, **vi** may be the only editor available.

In reality, current Linux distributions use an enhanced version of the **vi** editor, known as **vim**, in common use when the Linux+ objectives were released. You should know how to use the two basic modes of **vi**: command and insert. When you use **vi** to open a file, it opens in command mode. Some of the commands start insert mode. Opening a file is easy: just use the **vi** *filename* command. By default, this starts **vi** in command mode. An example of **vi** with the /etc/inittab file is shown in Figure 3.2.

This section provides only the briefest of introductions to the **vi** editor. For more information, there are a number of books available that cover **vi** in depth, and an online book available at www.vim.org. Alternatively, a tutorial can be found through the **vimtutor** command.

Exam Tip
Know how to work the **vi** command mode in detail.

vi Command Mode

In command mode, you can do just about everything you need to do to a text file, except add new text. The options in command mode are broad and varied, and they are the subject of a number of book-length texts. In summary, **vi** requires eight critical command skills:

- **Open** To open a file in the **vi** editor from the command-line interface, run the **vi** *filename* command.

- **Search** Start with a forward slash, followed by the search term. Remember, Linux is case sensitive, so if you're searching for "Michael" in /etc/passwd, use the **/Michael** (not **/michael**) command.

- **Write** To save your changes, use the **w** command. You can combine commands: for example, **:wq** writes the file and exits **vi**. Alternatively, **:x** is equivalent to **:wq**.

- **Close** To leave **vi**, use the **:q** command.

- **Abandon** If you want to abandon any changes that you've made, use the **:q!** command.

- **Edit** You can use a number of commands to edit files through **vi**, such as **x**, which deletes the currently highlighted character; **dw**, which deletes the currently highlighted word; and **dd**, which deletes the current line. Remember, **p** places text from a buffer, and **U** restores text from a previous change.

```
#
# inittab        This file describes how the INIT process should set up
#                the system in a certain run-level.
#
# Author:        Miquel van Smoorenburg, <miquels@drinkel.nl.mugnet.org>
#                Modified for RHS Linux by Marc Ewing and Donnie Barnes
#                Modified for TurboLinux by Christian Holtje
#                                         <docwhat@turbolinux.com>
#                Modified for TurboLinux by Go Taniguchi
#                                         <go@turbolinux.co.jp>
#

# Default runlevel. The runlevels used by RHS are:
#   0 - halt (Do NOT set initdefault to this)
#   1 - Single user mode
#   2 - Multiuser, without NFS (The same as 3, if you do not have networking)
#   3 - Full multiuser mode
#   4 - unused
#   5 - X11
#   6 - reboot (Do NOT set initdefault to this)
#
id:3:initdefault:

/etc/inittab                                        23.0-1           Top
```

FIGURE 3.2   The **vi** editor with /etc/inittab

- **Insert**   A number of commands allow you to start insert mode, including **i** to start inserting text at the current position of the editor, and **o** to open up a new line immediately below the current position of the cursor.

- **Replace**   What you know about the **sed** command should help here. For example, if you want to replace the first instance of bash with ksh for lines 40 through 45 in /etc/passwd, type **:40,45s/bash/ksh/**.

In addition, if you want to run a regular shell command from inside the **vi** editor, the colon and exclamation point can help. For example, the following command from the **vi** editor in command mode reads a list of configuration files in the /etc directory in long listing format (-l), without leaving the **vi** editor:

```
:! ls -l /etc | less
```

Basic Text Editing

In modern Linux systems, editing files with **vi** is easy. Just use the normal navigation keys (arrow keys, PAGE UP, and PAGE DOWN), and then one of the basic commands such as **i** or **o** to start **vi**'s insert mode, and type your changes directly into the file.

When you're finished with insert mode, press the ESC key to return to command mode. You can then save your changes or abandon them and exit **vi**.

Travel Advisory

There are several specialized variations on the **vi** command. Three are **vipw**, **vigw**, and **visudo**, which edit /etc/passwd, /etc/group, and /etc/sudoers, respectively.

 **Create Linked Files**

L inked files can save space. They can also represent files in directories expected by installation and build programs such as tarballs and even the Linux kernel. There are two types of linked files: hard and soft.

Exam Tip

When creating a linked file, the existing file comes first; the new file comes second.

Hard Links

Hard links represent a copy of the file. The file is still stored on the same location on the disc. As long as the hard link is made within the same partition, the inode numbers are identical. You could delete a hard-linked file in one directory, and it would still exist in the other directory. For example, the following command creates a hard link from the actual Samba configuration file to smb.conf in the local directory:

```
# ln /etc/samba/smb.conf smb.conf
```

Soft Links

A soft link serves as a redirect; when opening a file created with a soft link, you're directed to the original file. If the original file is deleted, the file is lost. While the soft link is still there, it has nowhere to go. The following command is an example of how to create a soft link:

```
# ln -s /etc/samba/smb.conf smb.conf
```

Modify Ownership and Permissions

Objective 3.05

One aspect of security is the control of files and directories, based on owner-ship and permissions. Ownership falls into three categories: the user, the group, and everyone else. Once ownership is established, permissions can be defined based on the different levels of file ownership. Remember, a directory is just a specialized kind of file, so everything in this section applies to directories as well.

Permissions are defined by three bits, associated with the user, the group, and everyone else. As computer code is binary, and $2^3 = 8$, this is known as the octal method for defining permissions, which can help redefine them with the **chmod** command, add the so-called sticky bits, and define default permissions for new files.

Of course, anything in this section can be overridden by the root administrative user.

File Ownership

Every file has two owners: a user and a group. Linux, like Unix, is configured with users and groups. Everyone who uses Linux is set up with a username, even if it's just "guest." Take a look at /etc/passwd. One version of this file is shown in Figure 3.3.

openSUSE

```
at:x:25:25:Batch jobs daemon:/var/spool/atjobs:/bin/bash
bin:x:1:1:bin:/bin:/bin/bash
daemon:x:2:2:Daemon:/sbin:/bin/bash
ftp:x:40:49:FTP account:/srv/ftp:/bin/bash
games:x:12:100:Games account:/var/games:/bin/bash
haldaemon:x:101:102:User for haldaemon:/var/run/hal:/bin/false
lp:x:4:7:Printing daemon:/var/spool/lpd:/bin/bash
mail:x:8:12:Mailer daemon:/var/spool/clientmqueue:/bin/false
man:x:13:62:Manual pages viewer:/var/cache/man:/bin/bash
messagebus:x:100:101:User for D-Bus:/var/run/dbus:/bin/false
news:x:9:13:News system:/etc/news:/bin/bash
nobody:x:65534:65533:nobody:/var/lib/nobody:/bin/bash
ntp:x:74:103:NTP daemon:/var/lib/ntp:/bin/false
postfix:x:51:51:Postfix Daemon:/var/spool/postfix:/bin/false
root:x:0:0:root:/root:/bin/bash
sshd:x:71:65:SSH daemon:/var/lib/sshd:/bin/false
suse-ncc:x:102:104:Novell Customer Center User:/var/lib/YaST2/suse-ncc-fakehome:/bin/bash
uucp:x:10:14:Unix-to-Unix CoPy system:/etc/uucp:/bin/bash
wwwrun:x:30:8:WWW daemon apache:/var/lib/wwwrun:/bin/false
michael:x:1000:100:Michael Jang:/home/michael:/bin/bash
donna:x:1001:100::/home/donna:/bin/bash
~
~
~
~
~
~
~
~
"/etc/passwd" 21L, 1090C
```
                                                    1,1   All

FIGURE 3.3   /etc/passwd

All kinds of usernames are listed in /etc/passwd. Even a number of Linux services, such as mail, news, ftp, and apache, have their own usernames. In any case, /etc/passwd follows a specific format, described in more detail in the Chapter 5 section "Manage User Accounts." For now, note that the only users shown in this file are michael and donna, their user IDs (UID) are 1000 and 1001, and their home directories match their usernames. Both users have a group ID (GID) of 100.

In this case, they happen to be members of the same group. For the other selected distributions, each user gets their own private group. In other words, the first regular user in Red Hat, Mandriva, and Turbolinux has both a UID and GID of 500. The next user gets both a UID and GID of 501, and so on.

Changing Ownership with chown and chgrp

Every file has a user and a group owner. Run the ls -l command. Every file is listed with these owners. For example, when I run the command in my openSUSE home directory, I get the output shown in Figure 3.4, where the user who owns the files (and directories) is michael, and the group owner is users.

The **chown** command can change the user and group owners. Normally, it's just used to change the owner; the following command changes ownership of file abc to donna:

```
# chown donna abc
```

To change both the user and group owners, add a colon or period between the user and group; for example, the following command changes the user and group owner of file abc to donna and project, respectively:

```
# chown donna:project abc
```

Naturally, the **chgrp** command is more limited, as it can only change the group owner of a file. As with the **cp** command, changes can be made recursively. If I wanted to change the user and group ownership of all files and directories within the Documents subdirectory to donna and project, I'd just add the -R switch:

```
# chown -R donna:project abc
```

```
michael@SUSEvmware:~> ls -l
total 16
-rw-r--r-- 1 michael users  553 2007-07-06 11:40 abc
drwxr-xr-x 2 michael users 4096 2007-06-29 14:41 bin
drwx------ 2 michael users 4096 2007-06-29 14:41 Documents
drwxr-xr-x 2 michael users 4096 2007-06-29 14:41 public_html
michael@SUSEvmware:~>
```

FIGURE 3.4   ls -l and file ownership

Exam Tip

One other way to modify group ownership is to remove a target owner from that group. For example, if user katie is no longer a member of the project group, use the **vigr** command to remove katie from that group in the /etc/group and /etc/gshadow files.

Defining Permissions, Octally

Linux file permissions are straightforward. Consider the following output from **ls -l /usr/sbin/useradd**:

```
-rwxr-xr-x  1 root   root    103064 Nov 29 2006  /usr/sbin/useradd
```

The permissions are shown on the left side of the listing. Ten positions are available for characters. The first character determines whether it's a regular or a special file. The remaining nine characters are grouped in threes, applicable to the file owner (user), the group owner, and everyone else on that Linux system. The letters are straightforward: r = read, w = write, x = execute. These characters are described in Table 3.7.

To define read, write, and execute permissions in octal format, more numbers are required. To avoid getting into details of translating base 2 to base 10, Table 3.8 simply describes the value associated with different combinations of permissions. For example, rx = 5 because r is associated with 4 and x is associated with 1.

Permissions on a Soft Link

One variation—when there's a soft link, that file may look like it has full permissions, as shown in this output:

```
lrwxrwxrwx 1 mike mike 19 Aug 29 21:33 smb.conf -> /etc/samba/smb.conf
```

TABLE 3.7 Description of File Permissions

Column	Description
1	Type of file; - = regular file, d = directory, b = device, l = linked file
234	Permissions granted to the owner of the file
567	Permissions granted to the group owner of the file
890	Permissions granted to all other users on the Linux system

TABLE 3.8	File Permissions Translated to Octal Format

Permission	Number
r	4
w	2
x	1
rx	5
wx	3
rwx	7

It seems to have full read, write, and execute permissions, and is owned by user and group mike. The *l* in the first column does indicate that the file is a link; and the arrow points to the original file, /etc/samba/smb.conf. But take a look at the permissions for this file:

```
-rw-r--r-- 1 root root 9861 Aug  2 17:30 /etc/samba/smb.conf
```

Note how ownership and permissions are different; when user mike opens the soft-linked smb.conf file, he doesn't get to write to that file. The permissions and ownership as applied to the soft-linked file are based on the permissions and ownership from the original file.

Permissions on a Hard Link

The change in permissions on a hard link are a bit more subtle. Actually, the change isn't to permissions, but check the difference in output from the **ls -l /etc/samba/smb.conf** command, before

```
-rw-r--r-- 1 root root 9861 Aug  2 17:30 /etc/samba/smb.conf
```

and after creating a hard link:

```
-rw-r--r-- 2 root root 9861 Aug  2 17:30 /etc/samba/smb.conf
```

The number that changed is a sign of the new hard link.

Changing Permissions with chmod

With the **chmod** command, it's possible to change permissions in octal format, or by directly citing the desired permissions. As one example, the **chmod 765** *filename* command provides:

- Read, write, and execute permissions for the user owner
- Read and write permissions for the group owner
- Read and execute permissions for everyone else

Alternatively, if the current permissions are as shown in this output to ls -l *filename*:

```
-r--r--r--  1 mike users  103064 Nov 29 2006  filename
```

you can set up the same permissions with the following command:

```
# chmod u+wx,g+w,o+x filename
```

In this case, u represents the user owner, g represents the group owner, and o represents everyone else (others). One option: if you wanted to make a file named *script* executable for all users, the a in the following command represents all users:

```
# chmod a+x script
```

Exam Tip

While you may not need to know specialized commands like **chmod a+x *script*** in practice, expect to know this level of detail for the Linux+ exam.

The SUID, SGID, and Sticky Bits

Specialized permissions are available, known as Set User ID (SUID), Set Group ID (SGID), and the sticky bit. To see files or directories associated with the SUID and sticky bits, run the **ls -l /usr/bin/passwd** and **ls -l /** commands. The *s* in the permissions column is the SUID bit.

```
-rwsr-xr-x 1 root root 28736 2007-04-05 01:54 /usr/bin/passwd
```

In contrast, the *t* in the permissions associated with the /tmp directory is the sticky bit:

```
drwxrwxrwt  11 root root  4096 2007-07-10 21:00 tmp
```

I know of no standard file or directory with the SGID bit. When configured, it includes an *s* in the group part of the permissions column. While SUID and SGID access reduces security for a specific file, it can help administrators avoid giving root-level access to more users.

The SUID Bit

The SUID bit allows normal users to run a script or program as the user who owns that script or program. For example, the **passwd** program has the SUID bit set by default and can be run by anyone as the root user. With Pluggable Authentication Modules, as discussed in the Chapter 8 section "Set Up Security Environment Files," regular users are allowed to change their own passwords.

To set the SUID bit on a file, run the following command:

```
# chmod u+s filename
```

Alternatively, if you're also setting rwx permissions for just the user (and read permissions for everyone else), the following command sets the SUID bit on the file:

```
# chmod 4744 filename
```

The SGID Bit

The SGID bit is commonly used for directories shared by a specific group of users. For example, the SGID bit set on a /home/supervisors directory, with a group owner of supervisors, allows each member of the supervisors group to add files to and read files from that directory. To set the SGID bit on a file, run the following command:

```
# chmod g+s directory
```

Alternatively, if you're also setting rwx permissions for just the group owner (and read permissions for everyone else), the following command sets the SGID bit on the file:

```
# chmod 2474 directory
```

The Sticky Bit

The sticky bit is usually applied to a directory. It allows files in the directory to be added and deleted by their owners. To set the sticky bit on a file, run the following command:

```
# chmod o+t directory
```

Alternatively, if you're also setting rwx permissions for all users, you can also set the sticky bit on a directory with the following octal command:

```
# chmod 1777 directory
```

Of course, variations are possible. For example, the following command sets read and write permissions for all users, with the SUID and sticky bits:

```
# chmod 5666 directory
```

Defining Default Permissions with umask

The way **umask** works in Linux may be surprising, especially if you're coming from a different Unix-style environment. The **umask** command cannot be configured to allow creation of new executable files. This promotes security: if fewer files are executable, fewer files pose a risk to your system.

Every time a new file is created, the permissions are based on the value of **umask**. In the past, the value of **umask** canceled out the value of numeric permissions on a file. For example, if the value of **umask** is 000, the default permissions for any file created by that user used to be $777 - 000 = 777$, which corresponds to read, write, and execute permissions for all users.

Run the **umask** command. You'll see a four-number output such as 0245. As of this writing, the first number in the **umask** output is always 0 and is not used. In the future, this first number may be usable to allow for new files that automatically include the SUID or SGID bit.

Also, no matter what the value of **umask**, new Linux files can no longer be automatically created with executable permissions. In other words, a **umask** value of 0454 leads to identical permissions on new files as a **umask** value of 0545. You need to use commands such as **chmod** to set executable permissions on a specific file.

So let us return to the original **umask** example of 000. In that case, default permissions for any file created with that value of **umask** are 666, which corresponds to read and write permissions for all users.

Objective 3.06   Shell Command Management

Linux uses three basic data streams. Data goes in, data comes out, and errors are sent in a different direction. These streams are known as standard input (stdin), standard output (stdout), and standard error (stderr).

Normally, input comes from the keyboard and goes out to the screen, while errors are sent to a buffer. Error messages are also sent to the display (as text stream 2). In the following example, *filename* is stdin to the **cat** command:

```
# cat filename
```

When you run **cat** *filename*, the contents of that file are sent to the screen as standard output. To help define standard input, it's helpful to understand how quotes work in the shell.

Standard Output

Standard output normally goes to the screen. It's easy to redirect. For example, the following command uses the right redirection arrow (>) to send the standard output of the **ls** command to the *filelist* file.

```
# ls > filelist
```

You can add standard output to the end of an existing file with a double redirection arrow with a command such as **ls** >> *filelist*.

Standard Input

You can redirect each of these streams to or from a file. For example, if you have a program named *database* and a data file with a lot of data, the contents of that data file can be sent to the database program with a left redirection arrow (<). As shown here, *datafile* is taken as standard input:

```
# database < datafile
```

Standard input can come from the left side of a command as well. For example, if you need to scroll through the boot messages, you can combine the **dmesg** and **less** commands with a pipe:

```
# dmesg | less
```

The output from **dmesg** is redirected as standard input to **less**, which then allows you to scroll through that output as if it were a separate file.

Error Output

If you believe that a particular program is generating errors, redirect the error stream from it with a command like the following:

```
# program 2> err-list
```

Quotes in the Shell

Linux shells typically read a command one word at a time. For example, when searching for a two-word term such as *Michael Jang*, quotes make sure that Linux looks for the complete term. For example, if you were to search for my name in /etc/passwd without quotes:

```
# grep Michael Jang /etc/passwd
```

the result would lead to an error:

```
grep: Jang: No such file or directory
/etc/passwd:michael:x:1000:100:Michael Jang:/home/michael:/bin/bash
```

In other words, the **grep** command searches for the term *Michael* in files named Jang and /etc/passwd. As there's no file named Jang in my directory, that's the error. For more information on the **grep** command, see the "Work with Files and Directories" section earlier in this chapter.

Quotes help define the standard input to a shell command. There are three types of quotes available in the bash shell: the single quote ('), the double quote ("), and the back quote (`).

Local Lingo

The back quote key is found directly above the TAB key on a standard U.S. keyboard.

Each type of quote has a distinct effect on variables such as **$PATH** and commands such as **date**. Specifically:

- **Single quotes**   The shell does not process any variables or commands inside the quotes.
- **Double quotes**   The shell processes variables but does not process commands.
- **Back quotes**   The shell processes all variables inside the quotes, and then tries to process every word inside the quotes as a command.

Before continuing on in this section, run the following commands:

```
$ NAME=michael
$ echo $NAME
$ date
```

The following examples illustrate the use of each type of quote. The **echo** command returns everything that follows as standard output. You should see *michael* in the output to **echo $NAME**, and the current date in the output to the **date** command. Now your system is ready for the following examples:

```
$ echo Welcome $NAME, the date is date
$ echo 'Welcome $NAME, the date is date'
$ echo "Welcome $NAME, the date is date"
$ echo "Welcome $NAME, the date is `date`"
```

Note the location and type of quote associated with each command. These commands return the following results, in order:

```
Welcome michael, the date is date
Welcome $NAME, the date is date
Welcome michael, the date is date
Welcome michael, the date is Wed Oct 11 11:57:33 PDT 2007
```

The first command has no quotes. The shell translated the **$NAME** variable, but did not run the **date** command. The result was sent as standard input to **echo**.

The second command used single quotes. Neither the **$NAME** variable nor the **date** command was processed before being sent as standard input to **echo**.

The third command used double quotes. While the result was the same as with no quotes, double quotes are still useful for commands such as **grep**.

The fourth and final command added back quotes around the **date** command, which runs the command, even if it's inside the double quotes. Then it sends the result as standard input to **echo**.

Interactivity

It is easy to interact with a history of Linux commands. At the command-line interface, type the **history** command. The result should be similar to what's shown in Figure 3.5. The list you see corresponds to the commands that have been run in that account, in order.

There are several ways to repeat previously used commands. The simplest way is to use the up and down arrow keys. At the command-line prompt, press the up arrow. You'll see the last command run on this account, at this console. Continue pressing the up arrow. You'll see more of the command history. You can reverse this process by pressing the down arrow.

If you know the command number, as shown in the output to the **history** command, you can run it again. For example, if I wanted to run command number 985 again (**find / -xdev -nouser** in Figure 3.5), I'd run

```
# !985
```

Alternatively, the first letter (or more) of a command in the history can help. Based on the history shown in Figure 3.5, the following command reruns **cp -r . /tmp/michael**:

```
# !c
```

```
981  find / -xdev -user michael -cmin +1000
982  find / -xdev -nouser
983  ls
984  chown 600 dkms-0-2.0.13-1.el5.rf.html
985  find / -xdev -nouser
986  find / -xdev -perm 777
987  ls -l /sbin/pvscan
988  find / -xdev -perm 777 | more
989  ls -l /bin/mailx
990  find / -xdev -size 1M
991  find / -xdev -size 1G
992  find / -xdev -type l
993  alias
994  cp . /tmp/
995  cp -r . /tmp/michael
996  ls -l /tmp/michael/
997  ls -la /tmp/michael/
998  ls .
999  echo $NAME
1000 exit
1001 history
[root@enterprise5hp ~]# █
```

FIGURE 3.5   Output from the **history** command

More letters can help. For example, based on the aforementioned history, the following command reruns **chown 600 dkms-0-2.0.13-1.el5.rf.html**:

```
# !ch
```

Command Completion

The bash shell allows you to use the TAB key to complete a command. For example, if you want to run the **xf86gammacfg** command, you don't have to type all 12 letters. In Red Hat distributions, all I need to type is

```
# xf8
```

and then press the TAB key, and bash completes the command:

```
# xf86gammacfg
```

If the letters you type correspond to the beginning of more than one command, you'll see a list. For example, in Mandriva 2007, when I type **ls** and press the TAB key twice, I see

```
ls    lsattr       lsdev    lsmod        lsof    lsscsi
ls-1  lsb_release  lshal    lsmod.static lspci   lsusb
```

This lists the commands that start with ls and returns to the command prompt with what was originally typed. In this case, type the third letter of the desired command and press the TAB key again to complete the command, or press TAB twice to narrow the choices.

Escaping Special Characters

There are a number of special characters described in this chapter, including the asterisk (*), the question mark (?), and even the space. While special characters such as the space can be managed with quotes, another method is to use the backslash.

For example, if you've mounted a Microsoft partition on /media/hda1, the following command would lead to errors:

```
# ls /media/hda1/Documents and Settings
```

but the following command would actually list the files and directories therein:

```
# ls /media/hda1/Documents\ and\ Settings
```

Consider one more example, based on the asterisks in the /etc/shadow file. If you tried searching for the asterisks with the following command, it would actually take the name of every file in the local directory as a search term for /etc/shadow:

```
# grep * /etc/shadow
```

In contrast, the backslash escapes the standard meaning of the asterisk as a wildcard, which allows it to be used as a search term:

```
# grep \* /etc/shadow
```

Objective 3.07 Create, Modify, and Run Basic Scripts

In essence, a shell script is a combination of commands, organized for a specific purpose. By definition, a shell script uses commands associated with the shell; for Linux, it's normally the default bash shell. This section describes some example scripts, and how to make them executable.

Shell Script Examples

All of the selected distributions include scripts in the /etc/cron.daily directory. As the name suggests, these scripts are run on a daily basis. (For more information, see the Chapter 5 section "Administrative Job Management.")

Those scripts using bash shell commands start with the following directive:

```
#!/bin/sh
```

This directive may be a bit misleading for some. In most cases, the # is associated with comments. While the **/bin/sh** is used to start the Bourne shell in some other distributions, it's generally soft linked to the bash shell, /bin/bash, in the selected distributions. In other words, the commands in the script can also be run at the bash command line.

Local Lingo
Shebang   The **#!** characters used together. Of course, it has nothing to do with a Latin pop star or a popular U.S. singing competition.

In addition to regular shell commands, stanzas can be constructed around conditional statements. This stanza from Red Hat's anacron script runs anacron if the anacron daemon isn't already running:

```
if [ ! -e /var/run/anacron.pid ]; then
    anacron -u cron.daily
fi
```

Of course, many **if** stanzas include an **else** and even **elseif** options if the conditional is not met. In any case, **if** stanzas end with an **fi**.

This next stanza from openSUSE's suse.de-backup-rpmdb script increments the RPM database filename until a new name is found. Note the **while** and **done** expressions bracketing this stanza. The presence of the **while** expression means the stanza is executed as long as the condition associated with the **while** directive is true.

```
while [ -e $NEWNAME -o -e $NEWNAME.gz ] ; do
    NEWNAME=$RPMDB_BACKUP_DIR/$PACKAGEDBFILE-$DATESTRING-$NUMBER
    NUMBER=`expr $NUMBER + 1`
done
```

Don't confuse Linux stanza scripts bounded by **while** and **done** with the **while** and **wend** directives commonly associated with the BASIC programming language.

Making a Shell Script Executable

Making a shell script executable is the easy part. You can do so with the **chmod** command, as described earlier in the "Modify Ownership and Permissions" section.

CHECKPOINT

✔**Objective 3.01: Work with Files and Directories**   When working with files and directories, there are basic concepts such as using the tilde for the current user's home directory and the dot for the current directory. Basic navigation commands include **cd**, **pwd**, and **ls**. Searches involve **find** and **locate**. Searches within files benefit from **grep**. Text file changes can be shown with **diff**.

✔**Objective 3.02: Create Files and Directories**   There are several different commands that can create, modify, and remove files and directories, including **touch**, **cp**, **mv**, **rm**, **mkdir**, and **rmdir**. With the right switches, the changes can apply to subdirectories.

✔**Objective 3.03: Manage Text Files**   Several different methods are available for managing text files. Key commands include **file**, **cat**, **more**, **less**, **head**, and **tail**. The stream editor, **sed**, can substitute text. The **awk** command can help manage database text files. And you need to know how to use a console text editor; **vi** is cited in the Linux+ objectives.

✔**Objective 3.04: Create Linked Files**   Linked files provide a second pointer to the same file. Hard links are like a copy; if you delete one link, the other link still works. Soft links don't work that way.

✔**Objective 3.05: Modify Ownership and Permissions** Files are owned by different users and groups. Ownership can be changed with the **chown** and **chgrp** commands. Permissions for each file, including SUID, SGID, and the sticky bit, can be changed with **chmod**. Default permissions are based on the **umask**.

✔**Objective 3.06: Shell Command Management** Commands send data in three directions, known as standard input, standard output, and standard error. Many command combinations redirect input and output using constructs such as left and right redirection arrows, as well as the pipe. Key shell skills also include interactivity, command completion, and the ability to escape special characters.

✔**Objective 3.07: Create, Modify, and Run Basic Shell Scripts** A shell script is a file with a combination of shell commands, which can include stanza constructs contained by **if** and **fi** as well as **while** and **done**. Some examples are available on most Linux systems, in directories such as /etc/cron.daily.

REVIEW QUESTIONS

Before leaving for the next chapter, take a few minutes to go through these questions. While doing so, take in both the content and the question format. Understanding what to expect on the exam can increase your chances for success.

1. Which of the following commands creates a hidden file?
   A. touch hide
   B. cp /etc/fstab .fstab
   C. mv file hiddenfile
   D. cp /etc/fstab /tmp

2. Which of the following commands adds the sticky bit to the /data directory?
   A. chown o+t /data
   B. chmod u+s /data
   C. chgrp o+s /data
   D. chmod 1777 /data

3. You've been told that the /etc/grub.conf and /boot/grub/grub.conf files are hard linked together. How can you verify this? Hint: The /boot and / directories are mounted on the same partition—in other words, they're part of the same filesystem.
   A. Run ls -l on each of these files; one should have an arrow pointing to the other.

    B. Compare the inode numbers of each file.

    C. Run the **ln -s /boot/grub/grub.conf /etc/grub.conf** command.

    D. Run the **ln /etc/grub.conf /boot/grub/grub.conf** command.

4. Based on the following output to **ls -l**, what's the size of the file abc?

```
-rw-r--r-- 1 root root 0 2007-07-10 23:36 abc
```

    A. 0

    B. 1KB

    C. 1MB

    D. 36KB

5. If you're going to change the user and group owner of the /home/ project directory to nobody and supervisors, which of the following commands works?

    A. **chown nobody /home/project**

    B. **chgrp supervisors /home/project**

    C. **chmod nobody.supervisors /home/project**

    D. **chown nobody.supervisors /home/project**

6. Which of the following commands sends data from file job1 to the script named bigjob in the local directory?

    A. **job1 | bigjob**

    B. **/local/bigjob < job1**

    C. **./bigjob < job1**

    D. **job1 > bigjob**

7. What command would you run to change only the first instance of chicken to fish in each line in the file named menu, and send the result to the file named newmenu?

    A. **sed 's/chicken/fish/g' menu > newmenu**

    B. **sed 's/fish/chicken/g' menu > newmenu**

    C. **sed 's/chicken/fish/' menu > newmenu**

    D. **sed 's/fish/chicken/' menu > newmenu**

8. If user owright has a **umask** of 011, and creates a new file named abc (without changing any permissions), what will you see in the first column if you run the **ls -l abc** command?

    A. -rwxrw-rw-

    B. -rw-rw-rw-

    C. ------x--x

    D. -rwxrwxrwx

9. What single command would create the /a/b/c/d/e/f/g directory? Hint: Directory /a (or the others) doesn't yet exist.

   A. touch /a/b/c/d/e/f/g

   B. mkdir /a/b/c/d/e/f/g

   C. mkdir -p /a/b/c/d/e/f/g

   D. touchdir -p /a/b/c/d/e/f/g

10. Which of the following commands searches through /etc/group for a group or groups named Mike?

   A. awk Mike /etc/group

   B. grep Mike /etc/passwd

   C. grep Mike /etc/group

   D. diff Mike /etc/passwd

REVIEW ANSWERS

1. **B** Hidden files have a dot in front, and are only shown with commands like ls -a.

2. **D** The command that can change permissions and add the sticky bit (as well as the SUID and SGID bits) is **chmod**. The **chmod 1777 /data** command adds the sticky bit (and applies rwx permissions for all users) to the /data directory.

3. **B** Hard links by definition have the same inode number, as long as they're on the same partition.

4. **A** The column after the ownership specifies the size of the file, in bytes.

5. **D** Answer D is the only answer that makes both changes with one command. While answers A and B would work together, you have to pick the best answer.

6. **C** The **./bigjob** command executes the bigjob script from the local directory, taking input from the file named job1. Answers A and D don't execute the bigjob script; and you don't know that the bigjob script is in the /local directory—or even if /local exists.

7. **C** The g option at the end of answers A and B would change all instances. Answer C has the options in the correct order.

8. **B**   Linux values of **umask** don't allow the automatic creation of executable files, so a umask of 011 creates octal permissions of 666 and rw permissions for all users.

9. **C**   The -p switch to **mkdir** supports creation of directories with as many levels as desired in the command.

10. **C**   The **grep** command searches, using the given search term (Mike), the file that follows (/etc/group) in the command.

Media, Process, and Package Management

	NEWBIE	SOME EXPERIENCE	EXPERT
ETA	80+ hours	8 hours	4 hours

This chapter is focused on how Linux administrators manage directories, storage media, runlevels, processes, and packages. Linux is organized into the Filesystem Hierarchy Standard (FHS). This chapter examines the basic structure of the FHS, as well as how associated partitions are created, maintained, and formatted. It then reviews several ways to mount local and remote directories, followed by a description of how Linux can be copied and backed up directory by directory, with a few variations when working with recordable media such as CD/DVD drives and flash devices.

Different sets of services are configured at each runlevel. Because the default is configured in /etc/inittab, runlevel management is part of the boot process, and is therefore related to other initialization scripts. Once services are started, they can be managed as processes. If there are problems, packages may need to be updated, with associated dependencies.

Manage Storage Devices and Filesystems

Objective 4.01

Before starting to manage any storage device in the Linux operating system, you need to understand the Filesystem Hierarchy Standard (FHS). Then you can intelligently create partitions with **fdisk**, format them with **mkfs**, and check the integrity of the resulting filesystems with **fsck**.

All hard disks can be configured with primary, extended, and logical partitions. Until the past few years, the /boot directory had to be configured on a partition below cylinder 1024; many distributions therefore configure /boot to mount separately on a primary partition below that cylinder. The following is a brief description of these types of partitions:

- **Primary partition**   You can create up to four different primary partitions on a hard drive.
- **Extended partition**   If you need more than four partitions, reassign one primary partition as an extended partition. That partition can then be further subdivided into logical partitions.
- **Logical partition**   Once an extended partition is available, it can be subdivided. The limit is 15 on a SCSI or SATA and 63 on an IDE/PATA hard disk. (However, not all such partitions may be recognized in Linux.)

The Filesystem Hierarchy Standard

The FHS is the official way to organize files in Unix and Linux directories. Several major directories are associated with all modern Unix/Linux operating systems. These directories organize user files, drivers, kernels, logs, programs, utilities, and more into different categories. The standardization of the FHS makes it easier for users of other Unix-based operating systems to understand the basics of Linux.

Every FHS starts with the top-level root directory (/). All of the other directories shown in Table 4.1 are subdirectories. Unless mounted separately, you can also find their files on the same partition.

Local Lingo

Filesystem A word with several different meanings. For example, a filesystem can refer to the FHS, a format such as ext3, a network filesystem such as NFS, or even an individual partition.

TABLE 4.1 Basic Filesystem Hierarchy Standard Directories

Directory	Description
/	The root directory, the top-level directory in the FHS. All other directories are subdirectories of root, which is always mounted.
/bin	Contains essential command-line utilities. Should not be mounted separately; otherwise, it could be difficult to get to these utilities when using a rescue disk.
/boot	Includes Linux startup files, including the Linux kernel. The default size of 100MB is usually sufficient for a typical modular kernel and additional kernels that you might install on test systems.
/dev	Designed for hardware and software device drivers for everything from floppy drives to terminals. Do not mount this directory on a separate partition.
/etc	Associated with basic configuration files.
/home	Created for home directories for almost every user.
/lib	Includes program libraries for the kernel and various command-line utilities. Do not mount this directory on a separate partition.
/media	The mount point for removable media, including floppy drives, DVDs, and Zip disks.
/misc	The standard mount point for local directories mounted via the automounter.
/mnt	A legacy mount point; formerly used for removable media.
/net	The standard mount point for network directories mounted via the automounter.
/opt	Common location for third-party application files.

[Handwritten margin notes: "command Line Utilities", "Device Drivers", "Basic Config files", "Program Libraries", "removable media", "Local Dir"]

[Handwritten note next to /home: "- USR"]

TABLE 4.1	Basic Filesystem Hierarchy Standard Directories *(continued)*
Directory	**Description**
/proc	Stores settings for currently running kernel-related processes, including device assignments such as IRQ ports, I/O addresses, and DMA channels, as well as kernel configuration settings such as IP forwarding.
/root	The home directory of the root user.
/sbin	Associated with system administration commands. Don't mount this directory separately.
/srv	Commonly used by various network servers on non–Red Hat distributions.
/tmp	Includes temporary files. By default, many Linux distributions periodically delete all files in this directory.
/usr	Designed for small programs accessible to all users. Includes many system administration commands and utilities.
/var	Storage for variable data, including log files and printer spools.

handwritten annotation: s Admin Commands

Configuring with fdisk

The Linux **fdisk** utility is a lot more versatile than its Microsoft counterpart. But to open it, you need to know the device file associated with the hard drive that you want to change. To identify attached hard drives (and USB keys, which is one easy way to test these commands), run the following command (as the root user):

```
# fdisk -l
```

For example, if you want to manage the partitions on the first SATA or SCSI hard disk, enter the following command:

```
# fdisk /dev/sda
```

As you can see in Figure 4.1, the **fdisk** utility is flexible. Press **m** for a list of commands. Some key **fdisk** commands are described in Table 4.2, and key partition types are described in Table 4.3.

Travel Advisory

There are important alternatives to **fdisk**. The most prominent open source option is **parted**. Third-party alternatives are also available; for example, Partition Magic can now be used to create and manage ext3 partitions.

```
Command (m for help): m
Command action
   a   toggle a bootable flag
   b   edit bsd disklabel
   c   toggle the dos compatibility flag
   d   delete a partition
   l   list known partition types
   m   print this menu
   n   add a new partition
   o   create a new empty DOS partition table
   p   print the partition table
   q   quit without saving changes
   s   create a new empty Sun disklabel
   t   change a partition's system id
   u   change display/entry units
   v   verify the partition table
   w   write table to disk and exit
   x   extra functionality (experts only)

Command (m for help): p

Disk /dev/sdb: 160.0 GB, 160041885696 bytes
255 heads, 63 sectors/track, 19457 cylinders
Units = cylinders of 16065 * 512 = 8225280 bytes

   Device Boot      Start         End      Blocks   Id  System
/dev/sdb1   *           1        2596    20852338+   83  Linux
/dev/sdb2            2597        5636    24418800    83  Linux
/dev/sdb3            5637       19457   111017182+   83  Linux

Command (m for help): ▮
```

FIGURE 4.1   Linux **fdisk** commands; **p** returns the partition table

Checking with fsck

The **fsck** command is functionally similar to the Microsoft **chkdsk** command. It analyzes the specified filesystem and performs repairs as required. For example, if you're having problems with files in the /var directory mounted on /dev/sda3, you may want to check that partition. But before running **fsck**, unmount that filesystem first. Except for the top-level root directory filesystem, you can go

TABLE 4.2   Important **fdisk** Options

fdisk Command	Description
a	Allows you to specify the bootable Linux partition (with /**boot**).
l	Lists known partition types; **fdisk** can create partitions that conform to any of these filesystems.
n	Adds a new partition; works only if there is free space on the disk that hasn't already been allocated to an existing partition.
q	Quits without saving any changes.
t	Changes the partition filesystem type; you still need to format appropriately.

TABLE 4.3	Major **fdisk** Patition Types
fdisk Type	**Description**
b	W95 FAT32—Microsoft's VFAT
f	Microsoft Extended Partition
7	Microsoft NTFS
82	Linux swap
83	Standard Linux
85	Linux extended
8e	Linux for Logical Volumes
fd	Linux for RAID

into single-user mode with the **init 1** command before you can unmount a filesystem. For the top-level root directory, you'll need a Live CD. To unmount, analyze, and then remount the filesystem noted in this section, run the following commands (the command is spelled **umount**, not unmount):

```
# umount /var
# fsck -t ext3 /dev/sda3
# mount /dev/hda7 /var
```

The **fsck** command also serves as a "front end," depending on the filesystem format. For example, if you're formatting an ext2 or ext3 filesystem, **fsck** by itself automatically calls the **e2fsck** command (which works for both ext2 and ext3 filesystems). Therefore, if you're checking an ext3 filesystem, once you unmount it with the **umount** command, the following command is sufficient:

```
# fsck /dev/hda7
```

Exam Tip

If you need to run the **fsck** command, know that you need to unmount the filesystem first. If you need an unmounted top-level root directory partition, you need to boot with a rescue or Live CD. A Live Linux CD loads a complete copy of Linux without mounting any local filesystems, making it safe to run **fsck** on that partition.

Formatting with mkfs

To format a Linux partition, apply the **mkfs** command. It allows you to format a partition to a number of different filesystems. To format a typical partition such as /dev/sdb2 to the current Red Hat standard, the third extended filesystem, run the following command:

```
# mkfs -t ext3 /dev/sdb2
```

The **mkfs** command also serves as a "front-end," depending on the filesystem format. For example, if you're formatting a Red Hat standard ext3 filesystem, **mkfs** automatically calls the **mkfs.ext3** command. Therefore, if you're reformatting an ext3 filesystem, the following command is sufficient:

```
# mkfs /dev/hda2
```

Travel Advisory

Be careful with the **mkfs** command. First, back up any data on the subject partition and computer. This command erases all data on the specified partition.

The **mkfs** command works with a number of filesystem formats, and works as a front-end to filesystem-specific commands such as **mkdosfs**, **mkfs.ext2**, **mkfs.ext3**, **mkfs.msdos**, **mkfs.reiserfs**, **mkfs.vfat**, and **mkswap**.

Tuning with tune2fs

You don't always have to run **mkfs** to change filesystem formats. For example, the ext3 filesystem is very similar to ext2. The only difference is a journal. For example, if you want to add a journal to /dev/sda1, unmount the filesystem first, and then run the following command:

```
# tune2fs -j /dev/sda1
```

To reverse the process, on an unmounted filesystem, run the following command (the carat, ^, disables the noted feature):

```
# tune2fs -O ^has_journal /dev/sda1
```

Objective 4.02

Mount Locally and Remotely

Mounting can be divided into two basic categories: local and remote. Local mounts are available from local media such as hard disks, CDs, USB keys, and so forth. Remote mounts are available from servers that share directories over a network, typically using the Network File System (NFS) and Samba/Common Internet File System (CIFS) formats.

Each of the mounts configured in this section can also be configured in /etc/fstab and related configuration files. For more information, see the Chapter 6 section "Configure Mounted Directories."

Mounting on Your Own

If a filesystem is not otherwise configured in /etc/fstab (or for those filesystems specified with **noauto** mount option), you'll need to mount filesystems on your own. The basic format is *Local Mount*

```
mount -t fstype device directory
```

where *fstype* is the filesystem type (such as ext3 or vfat), *device* is the device file (such as /dev/hda2), and *directory* is the mount directory (such as / or /boot). This applies for local and network filesystems.

mount Before mounting any filesystem, check currently mounted devices. The simplest way is with the **mount** command, without switches. It'll list all mounted devices, including any mounted from a shared network directory.

Mounting a Shared NFS Directory

If an NFS directory is properly shared, you should be able to see it with the **showmount** command. For example, if the NFS server is nfs.example.com, the following command lists the shared directories, assuming firewalls and other security measures aren't blocking access:

```
# showmount -e nfs.example.com
```

You can substitute the IP address for the domain name; doing so may be necessary if any local hostname database, such as DNS or /etc/hosts, is not working. Once you've identified a desired network directory (and a local directory for mounting purposes), you can mount it. For the purpose of the following command, the shared network directory is /inst, and the local directory is /nfs:

```
# mount -t nfs nfs.example.com:/inst /nfs
```

The **-t nfs** may not be required. NFS mounts can be included in /etc/fstab, as described in Chapter 6.

Mounting a Shared Samba/CIFS Directory

Mounting a shared Samba/CIFS directory is similar to mounting a shared NFS directory. If it's properly shared, you should be able to see it with the **smbclient** command. For example, if the Samba/CIFS server is samba.example.com, the following command lists the shared directories, assuming firewalls and other security measures aren't blocking access:

```
# smbclient -L samba.example.com
```

You can substitute the IP address for the domain name, especially if any local hostname database such as DNS or /etc/hosts is not working. You can add -U *username* for access to appropriate directories. Once you've identified a desired network directory (and a local directory for mounting purposes), you can mount it. For the purpose of the following command, assume the shared network directory is /inst, and the local directory is /smb:

```
# mount -t smbfs //samba.example.com/inst /smb -o username=user
```

The **-t smbfs** may not be required. If the user on the Samba server is the same as the current user, **username=***user* is not required; you're prompted for the user's password on the Samba server.

Travel Advisory

Later versions of Samba require substitution of **cifs** for **smbfs**. Some versions of Linux include an **smbmount** command, which can substitute for **mount -t smbfs** or **mount -t cifs**. The latest Red Hat distributions replace this with a **mount.cifs** command for shared Samba/CIFS directories, which can be given Set User ID (SUID) permissions for access by regular users.

Objective 4.03 Back Up and Restore Data

Historically, backups and restores in Linux are normally associated with the **tar** and **cpio** commands. While there are plenty of other commands in common use for backups, these are the two commands listed in the Linux+ objectives.

Travel Advisory

There are many other commands associated with backups, including **rsync**, **dd**, and even a Linux clone of Norton Ghost, known as Partimage. For more information, see www.partimage.org.

Tape Archives and Compression with tar

TAR

The **tar** command was originally developed for archiving data to tape drives. However, it's commonly used today for collecting a series of files, especially from a directory. For example, the following command backs up the information from the /home directory in the home.tar.gz file:

```
# tar czvf home.tar.gz /home
```

This is one of the few commands that does not require a dash in front of the switch. This particular command creates (**c**) an archive, compresses (**z**) it, in verbose (**v**) mode, with the filename (**f**) that follows. Alternatively, you can extract (**x**) from that file with the following command:

EXTRACT

```
# tar xzvf home.tar.gz /home
```

The compression specified (**z**) is associated with the **gzip** command; if you wanted to use bzip2 compression, substitute the **j** switch.

If you want to review a list of files without decompressing an archive, the --**list** or -**t** switch is helpful. For example, the following command would list the files in the linux-2.6.22.tar.gz kernel source code package:

LIST

```
# tar -tvf linux-2.6.22.tar.gz
```

Input and Output with cpio

The **cpio** command can make it easier to archive a whole group of files, because, unlike **tar**, it works with standard input and output. To understand the **cpio** command, break it down. It's the **cp** command that works with I/O, input and output. In other words, it takes the standard output from a search, such as that associated with the **find** command. For example, the following **find** command lists all *.conf files, and pipes the result to the **cpio** command:

```
# find / -name *.conf | cpio
```

But that's not enough. If you run this command, it returns a message suggesting a need for the -**o**, -**i**, -**p**, or -**t** switch. The -**o** switch is what matters, because it creates the archive—and can be piped as standard output to an archive as shown:

```
# find / -name *.conf | cpio -o > config.cpiobak
```

The -**i** switch restores files from the archive:

```
# cpio -i < config.cpiobak
```

Objective 4.04 # Use Recordable Media

Of course, all media (even Read Only Memory) is recordable in some fashion. The related Linux+ objective lists CDRW, hard drives, and flash memory devices. Writing to hard drives is addressed any time you write to a file on a regular partition.

However, as most data in Linux is written asynchronously, data to be written may be temporarily stored in volatile memory such as RAM. The latest Linux distributions automatically apply the **sync** command to flush such data when running the **umount** command on recordable media. However, if you write something to a "hot" removable device such as a USB key or floppy disk (or even a hot-swappable hard drive) and remove it before unmounting, the data that you thought you wrote could be lost.

The only specialized commands associated with writing to removable devices, at least those listed in the Linux+ objectives, relate to CD/DVD drives, which involve commands such as **mkisofs** and **cdrecord**.

Mounting Devices

Before Linux reads or writes data to a device, that device must be mounted. Some mount points are automatically mounted during the boot process, as described earlier in the "Mount Locally and Remotely" section. Modern Linux distributions and desktops may automatically mount a properly formatted removable device such as a CD or USB key when inserted in the proper location. But that feature was generally not available when the Linux+ objectives were released.

> **Travel Advisory**
>
> The Hardware Abstraction Layer (HAL) enables automounting of inserted devices such as CD media and USB keys. Although HAL is in common use on current Linux distributions, it was implemented after the Linux+ objectives were released.

So you need to mount and unmount drives. To mount a drive or partition, you need the device and an empty directory on which to mount the device. Ideally, detected recordable devices are listed in the output to the **fdisk -l** command (when run as the root user). Depending on what's detected, some trial and error may be necessary to find the right device. Typical device names are listed in Table 4.4.

Some soft links may simplify the task of finding the media device; for example, if you see the following output to **ls -l /dev/cdrom**,

```
lrwxrwxrwx 1 root root 3 Jul  3 16:48 /dev/cdrom -> hdc
```

you should be able to use the /dev/cdrom device to mount an inserted CD, with a command like:

```
# mount /dev/cdrom /mnt
```

TABLE 4.4	Typical Media Devices
Device	**Description**
/dev/fd0	First floppy drive (the second floppy drive is associated with /dev/fd1, and so on).
/dev/sda1	First partition on the first SCSI or SATA drive; may also be used for USB and even Secure Digital (SD) memory cards.
/dev/sr0, /dev/scd0	SCSI or SATA attached DVD or CD-ROM or writer.
/dev/hda1	First partition on the first PATA/IDE drive.
/dev/hdc	Primary drive on the secondary PATA/IDE channel; commonly used for CD/DVD drives. (The drives on the first PATA/IDE channel are associated with /dev/hda and /dev/hdb.)
/dev/mmcblk0	Typical SD memory card device.

To prevent the potential data loss associated with sudden removal of drives, run the **sync** command. Normally, the unmount command, **umount**, automatically syncs data before unmounting the drive. The **umount /dev/cdrom** command works just as well as the following:

```
# umount /mnt
```

Writing to CD/DVDs

While it may seem that all CD and DVD drives sold today have write capabilities, that's not always true. So if you're not familiar with the current system hardware and are having trouble writing to a CD/DVD, that's the first thing to check.

For practical purposes, Linux GUI CD and DVD writing tools have simplified the process of writing to CD/DVDs. They allow you to write a group of files, or an .iso file, such as those downloaded as installation CD/DVDs for various Linux distributions.

Creating a CD from the command line is a two-step process: create an .iso file from the desired files, and then write the .iso file to the writable CD. For example, to back up the files in my /home/michael/LinuxPlus directory, I first run

```
# mkisofs -J -r -T -o LinuxPlus.iso /home/michael/LinuxPlus
```

I can test the result by mounting the .iso file (with the **-o loop** option, this command works on any properly created .iso file—or even .img files created with the **dd** command):

```
# mount -t iso9660 -o loop LinuxPlus.iso /mnt
```

Once verified, don't forget to unmount the .iso file, before writing with the **cdrecord** command:

```
# cdrecord -v LinuxPlus.iso
```

Of course, if you use a GUI-based tool, both steps are automated. Furthermore, if you have more than one CD writer or the CD writer is on an SCSI drive, more complex switches are required, discussion of which is beyond the scope of this book.

Objective 4.05 Manage Runlevels

Linux services are organized by runlevel. Some runlevels can reboot and halt Linux. Other runlevels are configured to start Linux with or without networking. The default runlevel for modern Linux distributions boots into the GUI (assuming the GUI is installed).

To understand how runlevels work, you need a basic understanding of the boot process for a Linux system.

Travel Advisory

Runlevels work somewhat differently on Debian-based distributions, including Ubuntu Linux. But the Linux+ objectives are based on RPM-based distributions, so that's what is covered in this book.

The Boot Process

When powering up a computer, the first thing that starts is the BIOS, the Basic Input/Output System. The BIOS performs a series of diagnostics to detect and connect the CPU and key controllers. This is also known as the Power-On Self-Test (POST). If you hear beeps during this process, there may be a hardware problem such as loose connections. Once complete, the BIOS passes control to the master boot record (MBR) of the boot device, normally the first hard drive. At this point, you should see a boot loader menu, such as those described in the Chapter 2 section "Understand and Reinstall a Boot Manager."

Once you've selected an operating system kernel, Linux loads that kernel, mounts partitions on appropriate directories, and more. It then starts **init**, also known as the first process because it always has a Process Identifier (PID) of 1. The parameters associated with **init** are determined in the local /etc/inittab file.

Setting the Default Runlevel

The default runlevel is set in /etc/inittab, normally in the first active directive in this file. The directive is simple:

```
id:3:initdefault
```

The default runlevel in this case is 3. All of the selected Linux distributions have comments that describe the functionality of each of the basic runlevels. All you need to do to change the default runlevel is change this number in /etc/inittab. For more information, see Table 4.5.

There are several other runlevels available, which I believe are beyond the scope of the exam. Possible exceptions are **s**, **emergency**, and **init=/bin/sh**. The **s** runlevel is associated with single-user mode but does not start scripts in runlevel 1. The **emergency** runlevel does not run scripts like **rc.sysinit**. Finally, **init=/bin/sh** boots into a shell without loading any devices or services. If any partitions are unmounted, in these runlevels (or in runlevel 1), you may be able, with the **umount** command, to unmount said devices before checking their integrity with a command such as **fsck**.

Travel Advisory

Users of Debian and Ubuntu Linux will note that standard runlevels are different in those distributions. For example, the default GUI login runlevel for those distributions is 2. That's one reason for sticking with the selected distributions as described in the Introduction when studying for the Linux+ exam.

TABLE 4.5	Standard Runlevels

Runlevel	Description
0	Halt. Never set the default runlevel to 0, or Linux will shut down as soon as it reads /etc/inittab.
1	Single-user mode. This is an excellent option for maintenance, such as checking the integrity of partitions with a command like **fsck**.
2	Multiuser mode without NFS.
3	Multiuser mode with NFS.
4	Unused.
5	If you have a GUI, this starts the GUI login screen when you boot Linux.
6	Reboot. Never set the default runlevel to 6, or Linux will reboot as soon as it reads /etc/inittab—and then reboot again, and again....

Changing Runlevels

Changing runlevels is almost trivial. Just run the **init** *n* command, where *n* is the desired runlevel. For example, to go into single-user mode, run

```
# init 1
```

The **telinit** command is a synonym, soft linked to **init**. In other words, one way to halt the system is to run the **telinit 0** command.

Services in Each Runlevel

The services configured at each runlevel are available either in the /etc/rc*n*.d directory or, in SUSE's case, in the /etc/init.d/rc*n*.d directory, where *n* is the runlevel. Try it in your selected distribution. You'll see a group of services that start with a *K* or an *S*. Scripts that start with a *K* are killed and those that start with an *S* are started in that runlevel.

Scripts in these directories are soft linked to actual locations in the /etc/init.d or /etc/rc.d/init.d directory. Review a couple of these scripts. You'll see these scripts can be used to start, restart, and reload services. For example, as you'll see in Chapter 7, Apache can be restarted with the following command:

```
# /etc/init.d/httpd restart
```

Other Initialization Scripts

There are two other initialization scripts of consequence, rc.sysinit and rc.local, both in the /etc directory. The exception again is openSUSE, which includes a series of initialization scripts named boot.* in the /etc/rc.d directory. The rc.local script is run at the end of the boot process, making it an excellent location for user- and administrator-defined custom settings.

Objective 4.06

Learn Process Management

Everything running on a Linux system requires one or more processes, which can be identified with variations of the **ps** command. Each process is associated with a PID. As described earlier in the "Manage Runlevels" section, init is associated with a PID of 1.

Process Collections with ps

The **ps** command identifies currently running processes. When run without switches, **ps** identifies the processes associated with the current account, which usually includes the shell.

```
USER    PID %CPU %MEM   VSZ  RSS TTY   STAT START  TIME COMMAND
root      1  0.0  0.0 10312  672 ?     Ss   Jul03  0:00 init [3]

root      2  0.0  0.0     0    0 ?     S    Jul03  0:00 [migration/0]
root      3  0.0  0.0     0    0 ?     SN   Jul03  0:00 [ksoftirqd/0]
root      4  0.0  0.0     0    0 ?     S    Jul03  0:00 [watchdog/0]
root      5  0.0  0.0     0    0 ?     S<   Jul03  0:00 [events/0]
root      6  0.0  0.0     0    0 ?     S<   Jul03  0:00 [khelper]
root      7  0.0  0.0     0    0 ?     S<   Jul03  0:00 [kthread]
root      9  0.0  0.0     0    0 ?     S<   Jul03  0:00 [xenwatch]
root     10  0.0  0.0     0    0 ?     S<   Jul03  0:00 [xenbus]
root     48  0.0  0.0     0    0 ?     S<   Jul03  0:00 [kblockd/0]
root     49  0.0  0.0     0    0 ?     S<   Jul03  0:00 [kacpid]
root    151  0.0  0.0     0    0 ?     S<   Jul03  0:00 [cqueue/0]
root    156  0.0  0.0     0    0 ?     S<   Jul03  0:00 [khubd]
root    158  0.0  0.0     0    0 ?     S<   Jul03  0:00 [kseriod]
root    180  0.0  0.0     0    0 ?     S    Jul03  0:00 [pdflush]
root    181  0.0  0.0     0    0 ?     S    Jul03  0:00 [pdflush]
root    182  0.0  0.0     0    0 ?     S<   Jul03  0:00 [kswapd0]
root    183  0.0  0.0     0    0 ?     S<   Jul03  0:00 [aio/0]
root    301  0.0  0.0     0    0 ?     S<   Jul03  0:00 [kpsmoused]
root    326  0.0  0.0     0    0 ?     S<   Jul03  0:04 [ata/0]
root    327  0.0  0.0     0    0 ?     S<   Jul03  0:00 [ata_aux]
root    330  0.0  0.0     0    0 ?     S<   Jul03  0:00 [scsi_eh_0]
root    331  0.0  0.0     0    0 ?     S<   Jul03  0:00 [scsi_eh_1]
--More--
```

FIGURE 4.2   Currently running processes as defined by **ps aux**

In contrast, the **ps aux** command shows everything running on the local Linux system. It's impressive; there are 160 processes running on my Linux laptop system as I write. One example of the output from **ps aux** is shown in Figure 4.2. Note that I've stopped with one screen of output by running **ps aux | more**.

The columns in Figure 4.2 can tell you a lot about each process. Key columns, from left to right, are described in Table 4.6.

There are other variations on the **ps** command available. The **ps axl** command lists commands with a PPID, which is the parent of the PID. In the upcoming section "Stopping and Restarting a Job," you'll see that when a process refuses to die, you may be able to stop it by applying the **kill** command to the parent process, identified by the PPID.

To identify the processes associated with a specific user, the **-u** switch can help; for example, the following command identifies all processes associated with user crackerthief:

```
# ps -u crackerthief
```

Core Kernel and init Processes

There's more information available in the output to the **ps** commands. First, the most important process is init. As the parent of all other processes, it should never be killed or stopped. Second, kernel processes are identified in the output to commands.

TABLE 4.6	Columns in the Output from the **ps aux** Command

ps aux Column	Description
USER	The owner of the process.
PID	The Process Identifier; every process has a PID.
%CPU	The proportion of CPU used by the process, as a percentage of the total available.
%MEM	The proportion of RAM memory in use by the current process, as a percentage of the total available.
TTY	Terminal where the process was started. If ?, the process is not associated with any terminal; otherwise, it is a number such as tty1.
STAT	The status of the process. The four basic options are running (R), sleeping (S), low priority (N), and swapped (SW); sometimes S and N are combined.
START	The start time or, if the process is more than a day old, the start date.
TIME	The amount of time the associated process has actually run; in many cases, you'll see 0:00, which means it has run less than a minute.
COMMAND	The command or script associated with the process.

To review the process hierarchy, run the **pstree** command. In most cases the output will scroll too quickly on the screen; it can be better controlled with the **pstree | less** command. As you can see from the left side of the console, the process hierarchy starts with the **init** process. All other processes are children of **init**; in other words, **init** is the PPID of the process listed in the next column to the right.

Stopping and Restarting a Job

One of the reasons Linux is popular is that it rarely crashes. There are reports of Web servers powered by Linux that have been running without a reboot for months and even years at a time. One reason for this level of reliability is that system administrators can easily end most programs with the **kill** command, for which you need the PID of the program that is stuck.

Linux applications at the graphical user interface (GUI) have been known to freeze on occasion. For example, I sometimes have problems with plug-ins associated with the Firefox Web browser. When I do, I take the following steps to kill that application:

1. I open a command-line interface, with a GUI command utility such as **gnome-terminal**, **konsole**, or **xterm**.

2. I then look for the PID associated with the Web browser. To identify the PIDs associated with Firefox, I run the **ps axl | grep firefox**

command; the number in the third column of output is the PID; the number in the fourth column is the PPID.

3. I identify the PID number of the process to be killed. For example, if it's 7777, I run the **kill 7777** command. I recheck the result by running **ps axl | grep firefox** again. If the command worked as intended, the noted process will no longer be active.

4. If the **kill** command didn't work, stronger measures may be appropriate. One option is the **kill -9 7777** command, which might kill the bad program but leave so-called "orphan" processes. If I choose to run that command, I then recheck running processes again to see if it worked.

5. If the **kill -9 7777** command didn't work, one more option is to try to kill the parent of the PID, also known as the PPID. Remember, the PPID is in the fourth column in the output to the **ps axl** command.

If you're trying to kill a daemon such as Samba (**smbd**), Apache (**httpd**), or the Secure Shell server (**sshd**), there is a shortcut. When these processes are running, their PIDs are available in the /var/run directory; you could run a command like the following to identify the desired PID:

```
# cat /var/run/smbd
```

The PID isn't required to kill all processes. You don't even need to know the PID; for example, as described in the Chapter 3 section "Shell Command Management," back quotes can process the contents of a file before passing the information as standard input to another command; in other words, you could kill the Samba daemon as follows:

```
# kill `cat /var/run/smbd.pid`
```

Another shortcut is the **killall** command, which only requires the name of the daemon, such as **smbd**.

But the **kill** command doesn't always work, especially with persistent services. One more option, as described earlier in the "Manage Runlevels" section, is to just stop the service with a command such as this:

```
# /etc/init.d/smbd stop
```

While you can restart many processes through scripts in the /etc/init.d directory with commands such as **/etc/init.d/vsftpd restart**, such scripts aren't always available. There's one more helpful **kill** command that restarts daemons; if you want to restart a daemon that doesn't appear in /etc/init.d, say on PID 2222, run the following command:

```
# kill -HUP 2222
```

Load Monitoring with top

The **top** command is intended to display the load on the current system. As shown in Figure 4.3, it illustrates the current load on the CPU, the RAM as defined by the Mem (in the upper left of the figure), and the swap space. It also lists commands by their use; by default, the commands that are using the most CPU and RAM resources are listed at the top of the listing.

If your system is loaded by a number of users, pay attention to the USER column. Having many users loading your systems may justify the purchase of more RAM, the redistribution of load to other systems, or perhaps additional investigation.

Listing Open Files with lsof *List open files*

A process is essentially anything that's running on a computer. Since everything on Linux is some form of a file, most processes open up other files. The **lsof** command shows you the number of files opened by currently running processes. Depending on what you're running, it's not uncommon to have hundreds or even thousands of open files.

The value of **lsof** is as a tool, especially related to troubleshooting hardware. Each Linux hardware component is related to a device file. For example, if you're having trouble with a hardware telephone modem, one thing to check is active

```
top - 23:19:39 up  9:28,  2 users,  load average: 0.06, 0.02, 0.00
Tasks: 134 total,   2 running, 132 sleeping,   0 stopped,   0 zombie
Cpu(s):  0.7%us,  0.0%sy,  0.0%ni, 99.3%id,  0.0%wa,  0.0%hi,  0.0%si,  0.0%st
Mem:   1894208k total,   569548k used,  1324660k free,    99372k buffers
Swap:   987988k total,        0k used,   987988k free,   261392k cached

  PID USER      PR  NI  VIRT  RES  SHR S %CPU %MEM    TIME+  COMMAND
 3415 michael   15   0 74252 1904  984 S  0.3  0.1   0:00.45 sshd
 5259 root      15   0  283m  14m 8592 R  0.3  0.8   0:00.14 gnome-terminal
    1 root      18   0 10312  672  560 S  0.0  0.0   0:00.44 init
    2 root      RT   0     0    0    0 S  0.0  0.0   0:00.00 migration/0
    3 root      34  19     0    0    0 S  0.0  0.0   0:00.00 ksoftirqd/0
    4 root      RT   0     0    0    0 S  0.0  0.0   0:00.00 watchdog/0
    5 root      10  -5     0    0    0 S  0.0  0.0   0:00.00 events/0
    6 root      10  -5     0    0    0 S  0.0  0.0   0:00.00 khelper
    7 root      10  -5     0    0    0 S  0.0  0.0   0:00.02 kthread
    9 root      10  -5     0    0    0 S  0.0  0.0   0:00.00 xenwatch
   10 root      10  -5     0    0    0 S  0.0  0.0   0:00.00 xenbus
   48 root      10  -5     0    0    0 S  0.0  0.0   0:00.01 kblockd/0
   49 root      20  -5     0    0    0 S  0.0  0.0   0:00.00 kacpid
  151 root      20  -5     0    0    0 S  0.0  0.0   0:00.00 cqueue/0
  156 root      10  -5     0    0    0 S  0.0  0.0   0:00.00 khubd
  158 root      16  -5     0    0    0 S  0.0  0.0   0:00.00 kseriod
  180 root      25   0     0    0    0 S  0.0  0.0   0:00.00 pdflush
```

FIGURE 4.3   A view of the **top** command

serial ports. Try to start the modem. Run the following command to review open serial ports:

```
# lsof /dev/ttyS*
```

If there's no output, then there may be a problem with the modem, the connection, or perhaps the serial port hardware.

Changing Job Priorities

Many jobs are run at the console. As an administrator, you may need to prioritize. For example, if your supervisor accidentally erased his hard drive and wants his data restored from backup, you might want to give that job a higher priority.

To manage job priorities, Linux includes a number of command-line tools. If you've logged in remotely (and don't have enough consoles), you may want to move some jobs into the background. Related commands include **bg**, **fg**, and **jobs**. Sometimes you just need to raise or lower the priority of certain tasks; related commands include **nice** and **renice**.

Running Jobs in the Background: &, bg, jobs, fg

The simplest way to run multiple jobs in one console is by adding the ampersand (&) to the end of a command. For example, if you're processing some big database with the **./bigdb** command, the following command returns you to the command line, all the while running the job in the background:

```
# ./bigdb &
```

But if you forget the &, not all is lost. To send the job into the background, first suspend it by pressing CTRL-Z, and then enter the **bg** command. The job continues to run just as if you added the ampersand at the end of the command.

If you want to restore the command to the foreground—and it's the only job in the background—just run the **fg** command. But if you have more than one job in the background, that's where the **jobs** command can help. Here's one example of output from the **jobs** command on my system:

```
[1]-  Stopped   sudo /etc/cron.daily/mlocate.cron
[2]+  Stopped   sudo /etc/cron.daily/tmpwatch
```

If you see "Done" instead of "Stopped," the job is complete. Otherwise, you can specify the job to return to the foreground with the number of the job, as specified in the left column.

nice and renice

The **nice** and **renice** commands support adjusting priorities for the processes of your choice. The numbers associated with priorities are counterintuitive; while −20 is the highest priority, 19 is the lowest priority.

If you are ready to run a program, you can start it with the priority of your choice with the **nice** command. For example, the following command starts the program1 script with the lowest possible priority:

```
# nice -n 19 ./program1
```

If the job is already running, you need its PID to reprioritize it. For example, if the PID of a process restoring data to your supervisor is 3333, the **renice -10 3333** command raises its priority by ten notches.

Objective 4.07 Identify Package Problems and Solve with Updates

Sometimes packages break, or need to be updated. Sometimes dependencies are unresolved. Sometimes there are bugs that can be addressed if the relevant packages are updated. Because the selected distributions use RPMs for package management, this section examines RPM tools to identify problems with specific packages and files, and to update applications.

Importing the Keyfile

Before verifying the integrity of an RPM package, the encryption key must be installed. The file with the encryption key varies even among the selected distributions. Once you find the *keyfile* for your distribution, it can be installed with the following command:

```
# rpm --import keyfile
```

The *keyfile* supports verifying each package using the GNU version of Pretty Good Privacy (PGP) encryption, known as the GNU Privacy Guard (GPG). If you've updated packages from an updates repository, chances are good that you've already imported the appropriate GPG key.

If you don't currently have access to an updates repository, the GPG *keyfile* should be available from the installation CD; otherwise, just search for the RPM-GPG-KEY file, probably with some extension like **-redhat**, somewhere in the /usr/share/doc directory.

Travel Advisory

The GPG keyfiles on installation CDs/DVDs may be available in files named other than RPM-GPG-KEY. They may also be available on the installed system. For example, on current versions of Red Hat/Fedora, keyfiles can be found in the /etc/pki/rpm-gpg directory.

Identifying a Problem

To check a package, you can use the **rpm --checksig** *packagename* command. It checks the GPG signature of a package against the GPG *keyfile* just described. For example, if you've downloaded a distribution from a third-party mirror and have doubts about the integrity of its packages, you could check the signature of an individual package with a command such as this:

```
# rpm -K gimp-2.2.14-5.fc7.x86_64.rpm
```

The **-K** switch is synonymous with **--checksig**. If everything is OK, you'll see output like

```
gimp-2.2.14-5.fc7.x86_64.rpm: (sha1) dsa sha1 md5 gpg OK
```

which verifies that the package is OK, with a list of encryption algorithms. For example, *sha1* refers to a Secure Hash Algorithm; *dsa* refers to a Digital Secure Algorithm; *md5* refers to Message Digest algorithm 5; and *gpg* refers to the GNU Privacy Guard key.

Next, the **rpm -V** *packagename* command, with the right additional switch, can help you verify differences between packages as installed and as revised. For example, I can check the integrity of all files associated with the initscripts RPM package with the following command (you can substitute **--verify** for **-V**):

```
# rpm -V initscripts
```

If there's no output, then no file from this package has changed. If there are changes, you'll see output similar to

```
S.5....T c /etc/X11/prefdm
.......T c /etc/inittab
```

Numbers or letters in the first eight positions signify some sort of "failure." It may not be a problem; for example, a *T* may mean that the administrator has made a normal edit, such as changing the default runlevel in /etc/inittab. The failure codes associated with the **rpm -V** command are shown in Table 4.7.

The last letter (just before the filename) can be one of five codes, as described in Table 4.8. Note from the **rpm -V initscripts** output, both /etc/inittab and /etc/X11/prefdm have the code associated with configuration files.

If you want a comprehensive check, the **rpm -Vv** *packagename* command checks every file in the RPM package *packagename*. Alternatively, you can check individual files with the **rpm -Vf** *filename* command.

Dependency Resolution

There are several ways to manage dependencies. A common option for current distributions is to use commands that automatically install dependencies, such as

TABLE 4.7	**rpm -V** Failure Codes
Failure Code	**Description**
S	File size
M	Mode
5	MD5 checksum
D	Device
L	Symbolic link
U	User
G	Group
T	File modification time

yum, **apt**, and **urpmi**. But these are distribution specific; for example, **yum** was adapted for Red Hat distributions well after the Linux+ objectives were released.

If you use the **rpm** command to try to install a package, and there's a dependency, the package isn't installed. For example, if I haven't installed the Samba server on my system and try to install the samba-swat RPM, I get the following message:

```
# rpm -ivh samba-swat-3.0.23c-2.i386.rpm

warning: samba-swat-3.0.23c-2.i386.rpm: Header V3 DSA signature:
NOKEY, key ID 37017186
error: Failed dependencies:
  samba = 0:3.0.23c-2 is needed by samba-swat-3.0.23c-2.i386
```

For distributions with an RPM database such as Red Hat's old redhat-rpmdb package, the --**aid** switch can read dependency messages and install noted packages. But the --**aid** switch does not work with (and is not needed for) current update commands such as **yum**, **apt**, or **urpmi**.

TABLE 4.8	**rpm -V** File Codes
Code	**Description**
c	Configuration file
d	Documentation file
g	Ghost (In other words, this file shouldn't be there, and may be a sign of trouble.)
l	License file
r	Readme file

Package Updates

The package update process is straightforward. With the **rpm** command, packages can be updated with the **rpm -U** *packagename* command. For more information, see the Chapter 2 section "Perform Post-Installation Package Management."

Sometimes there are dependencies associated with updates. The dependencies can be handled in the same way as those for regular installations, with the options just described for regular package installations.

CHECKPOINT

✔**Objective 4.01: Manage Storage Devices and Filesystems** The Filesystem Hierarchy Standard (FHS) defines the structure of Linux directories. Important tools to help configure systems to the FHS include **fdisk** for partitions, **mkfs** for formatting, and **fsck** for integrity checking of the resulting filesystems.

✔**Objective 4.02: Mount Locally and Remotely** Local mounts define connections to local media such as hard disk partitions, CDs, USB keys, and so forth. Remote mounts define connections to shared directories over a network.

✔**Objective 4.03: Back Up and Restore Data** Two commands for backing up and restoring data are **tar** and **cpio**. The **tar** command helps create compressed archives; the **cpio** command can create archives from file lists.

✔**Objective 4.04: Use Recordable Media** Because data to be written may be temporarily stored in volatile memory such as RAM, writes to a "hot" removable device such as a USB key or floppy disk may be at risk. The Linux+ objectives define specialized commands associated with writing to removable devices such as CD/DVD drives.

✔**Objective 4.05: Manage Runlevels** Linux services are organized by runlevel; the default is defined in /etc/inittab. Services associated with each runlevel are configured by directory.

✔**Objective 4.06: Learn Process Management** Every process can be identified with variations of the **ps** command. Each process has a Process Identifier, or PID. All but one process have a parent process, with a parent PID, or PPID. The first process is init, which has a PID of 1.

✔**Objective 4.07: Identify Package Problems and Solve with Updates**
When packages break, or need to be updated, they can be verified against the source. Every distribution includes a *keyfile* with a GPG encryption key. Once imported, packages and individual files can be verified with certain **rpm** commands.

REVIEW QUESTIONS

Before leaving for the next chapter, take a few minutes to go through these questions. While doing so, take in both the content and the question format. Understanding what to expect on the exam can increase your chances for success.

1. What is the standard filesystem code in **fdisk** for a regular Linux partition?
   A. 82
   B. 83
   C. 85
   D. fd

2. If you need to run **fsck** on a standard root directory partition, what's the best option?
   A. Unmount the root directory.
   B. Boot in rescue mode.
   C. Boot from a Linux Live CD.
   D. Run **fsck** without unmounting the root directory partition.

3. If you're converting from an older version of Linux, from ext2 to ext3 formatted filesystems, which of the following actions is not appropriate?
   A. Change /etc/fstab formats from ext2 to ext3.
   B. Run the **mkfs.ext3** command on all ext2 formatted filesystems.
   C. Run the **tune2fs -j** command on all formatted filesystems, except floppy drives.
   D. Back up all data.

4. What standard runlevel automatically boots Linux with command-line login consoles?
   A. 1
   B. 2
   C. 3
   D. 5

5. What happens if you write a file to a USB key and remove it from its slot a few minutes later?

   A. The file is saved to the USB key.

   B. The file may not be saved to the USB key.

   C. The file is not saved to the USB key.

   D. The file is deleted from all media.

6. If you want to run a custom script for booting the local Linux system, which of these files is most appropriate?

   A. /etc/rc.local

   B. /etc/init

   C. /etc/profile

   D. /boot/grub/grub.conf

7. What command or command switch brings a process to the background?

   A. +

   B. &

   C. bg

   D. fg

8. If you see a noauto in /etc/fstab, what do you need to do to mount the filesystem just after Linux is booted?

   A. Nothing, it's done automatically.

   B. Apply the **mount** command to the device as defined in /etc/fstab.

   C. Run the **fsck** command to the device as defined in /etc/fstab.

   D. Configure appropriate permissions in /etc/group.

9. Which of the following commands reviews files from a test.tar.gz archive without extracting them?

   A. tar -tvf test.tar.gz

   B. tar -lvf test.tar.gz

   C. tar xzvf test.tar.gz

   D. tar xjvf test.tar.bz2

10. Which of the following commands can tell you if RAM is overloaded?

   A. ramload

   B. ps aux

   C. ls

   D. top

REVIEW ANSWERS

1. **B**   Type **83** corresponds to a standard Linux partition. Type **82** corresponds to a Linux swap filesystem. Type **85** corresponds to a Linux Extended filesystem. Type **fd** corresponds to a Linux RAID filesystem.

2. **C**   When booting from a Linux Live CD, you get a full set of tools, including **fsck**. If you run **fsck** without unmounting a partition, it may damage the filesystem (as noted by a warning message when you try). Even if you force unmounting of the top-level root directory, **fsck** still sees that directory as mounted. Rescue mode in some systems may also work, but booting from a Live Linux CD is more reliable.

3. **B**   It's not necessary to reformat any filesystem to convert from ext2 to ext3. The **tune2fs -j** command adds a journal, which is the only difference that makes an ext3 filesystem. It is appropriate to document the change in /etc/fstab to make sure the system is mounted with ext3. It's always appropriate to keep backups up to date.

4. **C**   Runlevel 3 is the standard associated with command-line login consoles. While runlevel 2 does the same thing, it does not include NFS networking. Runlevel 1 is single-user mode. Runlevel 5 boots into the GUI.

5. **B**   The file may or may not be saved to the USB key, depending on whether data in RAM has been flushed to disk. While running the **umount** command on the associated device should work, the way to make sure it is saved is by running the **sync** command before removing the USB key.

6. **A**   The /etc/rc.local script (or /etc/boot.local in openSUSE) is the most appropriate place for user-defined administrative scripts. While in some cases /etc/inittab may be appropriate, there is no /etc/init script in any of the selected distributions. The /etc/profile configuration file is associated with user settings, and scripts are not appropriate for the GRUB configuration file in /boot/grub/grub.conf.

7. **B**   The **&** after a command runs it in the background. The + after a command doesn't do anything (at least with the commands I know). The **bg** command does bring a command paused with CTRL-Z to the background. The **fg** command brings a background command to the foreground.

8. **B** The **noauto** directive prevents automatic mounting during the boot process.

9. **A** The -t switch is short for --**list** with the **tar** command. The -l switch remains in the local filesystem. The other two commands extract files from noted archives.

10. **D** The **top** command starts a screen that monitors the load on your system, including that associated with RAM.

User and Service Management

	NEWBIE	SOME EXPERIENCE	VETERAN
ETA	40+ hours	8 hours	4 hours

Managing Linux services requires a knowledge of network management. Basic network troubleshooting tools like **ping**, **netstat**, and **traceroute** can confirm connectivity and routing. Remote management tools allow administration from remote systems.

Other Linux services discussed in this chapter include printers, the Network Information Service (NIS), and mail services and clients. Services such as **cron** and **at** help automate jobs. This chapter also covers the basics of managing users and groups from the command-line interface.

Understand Network Troubleshooting
Objective 5.01

There are three basic network troubleshooting commands listed in the Linux+ objectives: **ping**, **netstat**, and **traceroute**. They can confirm connectivity, verify routing tables, and literally trace the route of data from source to destination. If you want to diagnose trouble with a network from a Linux system, you need to be familiar with these commands.

Confirming Connectivity with ping

The simplest way to test connectivity is with the **ping** command. If you know the right IP addresses (or have a working DNS or /etc/hosts database), you can use **ping** to check local and network connectivity. For the purpose of this section, assume your IP address is 10.11.12.13 and the gateway address on your network is 10.11.12.1. If you're having problems connecting to a network, you should use the **ping** command in the following order: In any case, to actually run these commands, you'll need the IP address of the local network card as well as the gateway address, which would then be substituted for 10.11.12.13 and 10.11.12.1, respectively.

1. Test the integrity of TCP/IP on your computer:

   ```
   # ping 127.0.0.1
   ```

2. Normally, **ping** works continuously on Linux; you need to press CTRL-C to stop this command. To see if networking is properly configured, **ping** your own IP address:

   ```
   # ping 10.11.12.13
   ```

3. If that works, **ping** the address of another computer on the local network. If you don't know the name or IP address of any other

system on the local network, try the broadcast address. For the given network, the command would be

```
# ping -b 10.11.12.255
```

4. Start tracing the route to the Internet. Run the **ping** command for more distant systems, such as the IP address for the local network gateway, in this case, 10.11.12.1. If known, **ping** the IP address of your network's connection to the Internet. And finally, **ping** the address of a computer that you know is *active* on the Internet.

Travel Advisory

To find the IP address of the local network gateway, run the **route -n** command. The Gateway IP address is associated with the 0.0.0.0 or *default* destination network.

You can substitute hostnames or fully qualified domain names, such as bobsdesktp or www.google.com, for an IP address. If the hostname doesn't work, there's a problem with the database of hostnames and IP addresses, such as /etc/hosts, or, more likely, with the DNS server. For more information, see the Chapter 6 section "Implement Name Resolution."

Local Lingo

BIND   Short for Berkeley Internet Name Domain, the most common DNS server in Linux. There are other DNS servers available for Linux, such as djbdns and dnsmasq.

Reviewing Network Connections with netstat

The **netstat** command can help you see the channels available for network connections, interface statistics, and more. It can even display routing tables with the **netstat -r** command. Run this command, and learn how to read a routing table, as shown below.

```
# netstat -r
Kernel routing table
Destination  Gateway      Genmask         Flags MSS Window irtt Iface
10.11.12.0   *            255.255.255.0   U     40  0         0 eth0
169.254.0.0  *            255.0.0.0       UH    40  0         0 lo
default      10.11.12.1   255.255.255.0   UG    40  0         0 eth0
```

Incidentally, the **route** command provides the same information. The Destination column lists networks by their IP addresses. The *default* destination is associated with all other IP addresses; if you run the **netstat -nr** or **route -n** commands, this is shown as 0.0.0.0. The Gateway column indicates gateway addresses. If the destination is on the LAN, no gateway is required, so an asterisk is shown in this column. The Genmask column lists the network mask. Networks look for a route appropriate to the destination IP address. The IP address is compared against the destination networks, in order. When the IP address is found to be part of one of these networks, it's sent in that direction. If there is a gateway address, it's sent to the computer with that gateway. The Flags column describes how this is done; descriptions of the more important flags are listed in Table 5.1.

Now for a bit of analysis. The routing table listed in this section is read from top to bottom; in other words, when this system is looking to send a message, it first looks to see if the destination IP address is on the 10.11.12.0/255.255.255.0 network. If it's there, the message proceeds through network card eth0. The second line refers to a common Zero Configuration Network address, available when there are no DHCP servers, or no static IP addresses. Microsoft refers to this address as Automatic Private IP Addressing (APIPA). The final line is for messages sent everyplace else on the Internet, which are sent out through the gateway system on 10.11.12.1.

Tracing a Network Path with traceroute

The **traceroute** command can help identify problems on the network. While it's intended for large internal networks, it's most easily illustrated over the Internet. For example, when I run the command

```
# traceroute www.bbc.co.uk
```

I see the results shown in Figure 5.1, which traces the route taken by the connection, through my ISP, on to Seattle, New York, and finally to the BBC website in the United Kingdom. But that's a successful connection.

TABLE 5.1	The **netstat** Flag Indicates the Route

Flag	Description
G	The route uses a gateway.
U	The network adapter is up.
H	Only a single host can be reached via this route.
D	This entry was created by an ICMP redirect message.
M	This entry was modified by an ICMP redirect message.

```
[root@enterprise5hp ~]# traceroute www.bbc.co.uk
traceroute to www.bbc.co.uk (212.58.240.110), 30 hops max, 40 byte packets
 1  * * *
 2  68.87.219.193 (68.87.219.193)  29.995 ms  31.916 ms  31.966 ms
 3  te-9-3-ar01.troutdale.or.bverton.comcast.net (68.87.216.89)  31.632 ms * *
 4  68.86.90.237 (68.86.90.237)  41.649 ms  44.832 ms  46.858 ms
 5  te-3-3.car1.Seattle1.Level3.net (4.79.104.109)  46.402 ms  46.523 ms  50.509
ms
 6  ae-2-54.mp2.Seattle1.Level3.net (4.68.105.97)  49.780 ms  27.464 ms ae-2-52.
mp2.Seattle1.Level3.net (4.68.105.33)  39.282 ms
 7  as-4-0.bbr2.NewYork1.Level3.net (64.159.0.238)  93.102 ms ae-0-0.bbr1.NewYor
k1.Level3.net (64.159.1.41)  97.978 ms as-4-0.bbr2.NewYork1.Level3.net (64.159.0
.238)  93.921 ms
 8  vlan79.csw2.NewYork1.Level3.net (4.68.16.126)  105.060 ms  99.600 ms  104.26
6 ms
 9  ge-10-0.hsa2.NewYork1.Level3.net (4.68.97.43)  104.573 ms  103.091 ms ge-9-0
.hsa2.NewYork1.Level3.net (4.68.97.11)  100.888 ms
10  (166.90.136.142)  95.775 ms  89.205 ms  86.207 ms
11  www10.thny.bbc.co.uk (212.58.240.110)  86.427 ms  87.734 ms  88.805 ms
[root@enterprise5hp ~]# █
```

FIGURE 5.1   Using **traceroute** to trace a connection

On the other hand, when I try to trace a route to www.wipro.com in India, there happens to be a problem, which is not a complete surprise, because India is on the other side of the globe. The problem may be located just before where you might see three asterisks, which is associated with a **ping** command that is not acknowledged:

```
12   * * *
13   * * *
```

If you run **traceroute** on a large local network, it can help you identify routers that may be down or are otherwise not functioning.

Objective 5.02 Administer with Remote Management Tools

There are three categories of remote management tools. The two included in the Linux+ objectives are the "r" commands, which support connections to remote systems, and the **ssh** command, which supports secure encrypted connections to remote systems. There are also the **telnet** commands, which support remote connections in clear text.

These commands will work only if the associated servers (rsh-server, openssh-server, and telnet-server) are installed and active on the target systems. Of course, this also assumes no network blocking by firewalls, TCP Wrappers, or system regulation by other security services such as SELinux.

Firewalls and TCP Wrappers are discussed in Chapters 8 and 9; SELinux was not included in Linux when the Linux+ objectives were released, and therefore is beyond the scope of this book.

Exam Tip

Practice remote logins with the noted commands; try different types of login commands such as **ssh user@remotepc** and **ssh -l user remotepc**.

The "r" Commands

There are three "r" commands: remote copy (**rcp**), remote shell (**rsh**), and remote login (**rlogin**). The **rcp** command copies from one system to another, in the following format:

```
# rcp source destination
```

This assumes that the source or destination is a remote system, configured in the format *user@remotehost:/path/to/file*. For example, if I want to copy the xorg.conf.new file to Donna's account and home directory on the remote enterprise5dl system, I'd run the following command, which prompts for Donna's password:

```
                 source                  destination
# rcp xorg.conf.new donna@enterprise5dl:/home/donna
```

The **rsh** command supports access to a remote system for a single command. Access may be controlled by a .rhosts file in each user's home directory. For example, I can check the current list of files in Donna's home directory on her computer named poohbear with the following command:

```
            username
$ rsh -l donna poohbear ls
```

To elaborate on this command, the -l specifies a username, in this case donna, on the system named poohbear. The **rsh** command prompts for donna's password on the system named poohbear; once verified, the ls command is run by default in her home directory. Of course, I could have specified a different directory, such as /etc.

If you just want to log into a different system, the **rlogin** command is appropriate. It follows the same basic format. For example, if you wanted to log into my account on the computer named poohbear, you could try with the following command:

```
# rlogin -l michael poohbear
```

Of course, you would need my password. But if you got it, you would have the privileges of my account on the noted system.

The Secure Shell

The Secure Shell is the more popular way to create remote connections on
Linux. It's more secure, as it encrypts data on the network. When you connect to
a remote system with a Secure Shell command, the password is encrypted, unlike a Telnet connection.

As with the "r" commands, access depends on the installation of an appropriate server. Access through the server depends on the directives in the governing
configuration file, /etc/sshd_config. For detailed information on this file, and
other commands mentioned in this section, see the Chapter 8 section "Set Up
Security Environment Files."

There are four basic Secure Shell client commands available. The **scp** command works like the **rcp** command. It supports copying from a source to a destination, one of which is on a remote system. The basic syntax is the same; just
substitute **scp** for **rcp** in the **rcp** command noted earlier in this objective.

The **sftp** command connects securely to FTP servers. Anonymous connections are not allowed with the standard **sftp** client. As with other FTP servers, if
you log in with a regular account, the **sftp** FTP client navigates to the associated
home directory by default.

The last two Secure Shell commands, **ssh** and **slogin**, are synonymous. In
fact, the **slogin** command on the selected distributions is soft linked to **ssh**
(which can be confirmed with the **ls -l /usr/bin/slogin** command). The **ssh** command permits encrypted logins to a remote server, assuming the **sshd** daemon is
running. It works with the same syntax used for the **rsh** command; for example,
the following command attempts to connect as the root user on the remote system named poohbear:

```
# ssh -l root poohbear
```

I often log in remotely with **ssh** in more of an "e-mail" style format:

```
# ssh root@poohbear
```

It's safer to log in with **ssh** as a regular user, and then use **su** or **sudo** to access
the root administrative account. A cracker can guess that a password is near the
beginning of a connection. Even better is to use a private-public key pair, which
can be created with a **ssh_keygen** command, and copied to the Secure Shell

server, in the target user's home directory, in the .ssh/ subdirectory, in a file like authorized_keys2.

Configure Printer Systems

Objective 5.03

There were two major printer systems in use when the Linux+ objectives were released: the Line Printer Daemon (LPD) and the Common Unix Printing System (CUPS). Several Linux distributions used a variation of LPD, known as Line Printer, next generation (LPRng).

CUPS is in more common use today. LPD/LPRng isn't even available on some of the selected distributions. There are legacy systems where LPD/LPRng is still in common use, so you do need to know some of the basics about this older print management system. And several related commands can be used to manage CUPS printers.

The CUPS and LPD/LPRng services are mutually exclusive; in other words, you can't have both services installed or running on the same system simultaneously. However, it is possible to network the two services, with one as a client and the other as a server.

As installed on Linux, CUPS and LPD/LPRng share several commands, which you'll read about after the basic sections on each service. For example, the **lpc status** command lists all configured printers, local and remote, which can give you information such as:

```
HPLaserJet4:
    printer is on device 'ipp' speed -1
    queuing is enabled
    printing is disabled
    no entries
    daemon present
```

For a printer to actually work, both the print service and the specific printer have to be configured and enabled. The "no entries" output means there are no waiting print jobs.

The Line Printer Daemon   *Berkeley*

The LPD/LPRng service is also known as the Berkeley printing system. It provides spooling and print server functionality. Printers installed under this service can be shared over a network.

The LPD/LPRng daemon is **lpd**; standard configuration files are /etc/lpd.conf and /etc/lpd.perms. Configured printers are documented with filters in

/etc/printcap. The language associated with this configuration file for LPD/ LPRng systems is obscure.

The LPD/LPRng service uses print filters to translate print data to a language that a printer can understand. The translated files are stored in printer spools until the printer is ready to handle the data. The key file for filters is /etc/ printcap. Here's an excerpt from a typical LPD-enabled version of this file:

```
lp|Printer1 auto:\
    :lp=/dev/lp0:\
    :if=/etc/apsfilter/basedir/bin/apsfilter:\
    :sd=/var/spool/lpd/lp:\
    :lf=/var/spool/lpd/lp/log:\
    :af=/var/spool/lpd/lp/acct:\
    :mx#0
    :sh:
```

Yes, these commands are cryptic. Not everyone wants to learn details about a print system that is essentially obsolete on current Linux distributions. So just keep the following two directives in mind:

- **lp** Line print, associated with a print device such as /dev/lp0. Normally, /dev/lp0 and /dev/lp1 correspond to the LPT1 and LPT2 ports associated with Microsoft operating systems.

- **sd** Spool directory, where print files are stored on the print server, until the printer is ready to process the data.

The Common Unix Printing System

CUPS is the default print service for the selected distributions. In most cases, it is the only print service available on the latest Linux releases. CUPS is built for the Internet Printing Protocol (IPP), which is the evolving cross-platform standard for network print services. It can also handle printers shared on other networks from LPD/LPRng, Samba/CIFS, AppleTalk, and several other print services. CUPS can use many of the same PostScript Printer Description (PPD) drivers used for Microsoft operating systems. In other words, with CUPS, Linux developers no longer have to spend so much time customizing drivers for the latest printers.

You can configure printers directly through CUPS configuration files in the /etc/cups directory. While the CUPS configuration files are complex, there is a Web-based interface that makes CUPS administration less intimidating for many; just direct your browser to http://localhost:631; one view using the command-line ELinks browser is shown in Figure 5.2.

Travel Advisory

If the http://localhost:631 URL does not work, you either haven't installed and activated CUPS or aren't running Linux.

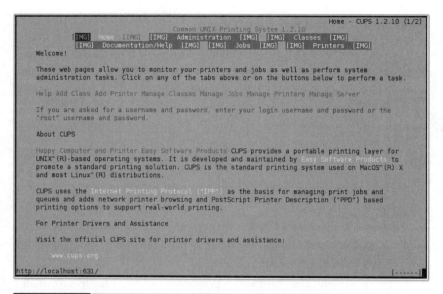

```
                                                    Home - CUPS 1.2.10 (1/2)
                            Common UNIX Printing System 1.2.10
      [IMG]  Home  [IMG]  [IMG]  Administration  [IMG]  [IMG]  Classes  [IMG]
      [IMG]  Documentation/Help  [IMG]  [IMG]  Jobs  [IMG]  [IMG]  Printers  [IMG]
  Welcome!

  These web pages allow you to monitor your printers and jobs as well as perform system
  administration tasks. Click on any of the tabs above or on the buttons below to perform a task.

  Help Add Class Add Printer Manage Classes Manage Jobs Manage Printers Manage Server

  If you are asked for a username and password, enter your login username and password or the
  "root" username and password.

  About CUPS

  Happy Computer and Printer Easy Software Products CUPS provides a portable printing layer for
  UNIX^(R)-based operating systems. It is developed and maintained by Easy Software Products to
  promote a standard printing solution. CUPS is the standard printing system used on MacOS^(R) X
  and most Linux^(R) distributions.

  CUPS uses the Internet Printing Protocol ("IPP") as the basis for managing print jobs and
  queues and adds network printer browsing and PostScript Printer Description ("PPD") based
  printing options to support real-world printing.

  For Printer Drivers and Assistance

  Visit the official CUPS site for printer drivers and assistance:

      www.cups.org

http://localhost:631/                                                    [-----]
```

FIGURE 5.2   The Web-based CUPS configuration tool

CUPS uses some of the same configuration files used by LPD/LPRng. For example, the /etc/printcap file lists shared printers. In both cases, the Samba configuration file, /etc/samba/smb.conf, refers to this file when sharing printers over Microsoft-based networks.

Running a Print Job

Most applications have print commands, which provide their own interfaces to the standard print command, **lpr.** In Linux, it's just another way of redirecting standard output, normally to a file in the associated spool directory. For example, if I wanted to print the Chapter5.pdf file, I could run the following command:

```
# lpr Chapter5.pdf
```

If the print system is not configured with appropriate filters or drivers, as described earlier in this objective, the printer produces a bunch of ASCII control characters. With the right filters, you can print out even complex PDF files with the **lpr** command.

Checking Print Queues and Spools

Print queues are maintained on clients. They can be checked with the **lpq** command. By itself, **lpq** checks the default printer as defined in /etc/printcap for

LPD/LPRng systems or /etc/cups/printers.conf for CUPS systems. To check a different printer, the -**P** switch can help:

```
# lpq -P differentprinter
```

Older versions of the **lpq** command actually required no space between the -**P** switch and the name of the printer, so the command looked like **lpq** -P*differentprinter*. Current versions of the **lpq** command aren't so limited.

Exam Tip

Don't be surprised to see a command such as **lpq** -**P***printername*; some exam candidates may be confused by the lack of a space between the -**P** and the name of the printer.

If you want to check all printers configured on the local system, run the **lpq** -**a** command. In any case, the **lpq** command can help check remote printers; for example, to check all printers on the computer with an IP address of 192.168.0.30, run the following command:

```
# lpq -a -h 192.168.0.30
```

If there are active print jobs, there will be output similar to this:

```
Rank     Owner    Job    File(s)              Total Size
1st      michael  413    passwd               2048 bytes
2nd      michael  414    Chapter Five: User and  1012736 bytes
```

Remember the job number; you'll need it if you want to cancel the associated print job.

Travel Advisory

CUPS can group printers in a class; the class name can then itself be administered as a separate printer.

Print spools are located on print servers and, depending on whether you're using LPD/LPRng or CUPS, are available in the /var/spool/lpd or /var/spool/cups directory.

Removing Print Jobs

The **lprm** command is designed to remove print jobs. By default, it removes the oldest print job first. To remove any other print job, you need the job number, available in the output to the **lpq** command.

Objective 5.04   Control Mail Servers

The Linux+ exam is designed for those who have 6 to 12 months of experience with Linux. Such users rarely have in-depth configuration experience with e-mail servers, so detailed configuration options are beyond the scope of this exam. Standard options for outgoing e-mail servers are sendmail and Postfix.

Mail servers such as sendmail, Postfix, Dovecot, and IMAP are categorized as Mail Transfer Agents (MTAs). Mail clients such as Evolution, Thunderbird, **mail**, and **elm** are known as Mail User Agents (MUAs). If you've installed both sendmail and Postfix, be aware that they're mutually exclusive. In other words, don't activate both services simultaneously on any system.

Outgoing mail servers use the Simple Mail Transfer Protocol (SMTP) service, and use a default TCP/IP port of 25. To check a list of current e-mail processed by sendmail or Postfix, the **mailq** command can help. Some distributions include the **mailq.sendmail** and **mailq.postfix** commands for each service.

Basic sendmail

Configuration files associated with sendmail are stored in the /etc/mail directory. The basic sendmail configuration file is complex; the latest version of this file on Red Hat distributions includes nearly 2000 lines. Several key files in /etc/mail are briefly explained in Table 5.2.

If you've edited a sendmail.mc file, it can then be processed into a sendmail.cf configuration file, as described in the opening comments to sendmail.mc. One option which processes just sendmail.mc uses the **m4** preprocessor:

```
# m4 /etc/mail/sendmail.mc > /etc/mail/sendmail.cf
```

Alternatively, courtesy of /etc/mail/Makefile, it's possible to use the **make** command to process sendmail.mc into sendmail.cf—and other configuration files in /etc/mail into appropriate database files, with .db extensions.

TABLE 5.2	Key sendmail Configuration Files
sendmail File	**Description**
sendmail.cf	The main sendmail configuration file
sendmail.mc	A group of macros that can be processed into sendmail.cf
domaintable	Provides a map of alternative domains
Makefile	A script that can help process files such as sendmail.mc
virtusertable	Supports e-mail forwarding for users outside the network

Basic Postfix

The Postfix mail server is a common option to sendmail. As it has over 600 lines, it's still beyond the scope of the Linux+ exam. Suffice to say that once configured and activated, it's as fully functional as sendmail for many configurations. There's no need to apply the **make** command to compile or process any edited files in the /etc/postfix directory.

Objective 5.05 Understand Text-based Mail Clients

G UI mail clients, even on Linux, are relatively trivial to configure, even for beginning Linux users. The Linux+ objectives specify the use of command-line interface-based mail clients such as **mail** and **mutt**.

Exam Tip

Learn basic commands associated with the **mail** and **mutt** e-mail clients.

The mail Client

To test a mail system, you can use the built-in command-line **mail** utility, which includes a simple text-based interface. The system keeps each user's mail in the /var/mail directory. Once users read a message, they can reply to, forward, or delete it. If they do not delete the message before quitting the **mail** utility, the system stores the message in a file named after the applicable username.

There are two basic methods to send e-mail to another user with the **mail** command-line utility. First, you can enter the subject and then the text of your message, press CTRL-D, enter another addressee in the Cc: line, if desired, and then press ENTER. The message is sent, and the **mail** utility stops and sends you back to the command line.

```
$ mail Michael@example.org
Subject: Test Message
This is only a test. If this had been an actual . . .
Cc: mjang@example.com
$
```

Alternatively, you can redirect a file as the text of an e-mail to another user. For example, the following command sends a copy of /etc/hosts to the root user on the abc.example.com system, with the Subject name of "hosts file":

```
$ mail root@abc.example.com -s "hosts file" < /etc/hosts
```

Here's one more example, which sends an e-mail containing the words "test message" under a subject name of "test subject":

```
$ echo "test message" | mail -s "test subject" root@abc.example.com
```

The mutt Client

Another way to test a mail system is with the **mutt** utility, which supports creating messages in text editors such as vi. The system keeps each user's mail in their home directory, in the Mail/ directory. The low-level graphical console interface lists options, as shown in Figure 5.3.

```
q:Quit  d:Del  u:Undel  s:Save  m:Mail  r:Reply  g:Group  ?:Help
    1 O   Jul 12 Michael Jang    (   1) another email
    2 O   Jul 12 root            (   1) test subject
```

```
---Mutt: /var/mail/michael [Msgs:2 Old:2 1.3K]---(reverse-date/date)----(all)---
```

FIGURE 5.3 Running **mutt** for e-mail

As you can see from the top row of **mutt**, there are a series of letters that correspond to standard mail client commands, such as **m** to start a new e-mail message, and **r** to reply to a highlighted message. When addressing a message, you're prompted for an e-mail address and subject. You're then taken to a message interface, which by default uses the vi editor. After you complete the message text, you're taken to a similar screen, where options are available to add a Cc:, attach a file, modify the subject, and more.

Objective 5.06 Administrative Job Management

The *cron* system is an alarm clock that can start any jobs that you or other administrators may schedule. When the alarm sounds, Linux runs associated commands and scripts automatically. The **cron** system can be set to run at all sorts of regular time intervals. Alternatively, the *at* system allows you to run the command of your choice, once, at a specified time in the future.

Exam Tip
Recognize the functionality of basic **crontab** and **at** commands, as well as their directory locations.

Standard and User cron Jobs

Standard **cron** jobs are configured in /etc/crontab, which refers to specific files in several /etc/cron.* directories. Each **cron** file is set up in a specific format. Lines in **cron** can be blank, a comment (which begins with #), a variable, or a command.

When you run a regular command, the actions of the shell are based on environmental variables. To see the environmental variables, run the **env** command. Some of the standard variables on the selected Linux distributions include **HOME** as the current user's home directory, **SHELL** as the default shell, and **LOGNAME** as the username.

To set environment variables within the crontab file, use the following syntax:

```
Variable=Value
```

Some variables are already set for you. For example, **MAIL** for me is /var/spool/mail/michael, **LANG** is en_US.UTF-8, and **PATH** specifies directories where the shell looks for commands. You can set these variables to different values in your crontab file. For example, the default /etc/crontab file on three of the selected distributions include the following variables:

```
SHELL=/bin/bash
PATH=/sbin:/bin:/usr/sbin:/usr/bin
MAILTO=root
HOME=/
```

Note that the values of **PATH, MAILTO,** and **HOME** are different from those for the standard environment variables.

The following describes the format of a line in crontab. Each of these columns is explained in more detail in Table 5.3.

```
#minute, hour, day of month, month, day of week, command
*        *    *              *      *             command
```

If you see an asterisk in any column, **cron** runs that command for all possible values of that column. For example, an * in the minute field means that the command is run every minute during the specified hour(s). Consider another example:

```
5   4   3   2   *   ls
```

This line runs the **ls** command every February 3 at 4:05 A.M. The asterisk in the day of week column simply means that it does not matter what day of the week it is; the **crontab** script still runs the **ls** command at the specified time.

The crontab file is flexible. For example, if you see 13–16 in the hour field, the **cron** daemon runs the associated command at 1:00 P.M., 2:00 P.M., 3:00 P.M., and 4:00 P.M. The list 0,10,20,30,40,50 in the minute field would run the specified command every ten minutes. The **cron** daemon also recognizes *lowercase* abbreviations for months and the day of the week. The actual command is the sixth field.

Each user can use the **crontab** command to create and manage **cron** jobs for their own accounts. There are four switches associated with the **crontab** command:

- **-u** *user* Allows the root user to edit the crontab of another specific user; requires one of the other switches.
- **-l** Lists the current crontab file.
- **-r** Deletes the specified user's crontab file.
- **-e** Edits an existing crontab file. By default, the **crontab** command opens the file in the vi editor.

If you want to set up **cron** entries on the local account, start with the **crontab -e** command. It opens the vi editor by default, for easy editing of the variables and commands of your choice, per the guidelines in this section. Entries for each user are saved under the username in the /var/spool/cron directory (except the SUSE distribution, which saves them in the /var/spool/cron/tabs directory).

| TABLE 5.3 | Entries in a **crontab** Command Line |

Field	Value
minute	0–59
hour	Based on a 24-hour clock; for example, 23 = 11 P.M.
day of month	1–31
month	1–12, or jan, feb, mar, etc.
day of week	0–7; where 0 and 7 are both Sunday; or sun, mon, tue, etc.
command	The command to be executed

Creating an at Job

Like **cron**, the **at** daemon supports job processing, and is suitable for one-time tasks. The **at** daemon works similarly to the print process; jobs are spooled in the /var/spool/at directory and run at the specified time.

You can use the **at** daemon to run the command or script of your choice. For the purpose of this section, assume that user michael has created a script named 7x7 in his home directory to process some airplane sales database to another file in the same directory called sales.

From the command line, you can run the **at** *time* command to start a job to be run at a specified *time*. That *time* can be now; in a specified number of minutes, hours, or days; or at the time of your choice. Several examples are illustrated in Table 5.4.

To open an **at** job, use a command similar to those shown in Table 5.4. It starts an *at>* prompt, where you can specify the command of your choice. For this example, assume you're late for a personal appointment, and want to start the job in an hour. From the conditions previously specified, run the following commands:

```
$ at now + 1 hour
at> /home/michael/7x7 > /home/michael/sales
at> Ctrl-D
```

| TABLE 5.4 | Examples of the **at** Command |

Time Period	Example	Description
Minutes	**at now + 20 minutes**	Associated jobs will start in 20 minutes.
Hours	**at now + 3 hours**	Associated jobs will start in 3 hours.
Days	**at now + 1 day**	Associated jobs will start in 24 hours.
Weeks	**at now + 1 week**	Associated jobs will start in 7 days.
n/a	**at teatime**	Associated jobs will start at 4:00 P.M.
n/a	**at 3:00 7/13/08**	Associated jobs will start on July 13, 2008, at 3:00 A.M.

The CTRL-D command exits the **at** command shell and returns to your original command-line interface. To check the status of your jobs, so you can see if it will work, run the following job queue command:

```
$ atq
1        2008-4-12 16:18 a michael
```

If there's a problem with the job, you can remove it with the **atrm** command. For the output shown, you'd remove job number 1 with the following command:

```
$ atrm 1
```

 **Manage User Accounts**

U sers and groups can be managed directly through configuration files, with utilities at the command-line interface, and with distribution-specific tools. As the coverage of the Linux+ exam is not limited to a specific distribution, this book does not address such tools; instead, it focuses on direct editing and command-line tools. To understand user account management, you need to know what's in the associated configuration files.

Users and groups can also be regulated by quotas, which can limit the space and number of files allocated to each account.

Exam Tip

Recognize what user and group management commands actually do, especially with detailed switches.

User and Group Configuration Files

There are several files associated with user and group configuration. The basic files are /etc/passwd and /etc/group. As you can see in /etc/passwd, users and groups are associated with user ID (UID) and group ID (GID) numbers. Review it for yourself in /etc/passwd. The third and fourth numbers in each row correspond to the UID and GID, respectively. In general, UIDs below 100 are reserved for system accounts, and the selected distributions (except SUSE) start regular UIDs at 500. There are seven columns in /etc/passwd, described in Table 5.5.

TABLE 5.5	Columns in /etc/passwd	
Column	**Category**	**Description**
1	Username	What's entered at the Login: prompt
2	Password	May contain an encrypted password, an x, which points to /etc/shadow for the password, or an *, which means the account is disabled
3	User ID	The UID number
4	Group ID	The GID number
5	User info	Text info commonly used for real names, location, and more
6	Home directory	Normally /home/*username*
7	Default shell	The shell started upon login

Similarly, /etc/group specifies a list of group names. There are four columns in this file, as described in Table 5.6.

The selected distributions also conform to the Shadow Password Suite, which encrypts passwords and other account configuration data in more secure files, specifically /etc/shadow and /etc/gshadow. (If these files don't exist on your system, the Shadow Password Suite is disabled.) There are eight columns in /etc/shadow, as described in Table 5.7.

Finally, the /etc/gshadow file documents the Shadow Password Suite implementation of groups. As shown in Table 5.8, it can specify a group password as well as a special group administrator.

As you read through the following sections associated with this objective, observe what the commands do to these files. I believe it's the best way to learn how to answer test questions associated with administering users and groups—and in real life.

TABLE 5.6	Columns in /etc/group	
Column	**Category**	**Description**
1	Group name	Some distributions use the name for user and group
2	Password	Some groups are password protected; if there's an x in this column, check /etc/gshadow
3	Group ID	The GID number
4	Members	Usernames of members of the group

	TABLE 5.7	Columns in /etc/shadow

Column	Category	Description
1	Username	Login name
2	Password	Encrypted password
3	Number of days	Time since the password was last changed, in days, after January 1, 1970
4	Min password life	Time, in days, during which a password must stay the same
5	Max password life	Time, in days, after which a password has to change
6	Warning period	Number of days before password expiration at which a warning is given
7	Disable account	Account is disabled if unused this many days after password expiration
8	Account expiration	Specifies an expiration date in YYYY-MM-DD format, or number of days after January 1, 1970; great for temporary accounts

Adding User Accounts in Configuration Files

When I first learned Linux, one of my first lessons was on the password configuration file, /etc/passwd. I learned to create users by editing this file directly. While you could open these files directly in the vi editor, the standard commands to open /etc/passwd and /etc/group are **vipw** and **vigr**, respectively.

If you've already created a regular user, use it as a model for creating a second user. Just make sure the username, UID, GID, user info, and home directories are appropriate for the new user.

Once you've configured /etc/passwd and possibly /etc/group with a new user, assign a password with the **passwd** *newuser* command. If the system is set up

	TABLE 5.8	Columns in /etc/gshadow

Column	Category	Description
1	Group name	Some distributions use the name for user and group
2	Password	The encrypted group password; set by **gpasswd**
3	Group administrator	The user allowed to manage users in this group
4	Members	Usernames of members of the group

with the Shadow Password Suite, with the /etc/shadow and /etc/gshadow files, you need to translate the new entries to that file with the **pwconv** and **grpconv** commands.

Adding Users and Groups from the Command Line

Alternatively, this process can be automated with the **useradd** command. If you wanted to add a new user named labrador, just type **useradd labrador** to add this user to the /etc/passwd file. By default, it creates a home directory, /home/labrador; adds standard files from the /etc/skel directory; and assigns the default shell, /bin/bash. But the **useradd** command can do more, as depicted by the options listed and described in Table 5.9.

However, creating a user is not enough; unless you run **passwd labrador** and tell him what password you've set, that user can't log in. After he logs into his account, he can then change his own password with the **passwd** command.

When needed, the **groupadd** command can be as elaborate. But in general, if you're creating a special group such as supervisors, the first step is to add the group with a command like **groupadd supervisors**, find the GID in /etc/group, and then add users to that group directly in /etc/group. Future supervisors can then be added with the **useradd -g GID** *newsupervisor* command.

Naturally, the **userdel** and **groupdel** commands reverse the process. But the **userdel** *username* command isn't a complete opposite to **useradd** *username*; without an -r switch, that command does not delete the /home/*username* directory.

User and Group Management Commands

Based on the Linux+ objectives, there are three commands associated with managing users and groups: **usermod**, for changing account settings, **chage**, for managing password expiration, and **groupmod**, for modifying group account settings.

TABLE 5.9	Command-line Options for **useradd**
Option	**Purpose**
-u *UID*	Assigns a specific *UID*.
-g *GID*	Assigns a specific *GID*.
-c *info*	The *info* is a comment about the user, such as name, phone, etc.
-d *dir*	Sets a home directory for the user.
-s *shell*	Sets a shell for the user.

usermod

The **usermod** command changes user account information in /etc/passwd and /etc/shadow. It can also set an expiration date for an account. For example, the following command sets the account associated with user tempworker1 to expire on April 15, 2008:

```
# usermod -e 2008-04-15 tempworker1
```

As a second example, the following command makes user tempworker1 a member of the *shorttime* group:

```
# usermod -G shorttime tempworker1
```

One more example: the following command changes the comment field in the /etc/passwd configuration file. It's often used to add human-readable information, such as:

```
# usermod -c "The supervisor is immature" supervisor
```

Of course, as an administrator, you'd want to include more relevant information.

chage

The **chage** command can be used to regulate when passwords have to change, as stored in the /etc/shadow file, as depicted by the options listed and described in Table 5.10.

groupmod

The **groupmod** command can modify the GID number:

```
# groupmod -g newGID -o groupname
```

And it can also change the group name:

```
# groupmod -g GID -n newgroupname groupname
```

TABLE 5.10	Command-line Options for **chage**
Command	**Description**
chage -m *num user*	Assigns a minimum password life of *num* days to *user*
chage -M *num user*	Assigns a maximum password life of *num* days to *user*
chage -I *num user*	Sets *num* days of inactivity before canceling an account
chage -E *date user*	Sets a *date* after which the account is inaccessible

Managing Users and Groups with Quotas

Quotas can be applied to users and groups. But first, appropriate filesystems must be mounted with usrquota and/or grpquota settings. They can be added to the appropriate line in /etc/fstab; for example, if /dev/sda5 is associated with the /home directory partition, an appropriate quota-based setting would look like this:

```
/dev/sda5    /home    ext3    defaults,usrquota,grpquota  1 2
```

If you don't want to reboot, remount /dev/sda5 with quota settings with the following command, which uses the settings in /etc/fstab:

```
# mount -o remount /dev/sda5 /home
```

You can then create appropriate quota configuration files (aquota.user and aquota.group) in the /home directory with the following command:

```
# quotacheck -cugm /home
```

In this command, the -c scans the filesystem, the -u scans for user quotas before adding aquota.user, the -g scans for group quotas before adding aquota.group, and the -m remounts the scanned filesystems. Naturally, if you're only creating user or group quotas, the -u or -g is not required, respectively.

Quotas can be created with the **edquota -u** *user* command. This opens the *user*'s quota settings in the vi editor; soft and hard limits for blocks and inodes are documented in Table 5.11.

Once quotas are configured, every user can check his or her own with the **quota** command. The root user can check quotas for a regular *user* with the **quota -u** *user* command.

TABLE 5.11	Categories When Configuring User Quotas
Quota Setting	**Description**
Blocks	Amount of data associated with the user, in KB
Inodes	Number of file handles associated with the user
Soft	Basic limit for the user
Hard	Temporary limit for the user

Objective 5.08   Configure the Network Information Service

Network Information Service (NIS) servers can use one set of configuration files for multiple computers on a network. For example, an NIS server can set up a single /etc/passwd file as a single database of usernames for a network. While detailed configuration of an NIS server is beyond the scope of the Linux+ exam, you are expected to know basic NIS domain management commands for working with that server.

The NIS service requires connections through the so-called RPC Portmapper. RPC refers to the Remote Procedure Call, which supports NIS communications on a TCP/IP network.

Basic NIS Client Configuration

NIS domains are unrelated to the domains associated with computer networks, such as example.com. If your system already has an NIS domain name, run the **domainname** command. If you see *(none)* in the output, you can assign a domain name with the following command:

```
# domainname nisdomain
```

The change to the /etc/yp.conf configuration file is simple. All you need in that file is a command such as the following, which specifies the name of the NIS domain as *nisdomain*, and the name of the NIS server as *nislinux*:

```
domain nisdomain server nislinux
```

NIS Commands

There are several "yp" commands that can help you monitor and maintain a domain, as described in Table 5.12. These commands work only if you've configured and started NIS server (using the **ypserv** daemon) as well as a local NIS client (the **ypbind** daemon), and, finally, have set an NIS domain name on the local system. While it would be helpful to configure an NIS server to test these commands, that process is not listed in the Linux+ objectives (all that's mentioned are the *yp** commands for NIS domain management). If you want to configure your own NIS server, one reference is The Linux NIS(YP)/NYS/NIS+ HOWTO, available from www.linux-nis.org/nis-howto/HOWTO/index.html.

TABLE 5.12	NIS Commands

NIS Command	Description
ypcat	Reads file information from an NIS server database; e.g. **ypcat passwd**.
ypchfn	Changes *finger* (information for a specific user) in the NIS password database; the **finger** command is no longer in common use.
ypchsh	Changes the default shell for a specific user.
ypdomainname	Synonym for **domainname**.
ypmatch	Searches within an NIS database file; e.g. **ypmatch** *username* **passwd**.
yppasswd	Supports changes to a user's password in the NIS database.

Common File Management

The Name Service Switch file, /etc/nsswitch.conf, governs how your computer searches for key files such as password databases. You can configure it to look through NIS and LDAP server databases. For example, when an NIS client looks for a computer hostname, it might start with the following entry from /etc/nsswitch.conf:

```
hosts: files nis dns
```

This line tells your computer to search through name databases in the order shown. The *files* look at local files. The *nis* searches through the NIS server based on the aforementioned *nisdomain*. DNS services are described briefly in Chapters 6 and 7.

NIS password information from the server is stored in /etc/passwd. If account lookups are enabled on the client, you see the following in that file:

```
+::::::
```

The following lines enable login access to specific users, in this case, john, jane, and jim:

```
+john::::::
+jane::::::
+jim::::::
```

Conversely, the following lines added to /etc/passwd disable access:

```
-guest::::::
-ftp::::::
-michael::::::
```

CHECKPOINT

✔**Objective 5.01: Understand Network Troubleshooting**   Network trouble-shooting commands such as **ping, netstat,** and **traceroute** can help diagnose network problems.

✔**Objective 5.02: Administer with Remote Management Tools**   Remote management commands relate to the Remote and Secure Shells. The Secure Shell is preferred because it encrypts connections.

✔**Objective 5.03: Configure Printer Systems**   While the LPD/LPRng and CUPS print systems are mutually exclusive, they share some common control commands.

✔**Objective 5.04: Control Mail Servers**   The sendmail and Postfix services are mutually exclusive and both support outgoing e-mail through TCP/IP port 25.

✔**Objective 5.05: Understand Text-based Mail Clients**   Text mail clients work from the console; examples include **mail** and **mutt.**

✔**Objective 5.06: Administrative Job Management**   Administrative jobs can be run on a regular schedule using **cron,** or on a one-time basis using the **at** daemon.

✔**Objective 5.07: Manage User Accounts**   Users and groups can be configured directly through their configuration files, or with commands such as **useradd, groupadd, chage,** and **passwd.**

✔**Objective 5.08: Configure the Network Information Service**   The NIS service supports common configuration files, such as /etc/passwd for usernames, for a network.

REVIEW QUESTIONS

Before leaving for the next chapter, take a few minutes to go through these questions. While doing so, take in both the content and the question format. Understanding what to expect on the exam can increase your chances for success.

   1. Which of the following is a print daemon?

    A. printd

    B. cupsd

    C. lprngd

    D. printcapd

2. Which of the following commands lists the **cron** jobs for user michael?

    A. crontab michael

    B. crontab -l michael

    C. crontab -u michael -l

    D. crontab michael -l

3. You've just created the bcollie account. What do you need to do before bcollie can log in?

    A. Run **passwd bcollie** and tell him the password that you've set.

    B. Run **password bcollie** and tell him the password that you've set.

    C. Run **pwconv** and tell him the password that you've set.

    D. Reboot the system.

4. Which of the following mail clients stores e-mail outside a user's home directory?

    A. mutt

    B. Evolution

    C. mail

    D. mta

5. Which of the following commands verifies that TCP/IP is properly configured on the local system? The local IP address is 192.168.0.2, and the gateway is 192.168.0.1.

    A. ping 127.0.0.1

    B. ping 192.168.0.2

    C. ping 192.168.0.1

    D. traceroute 127.0.0.1

6. If you run the **userdel** *michael* command, what happens to the /home/michael directory?

    A. It's made inaccessible.

    B. It's archived in /home/lost+found.

    C. It's deleted.

    D. Nothing.

7. Which of the following commands connects securely to donna's account on host remoteserver?

   A. rsh -l donna remoteserver

   B. rsh donna@remoteserver

   C. ssh -l donna remoteserver

   D. ssh -u donna@remoteserver

8. If you see a usrquota in /etc/fstab, which of the following commands can change the quota for user dickens?

   A. quota dickens

   B. edquota dickens

   C. usrquota dickens

   D. grpquota dickens

9. Which of the following commands sends a copy of /etc/passwd to michael@example.net, with subject "cracker"?

   A. mail michael@example.net -s "cracker" > /etc/passwd

   B. mail michael@example.net -s "cracker" < /etc/passwd

   C. mail /etc/passwd michael@example.net -s "cracker"

   D. cat /etc/passwd | mail michael@example.net

10. What file contains more secure encrypted passwords for users?

   A. /etc/passwd

   B. /etc/gpasswd

   C. /etc/shadow

   D. /etc/gshadow

REVIEW ANSWERS

1. **B**   The print daemons most commonly associated with Linux are **cupsd** and **lpd**.

2. **C**   Unless you're in michael's account, **-u michael** is required; the -l lists jobs for the specified user. They're also stored in the /var/spool/cron directory, in text files named after each user.

3. **A**   After setting the password with the **passwd bcollie** command, bcollie can log in with that password and change it with the **passwd** command.

4. **C**   The **mail** client stores e-mail in the /var/spool/mail directory, in a file named for the user.

5. **A** A **ping** command to the loopback address (127.0.0.1) verifies proper installation of TCP/IP on the local system.

6. **D** Unless you use the **-r** switch, the **userdel** command does not do anything to the home directory of the account being deleted.

7. **C** The **ssh** command connects with encryption. The -l switch specifies the login name. There is no -u switch; without it, answer D would work as well.

8. **B** The **edquota** command edits quotas for the specified user.

9. **B** A specific format for the message and e-mail address is required.

10. **C** The /etc/shadow file contains encrypted passwords in a more secure file.

Configuring Linux Clients and Servers

Basic Client Configuration

	NEWBIE	SOME EXPERIENCE	EXPERT
ETA	80+ hours	16 hours	4 hours

147

This chapter is focused on the configuration of Linux client systems. Environment variables set initial defaults upon login. Local and network mounted directories can be configured in /etc/fstab. Network clients can be customized from the command line. Name resolution supports easier connections to other networks, including the Internet. Log files can help maintain clients. Makefiles can compile the source code for drivers, kernels, and more. Finally, administrators need to know the commands to configure the X Window System on Linux client systems.

Objective 6.01 Set Up Environment Variables

To see the environment variables associated with the current account, run the **env** command. Which variables are active depends on the account, activation of the GUI, and /etc/profile and related configuration files in user home directories. For example, the **$DISPLAY** variable isn't active unless the current distribution is in the GUI, or you've logged in with some console (such as SSH) associated with remote GUI access.

Environment variables are listed without the **$** in the output to the **env** command. But to find the value of a specific environment variable such as **$DISPLAY**, run the **echo $DISPLAY** command. Try the **env** command from a command-line console and a GUI command line. Note the differences.

Even the selected Linux distributions have some variations in environment variables. Key variables listed in the Linux+ objectives include **$PATH**, **$DISPLAY**, **$TERM**, **$PROMPT**, and **$PS1**.

For detailed information on the **$PATH** variable and the interaction with directory paths, see the Chapter 3 section "Work with Files and Directories." Some typical variables are listed and described in Table 6.1.

Exam Tip
Understand the function of default environment variables such as **$HISTSIZE**, **$HOME**, **$PATH**, **$PS1**, and **$TERM**.

TABLE 6.1	Common Environment Variables

Environment Variable	Description
$PATH	The directories searched when typing a command without the directory path.
$DISPLAY	The default for a local GUI is :0.0; a second GUI console may be available when $DISPLAY=:1.0 (available by pressing CTRL-ALT-F8).
$TERM	The default command-line terminal.
$PROMPT	Formerly used to define the prompt; superseded by $PS1.
$PS1	As defined in a configuration file like /etc/profile, /etc/bash.bashrc, or /etc/bashrc; default definition is \u@\h \W; short for User@Host, followed by the current directory.
$MANPATH	A $PATH for man pages.
$HOSTNAME or $HOST	The name associated with the system in files such as /etc/hosts.
$HISTSIZE	The number of commands to store in the command-line history; typically stored each user's .bash_history.
$SHELL	Default command-line shell.
$USER	Current username.
$XAUTHORITY	Lists systems authorized to access local GUI applications; does not include SSH access.
$HOME	Notes the current user's home directory.

Objective 6.02

Configure Mounted Directories

While you could just run the **mount** command to connect local partitions and remotely shared directories, it's time consuming. If you need to connect to a partition on a regular basis, it's best to configure it in /etc/fstab.

If you want a regular connection to remotely mounted directories, they can also be configured in /etc/fstab, or in user-specific configuration files. This assumes a reliable network connection. Connection problems, especially to shared NFS directories, have been known to hang Linux systems so severely as to require power cycling. So the right setting of a shared NFS directory in /etc/fstab can prevent trouble during the boot process.

For detailed information on using the **mount** command to access local and remote directories, see the Chapter 4 section "Mount Locally and Remotely."

Editing /etc/fstab

The /etc/fstab configuration file includes several partitions that are automatically mounted when you start Linux. A typical /etc/fstab configuration file might look like Figure 6.1.

The regular partitions are mounted when you boot Linux. In this case, it's the top-level root directory, /, on /dev/sda3, and /boot on /dev/sda2. Other filesystems can be mounted at will; for example, based on the given /etc/fstab configuration file, if you insert a CD into the drive, it can be mounted with either of the following commands:

```
# mount /dev/cdrom
# mount /mnt/cdrom
```

When the **mount** command is run, it searches through /etc/fstab for other required information. For more information on each column in /etc/fstab, see Table 6.2, which lists the columns from left to right.

If you forget to add a configured filesystem to /etc/fstab, and it isn't mounted when Linux boots, you need to mount it separately after Linux starts.

```
/dev/sda3       /               ext3     defaults            1 1
/dev/sda2       /boot           ext3     defaults            1 2
/dev/cdrom      /mnt/cdrom      iso9660  noauto,owner,ro     0 0
/dev/fd0        /mnt/floppy     auto     noauto,owner        0 0
none            /proc           proc     defaults            0 0
none            /dev/pts        devpts   gid=5,mode=620      0 0
sysfs           /sys            sysfs    defaults            0 0
/dev/sda1       swap            swap     defaults            0 0
~
~
~
~
~
~
~
                                             1,44            All
```

FIGURE 6.1   Typical /etc/fstab configuration file

TABLE 6.2	/etc/fstab Columns, Left to Right
Field Name	**Description**
Device or Label	The device to be mounted. If you see a **LABEL** in this column (as is done by Red Hat), some trial and error is required with the **e2label** command to determine the actual device file.
Mount Point	The directory where the filesystem is mounted.
Filesystem Type	Describes the filesystem type, such as ext2, ext3, msdos, vfat, devpts, proc, tmpfs, udf, iso9660, nfs, smb, cifs, or swap.
Mount Options	See Table 6.3.
Dump Value	If **1**, data is automatically saved to the disk when you exit Linux.
Filesystem Check Order	Determines the order applied by **fsck** during the boot process.

Travel Advisory

With the latest developments in hardware detection, many portable devices such as DVD drives and USB keys are configured and mounted automatically, without any configuration in /etc/fstab. These hardware detection features were developed well after the Linux+ objectives were released.

Options for the **mount** command are numerous. The most typical option is *defaults*; this and other options are described in Table 6.3. Opposites are often available, such as *auto* and *noauto*, *dev* and *nodev*, *suid* and *nosuid*, and *exec* and *noexec*.

Exam Tip

Minor errors in /etc/fstab are possible. For example, if an ext3 filesystem is configured as ext2 in /etc/fstab, it's mounted without a journal when Linux boots. In contrast, if an ext2 filesystem is configured as ext3 in /etc/fstab, it's mounted as ext2 (no journal).

TABLE 6.3	/etc/fstab Mount Options

Mount Option	Description
async	Leads to asynchronous reads and writes.
auto	Searches through /etc/filesystems for the appropriate format before mounting a filesystem; normally associated with a floppy or removable drive.
defaults	Uses mount options *rw, suid, dev, exec, auto, nouser,* and *async.*
dev	Permits access to character devices such as terminals or consoles and block devices such as drives.
exec	Allows binaries (compiled programs) to be run on this filesystem.
grpquota	Supports group quotas on the noted filesystem.
noauto	Requires explicit mounting. Common option for removable media such as CD/DVD and floppy drives.
nouser	Allows only the root user to mount the specified filesystem.
owner	Allows the owner of the device file to mount.
remount	Remounts a currently mounted filesystem. Also an option for the **mount** command.
ro	Mounts the filesystem as read-only.
rw	Mounts the filesystem as read/write.
suid	Allows SUID or SGID permissions on programs on this filesystem.
sync	Leads to reads and writes being performed at the same speed at the same time.
user	Allows nonroot users to mount this filesystem. By default, this also sets the **noexec, nosuid,** and **nodev** options.
usrquota	Supports user quotas on the noted filesystem.

If you make changes to /etc/fstab, one way to test the result is with the **mount -a** command. It automatically mounts all filesystems described in /etc/fstab, unless the *noauto* mount comption is specified.

Exam Tip

Know the more common mount options, such as *auto, defaults, owner, remount, rw, suid,* and *user.* For example, if *nosuid* is associated with a filesystem, SUID permissions aren't allowed when the filesystem is mounted.

Configuring Local Mounts in /etc/fstab

Administrators configure and install new partitions. They may be dedicated to certain directories such as /home and /var. They could provide more space for associated files. Once you've created a new partition with a tool such as **fdisk**, and formatted it with a command such as **mkfs.ext3**, you'll want to configure it in /etc/fstab to make sure it's mounted on the desired directory the next time Linux is booted.

> **Travel Advisory**
>
> If you're configuring a larger partition for a dedicated directory such as /home, back up the contents of that directory first. Once the new partition is mounted, restore the saved data to the new location.

If you've created a new partition, it'll be visible in the output from the **fdisk -l** command—if run with root administrative account privileges. The new partition will have a device filename such as /dev/hda5 or /dev/sdb6.

To set up a mounted directory in /etc/fstab, use the pattern established by currently configured mount points. Based on the information in Tables 6.2 and 6.3, assume you're configuring /home on a newly formatted /dev/sdb6 partition. The first column is associated with the filename of the partition. The second column is the directory that you want mounted on that partition. So far, we have

```
/dev/sdb6    /home
```

The third column is associated with the filesystem format, normally *ext3*. Unless there are specialized requirements such as quotas, the best choice for a mount option is *defaults*. The final two columns are associated with the dump value and filesystem check order. As noted in Table 6.2, a dump value of 1 means that files are saved when Linux is stopped, and a filesystem check order of 2 means that the partition is checked after the top-level root directory (which has a filesystem check order of 1):

```
/dev/sdb6    /home    ext3    defaults    1 2
```

> **Travel Advisory**
>
> Some distributions, including Red Hat and Fedora, substitute a **LABEL** directive for the partition device file in their versions of /etc/fstab. Device files such as /dev/sdb6 work just as well.

Configuring Network Mounts in /etc/fstab

The Chapter 4 section "Mount Locally and Remotely" explored a couple of examples for mounting shared network directories. First, examine the mounting of a shared NFS directory. For the purpose of the following command, the shared network directory is /inst and the local directory is /nfs:

```
# mount -t nfs nfs.example.com:/inst /nfs     LOCAL
```

The **-t nfs** may not be required, as NFS mounts transparently; in other words, once mounted, it looks like a local filesystem. NFS mounts can be included in /etc/fstab. The following entry in that file corresponds to the previous command:

```
nfs.example.com:/inst  /nfs  rw,noauto,user 0 0
```

I prefer *noauto* for directories shared over a network, just in case of network problems. Attempted NFS mounts where the network or server is troubled have been known to hang systems so badly that administrators have had to power cycle the machine.

> **Travel Advisory**
>
> Future versions of NFS, namely NFS version 4, should address the "hang" issue.

Next, examine the mounting of a shared Samba directory. For the purpose of the following command, assume the shared network directory is /inst and the local directory is /smb:

```
                                          LOCAL
# mount -t smbfs //samba.example.com/inst /smb -o username=user
```

The **-t smbfs** may not be correct. For the latest versions of Samba that use the Common Internet File System, the **-t cifs** switch might be more appropriate. If the user on the Samba server is the same as the current user, **username=user** is not required; you're prompted for the user's password on the Samba server. Samba mounts can be included in /etc/fstab. The following entry in that file corresponds to the previous command:

```
//samba.example.com/inst /smb smbfs username=user,password=pw 0 0
```

The information in /etc/fstab is visible to all users, so if you'd rather hide the username and password, substitute *.credentials=file* for the *username* and *password* entries. The credentials file is hidden with a dot in front, and given appropriate permissions such as 600, which limits read and write access to the root user.

/etc/mtab

The /etc/mtab configuration file is slightly different from /etc/fstab. It includes all currently mounted directories, which may vary from the information in /etc/fstab. The following example notes the top-level root directory mounted on /dev/sdb2, to the ext3 filesystem, in read-write mode. In this case, the last two numbers aren't important, at least for the Linux+ exam.

```
/dev/sdb2 / ext3 rw 0 0
```

The following is a second example of an ISO file, mounted on the first loop device (/dev/loop0), in read-write mode:

```
/inst/FC-6-i386-DVD.iso /FC6 iso9660 rw,loop=/dev/loop0 0 0
```

Objective 6.03

Work Client Network Settings

While there are several different GUI tools that can help you configure clients on networks, they are distribution specific, and beyond the scope of the Linux+ exam. Therefore, it's important to know the commands and configuration files used to configure clients on a network.

Network Client Commands

There are several different commands available for configuring a client on a network, mostly associated with the net-tools RPM package. The **domainname** command, which assigns an NIS domain to a client, was discussed in the Chapter 5 section "Configure the Network Information Service." Related commands that read or set names of some sort are listed in Table 6.4.

TABLE 6.4	Network Name Commands
Command	**Description**
hostname	Sets or reads the system hostname. The **hostname --fqdn** command returns the fully qualified domain name (FQDN).
domainname nisdomainname ypdomainname	Sets or reads the system NIS domain name; all three commands are synonymous.
dnsdomainname	Reads the system domain name, such as example.org.

The **netstat** command can check detailed status information on the local network. The **netstat -nr** command is synonymous with **route** and is discussed in the Chapter 5 section "Reviewing Network Connections with netstat." The **netstat -a** command lists connections, established and potential. For example, Figure 6.2 lists potential connections with a **LISTEN** label, and established connections with an **ESTABLISHED** label. The **ESTABLISHED** connection to IP address 12.26.55.108 happens to be a connection to the McGraw-Hill website. The **ssh** connection to IP address 192.168.0.4 is a connection from my Ubuntu Linux system.

```
Active Internet connections (servers and established)
Proto Recv-Q Send-Q Local Address              Foreign Address            State
tcp        0      0 localhost:irdmi            *:*                        LISTEN
tcp        0      0 localhost:2208             *:*                        LISTEN
tcp        0      0 *:nfs                      *:*                        LISTEN
tcp        0      0 *:silc                     *:*                        LISTEN
tcp        0      0 *:vmware-authd             *:*                        LISTEN
tcp        0      0 *:netbios-ssn              *:*                        LISTEN
tcp        0      0 192.168.122.1:domain       *:*                        LISTEN
tcp        0      0 *:ftp                      *:*                        LISTEN
tcp        0      0 *:44597                    *:*                        LISTEN
tcp        0      0 *:ipp                      *:*                        LISTEN
tcp        0      0 localhost:x11-ssh-offset   *:*                        LISTEN
tcp        0      0 localhost:6011             *:*                        LISTEN
tcp        0      0 *:microsoft-ds             *:*                        LISTEN
tcp        0      0 *:vacdsm-app               *:*                        LISTEN
tcp        0      0 *:msdp                     *:*                        LISTEN
tcp        0      0 localhost:2207             *:*                        LISTEN
tcp        0      0 localhost:x11-ssh-offset   localhost:37176            ESTABLISHED
tcp        0      0 enterprise5fc6d:56461      12.26.55.108:http          ESTABLISHED
tcp        0      0 enterprise5fc6d:56460      12.26.55.108:http          ESTABLISHED
tcp        0   4884 localhost:37176            localhost:x11-ssh-offset   ESTABLISHED
tcp        0      0 *:sunrpc                   *:*                        LISTEN
tcp        0      0 *:http                     *:*                        LISTEN
tcp        0      0 *:ssh                      *:*                        LISTEN
tcp        0      0 *:ipp                      *:*                        LISTEN
tcp        0      0 localhost:x11-ssh-offset   *:*                        LISTEN
tcp        0      0 localhost:6011             *:*                        LISTEN
tcp        0      0 enterprise5fc6d:ssh        ::ffff:192.168.0.4:51056   ESTABLISHED
tcp        0      0 enterprise5fc6d:ssh        ::ffff:192.168.0.4:38522   ESTABLISHED
udp        0      0 *:filenet-tms              *:*
udp        0      0 *:nfs                      *:*
--More--
```

FIGURE 6.2	netstat -a output

Next, there's the **arp** command, associated with the Address Resolution Protocol (ARP). It translates IP addresses to the hardware address associated with a specific network card. The hardware address of a network card is associated with the Media Access Control (MAC) layer of the TCP/IP protocol suite; therefore, hardware addresses are often known as MAC addressees.

Recent communications between network cards are stored in an ARP cache, as documented in the output to the **arp** command. For example, the following output documents connections through the second Ethernet card (eth1) to the hardware address of cards associated with IP addresses 192.168.0.1 and 192.168.0.4:

```
Address         HWtype  HWaddress          Flags Mask  Iface
192.168.0.4     ether   00:18:DE:38:44:71  C           eth1
192.168.0.1     ether   00:09:5B:FA:BB:76  C           eth1
```

But ARP caches are limited to a local network; as hardware addresses don't cross networks, the cache shows connections to outside systems only as far as the hardware address of the local gateway. There are other ARP caches which eventually connect to the external system with the website.

A couple of other client commands are detailed later in this chapter, including **ifconfig** in "Manage a Network Card" and **dig** in "Implement Name Resolution."

Exam Tip

Know that the Linux **arp** command associates an IP address such as 192.168.0.22 with the hardware address, also known as the MAC address.

Network Client Configuration Files

In the selected distributions, network client configuration files are stored somewhere in the /etc/sysconfig directory. Information on whether networking is active by default is normally made available in /etc/sysconfig/network. As usual, SUSE is the exception, and as the exception, the details of such are beyond the scope of the Linux+ exam.

If networking is active, you'll see a simple directive in the appropriate configuration file, such as:

```
NETWORKING=yes
```

 **Objective 6.04** **Manage a Network Card**

Networking and the command line are important in Linux; you must know how to configure a network card from the command line. You can do so directly with the **ifconfig** command, or indirectly by modifying the associated configuration file. Alternatively, it's common to use the Dynamic Host Configuration Protocol (DHCP) to configure network cards.

Running ifconfig

The **ifconfig** command is versatile. Without switches, the command lists the current configuration of all network interfaces. A simple output is shown in Figure 6.3, which lists the configuration of one Ethernet card (eth0) and the local Loopback (lo) adapter. As you can see, there's a lot of information available for the first Ethernet card, as described in Table 6.5.

More recent Linux distributions may include more information, such as the IPv6 address, as labeled by **inet6 addr**.

The **ifconfig** command can also activate network cards. To activate or deactivate, say, the first Ethernet network card on the local network, run one of the following commands:

```
# ifconfig eth0 up
# ifconfig eth0 down
```

```
[michael@TurboLinux michael]$ /sbin/ifconfig
eth0      Link encap:Ethernet  HWaddr 00:0C:29:CF:B7:11
          inet addr:192.168.0.60  Bcast:192.168.0.255  Mask:255.255.255.0
          UP BROADCAST RUNNING MULTICAST  MTU:1500  Metric:1
          RX packets:1676 errors:0 dropped:0 overruns:0 frame:0
          TX packets:157 errors:0 dropped:0 overruns:0 carrier:0
          collisions:0 txqueuelen:1000
          RX bytes:271962 (265.5 Kb)  TX bytes:19844 (19.3 Kb)
          Interrupt:9 Base address:0x1080

lo        Link encap:Local Loopback
          inet addr:127.0.0.1  Mask:255.0.0.0
          UP LOOPBACK RUNNING  MTU:16436  Metric:1
          RX packets:0 errors:0 dropped:0 overruns:0 frame:0
          TX packets:0 errors:0 dropped:0 overruns:0 carrier:0
          collisions:0 txqueuelen:0
          RX bytes:0 (0.0 b)  TX bytes:0 (0.0 b)

[michael@TurboLinux michael]$
```

FIGURE 6.3   Output from **ifconfig**

TABLE 6.5 **ifconfig** Output

ifconfig Information	Description
HWaddr	Hardware address
inet addr	IP address
Bcast	Broadcast address for the local network
Mask	Network mask, also known as a subnet or subnetwork mask
UP	Signifies an active interface
BROADCAST	Associates with a card that broadcasts its existence
RUNNING	Refers to a network card with some external connection to other cards
MULTICAST	Receives multicast packets
MTU	Maximum transfer unit; normally 1500 packets for Ethernet
Metric	Unused for Linux networks
RX packets	Received packets (watch the "errors" in this line)
TX packets	Transmitted packets (watch the "errors" in this line)
collisions	Packets that interfere with transmissions from other network cards
Interrupt	IRQ address assigned to the card
Base address	I/O address assigned to the card

Alternatively, the **ifup** and **ifdown** commands, applied to a specific network card, have the same effect. For example, the following commands activate and deactivate the second Ethernet network card:

```
# ifup eth0
# ifdown eth0
```

Associated Configuration Files

The configuration file for the first Ethernet card probably has a name like ifcfg-eth0. The configuration file associated with the network card will have information either on the static IP address configuration, or on an IP address acquisition protocol such as DHCP.

Of course, with the **ifconfig** command, you can specify different options for many of the parameters specified in Table 6.5. The simplest includes the name of the adapter, which can be useful when there are a lot of network connections. For example, the following command limits the output to information associated with the third Ethernet adapter on the local system:

```
# ifconfig eth2
```

Some of the more popular configuration options are shown in Table 6.6. Just make sure to apply the option to the desired interface; for example, to set an MTU of 1400 to the second Ethernet card, run the following command:

```
# ifconfig eth1 mtu 1400
```

Here are a couple more examples of what you can do with the **ifconfig** command. The following command assigns the given IP address to the first Ethernet card:

```
# ifconfig eth0 10.11.12.13
```

Assign static IP address

This command assigns the same IP address with a nonstandard network mask to the first Ethernet card:

```
# ifconfig eth0 10.11.12.13 netmask 255.255.254.0
```

There's more. As Ethernet is not inherently a point-to-point protocol, any network card on a system can read all traffic on a local network, if configured in promiscuous mode.

TABLE 6.6	**ifconfig** Configuration Options

ifconfig Configuration Option	Description
-arp	Disables ARP database access; opposite of **arp**
promisc	Enables promiscuous mode; intercepts all information on the network, including data between other systems; opposite of **-promisc**
mtu *n*	Sets a different maximum transfer unit (MTU); 1500 is the standard for Ethernet
netmask *addr*	Assigns a network mask; often used for nonstandard network masks such as 255.255.255.0 for a Class A network such as 10.0.0.0
irq *channel*	Sets a different IRQ channel; can solve hardware interference issues
io_addr *addr*	Sets a different I/O address; can solve hardware interference issues
ipaddr	Sets a different IP address; for example, **ifconfig eth0 192.168.0.100** assigns that IP address to the first Ethernet card

> **Exam Tip**
>
> Know how to use the **ifconfig** command to modify various settings associated with a local network card, including those listed in Table 6.6.

Dynamic IP Configuration

One common option for IP configuration is through a DHCP server. While the Linux+ objectives do not require configuration of a DHCP server, it's available on the router installed on many home networks. If the DHCP server is remote, the Bootstrap Protocol, also known as BOOTP, is required to transmit DHCP data across a router or gateway.

Normally, DHCP servers assign IP addresses for a certain period of time. The client command that contacts a DHCP server varies; some DHCP client commands on the selected distributions include the following:

- **pump**
- **dhcpcd** (don't confuse with **dhcpd**, the DHCP server daemon)
- **dhclient**

When the client command is run, a broadcast message is sent over the network. On an IPv4 network, that address is 255.255.255.255. When a DHCP server sees the message, it responds to the client, with an IP address, leased for a specific period of time. Unless renewed, that IP address expires after that period.

Objective 6.05 Implement Name Resolution

People remember websites by their names, not by their IP addresses. Remembering www.mcgraw-hill.com is much easier than remembering 12.26.55.108, the IP address of the website. But computers work with numbers. Translating names such as www.mcgraw-hill.com to IP addresses such as 12.26.55.108 requires name resolution services.

There are two categories of name resolution services available for Linux. The first is based on a static database in /etc/hosts. The second is based on the Domain Name System (DNS), which is a distributed database of hostnames and IP addresses.

A computer hostname can be a single name, such as homepc1, or a fully qualified domain name (FQDN), such as www.mcgraw-hill.com. The FQDN, with a corresponding IP address, provides enough information to be included in a DNS database.

The DNS service most commonly used in Linux is the Berkeley Internet Name Domain (BIND), associated with the **named** daemon.

Travel Advisory

There are other name resolution services available, such as the Windows Internet Name Service (WINS), which translates Microsoft computer NetBIOS names to IP addresses. One common alternative for DNS services on Linux is D. J. Bernstein's djbdns, available online at http://cr.yp.to/djbdns.html.

/etc/hosts

The first database of hostnames and IP addresses was set up in a static text file, /etc/hosts. When there were just a few nodes on the network that eventually turned into the Internet, it was possible to maintain identical /etc/hosts files on each computer. Some networks still maintain identical versions of this file on each system using NIS, which was described in the Chapter 5 section "Configure the Network Information Service."

Here's a typical line in /etc/hosts, which lists the IP address, FQDN, and hostname alias for one computer connection:

```
192.168.13.3      linux1.mommabears.com  linux1
```
IP ADDRESS   FQDN   HOSTNAME ALIAS

Name Resolution Order

When there's more than one name resolution database, conflicts are possible. So operating systems specify a search order. For example, if my system is looking for the linux1.mommabears.com computer, does it look for the IP address in /etc/hosts or in a DNS database?

When the Linux+ objectives were released, the name resolution search order was determined by the /etc/host.conf configuration file. The contents of this file are simple:

```
order hosts,bind
```

In other words, this Linux system first searches through /etc/hosts for the IP address for linux1.mommabears.com. If it isn't found, that system searches through bind, short for the Berkeley Internet Name Domain, the DNS server most commonly associated with Linux.

Modern Linux systems specify the name search order in /etc/nsswitch.conf. The key line is almost as simple. The following line is functionally equivalent to **order hosts,bind** from /etc/host.conf:

```
hosts: files dns
```

Exam Tip
Understand the settings in /etc/host.conf and /etc/nsswitch.conf and how they affect the way networks search for name resolution databases.

Remote DNS Services

However, DNS databases don't just show up on Linux systems. They may need to be configured in appropriate files. If you've configured the IP address of DNS services statically, you'll find them in the /etc/resolv.conf configuration file. The basic format is straightforward:

```
nameserver 192.168.0.1
```

A *nameserver* is another name for a DNS server. It can be helpful to have more than one nameserver listed in /etc/resolv.conf, especially when connecting to remote DNS servers. If one DNS server is down or inaccessible, the second (or third) DNS server can fulfill the function of the database.

While no DNS server contains a complete database of hostnames and IP addresses, properly configured DNS servers can forward requests to other DNS servers. If the hostname or FQDN is available in a properly networked DNS server, the associated IP address will eventually be found.

Testing DNS Databases

If you have a good connection to the Internet, it's fairly easy to test DNS databases. There are three commands that can help: **host**, **dig**, and **nslookup**.

The **host** command is simple; it returns the IP address, alias(es), and, if so configured, associated mail servers. Here's the output when the command is applied to my personal domain:

```
$ host www.mommabears.com
www.mommabears.com is an alias for mommabears.com.
mommabears.com has address 67.19.74.18
mommabears.com mail is handled by 0 mommabears.com.
```

If you want more information, try the **host -v www.mommabears.com** command. As you read through this section, you'll see similarities with the **dig** command. Next, try the **nslookup www.mommabears.com** command, which uses the local DNS server to find the IP address of my personal domain:

```
Server:        192.168.0.1
Address:       192.168.0.1#53

Non-authoritative answer:
www.mommabears.com      canonical name = mommabears.com.
Name:   mommabears.com
Address: 67.19.74.18
```

The IP addresses associated with the Server and Address output are the same, in this case, the address associated with the local DNS server. The "Non-authoritative answer" means that mommabears.com is not in the "zone of authority" for the given DNS server. Finally, the canonical name is the real name of the host. Note the period at the end of mommabears.com., which is the so-called "root" domain. The IP address is the one assigned to mommabears.com; it happens to be a shared IP address on a virtual server.

Finally, try the **dig www.mommabears.com** command, with output shown in Figure 6.4, which gets answers directly from the DNS database (the data is from a BIND database).

The **A** is the address record for the domain. The **CNAME** is the canonical name of the system with the FQDN, in this case, www.mommabears.com. Finally, the actual domain is mommabears.com.

```
[michael@enterprise5hp ~]$ dig www.mommabears.com

; <<>> DiG 9.3.3rc2 <<>> www.mommabears.com
;; global options:  printcmd
;; Got answer:
;; ->>HEADER<<- opcode: QUERY, status: NOERROR, id: 27907
;; flags: qr rd ra; QUERY: 1, ANSWER: 2, AUTHORITY: 0, ADDITIONAL: 0

;; QUESTION SECTION:
;www.mommabears.com.            IN      A

;; ANSWER SECTION:
www.mommabears.com.    14400   IN      CNAME   mommabears.com.
mommabears.com.        14400   IN      A       67.19.74.18

;; Query time: 92 msec
;; SERVER: 68.87.69.146#53(68.87.69.146)
;; WHEN: Mon Jul 30 10:40:58 2007
;; MSG SIZE  rcvd: 66

[michael@enterprise5hp ~]$
```

FIGURE 6.4   Output from the **dig** command

One more use for the **dig** command is the reverse lookup. If all you have is the IP address, try the **dig -x** *ipaddress* command. For example, when I try the command as follows:

```
$ dig -x 208.252.144.4
```

it finds a pointer, as shown with the **PTR** label and reverse IP address datapoint, shown here:

```
;4.144.252.208.in-addr.arpa.    IN      PTR
```

The next stanza lists the reverse network IP address along with the governing systems:

```
144.252.208.in-addr.arpa. 900    IN    SOA
mustang.comptia.net. hostmaster.comptia.net.
83 900 600 86400 3600
```

So now you know, at least as of this writing, that IP address 208.252.144.4 is associated with the CompTIA website.

Exam Tip
Know what you get when running the **dig**, **host**, and **nslookup** commands (as well as the more important switches).

 **Work with Log Files**

For the selected distributions (except SUSE), the way log files collect information is governed by the /etc/syslog.conf configuration file. Most log files are stored in the /var/log directory (and subdirectories). Regular log file rotation means that new log files are created either after a certain period of time or when they reach a certain size. When administering many systems, it can be helpful to have a dedicated log server. By definition, that log server would be remote to all other systems.

As Defined in /etc/syslog.conf

The system log configuration file defines the level of information collected and stored in log files. Each service is associated with several different levels of priorities. Higher-priority log messages are sent less frequently.

From least to most important, log priorities are divided into the following levels:

- debug
- info
- notice
- warn (or warning)
- err (or error)
- crit
- alert
- emerg (or panic)

In other words, the *debug* log level means all messages are logged; the *emerg* log level refers only to the most critical issues. There's also a *none* priority level, which does not log messages at any level. What follows are some typical examples. The following directive, if active (the # is a comment character), logs all messages to the command-line console:

```
#kern.*    /dev/console
```

One common directive collects log messages of at least *info* priority in /var/log/messages. The Red Hat version of this directive from /etc/syslog.conf specifically leaves out log information associated with mail, news, authentication, and administrative cron jobs from the noted log file:

```
*.info;mail.none;news.none;authpriv.none;cron.none   /var/log/messages
```

Naturally, those services with logging information not collected in /var/log/messages should be collected elsewhere. The following directive collects all authentication information (note the * used as a wildcard, for all log messages) in /var/log/secure:

```
authpriv.*    /var/log/secure
```

There are variations; while the following directive sends log messages of error level or higher from the **cron** daemon to /var/log/cron/errors:

```
cron.err   -/var/log/cron/errors
```

the following directive limits messages sent to /var/log/cron/warnings to those at the **warn** level. Messages of greater or lesser severity are not included.

```
cron.=warn   -/var/log/cron/warnings
```

If any of these logs is inadvertently deleted, the next restart of the **syslog** service will re-create that log file. For example, if I moved the /var/log/secure file to

my home directory, to help investigate a possible login problem, restarting the
syslog service would re-create that file as follows:

```
# mv /var/log/secure ~
# /etc/init.d/syslog restart
```

Exam Tip	
Know the priorities associated with logging information, and how to re-create deleted log files.	

Logs in the /var/log Directory

Logs are often individually configured and dedicated to specific services. For
example, logs for the Apache Web server are most commonly stored in the
/var/log/httpd directory. Common log files and the kinds of messages they
collect are listed and described in Table 6.7.

Table 6.7 is far from a complete list, even for the selected distributions. Some
log files, such as /var/log/anaconda.*, are distribution specific. In several cases,
log files have their own dedicated directories; for example, Mandriva cron jobs
are logged individually in the /var/log/cron directory.

TABLE 6.7   Typical /var/log Log Files

Log File	Description
acpid	Specifies events related to the Advanced Control and Power Interface (ACPI) daemon; events indicate ACPI activity
boot	Associated with services that start and shut down processes
cups	Normally a directory of files associated with printer access, page, and error logs
dmesg	Collects basic boot messages
httpd	Normally a directory of files associated with the Apache Web server (/var/log/apache2 in SUSE)
lastlog	Lists login records, readable with the **lastlog** command
mail*	Collection of mail log statistics; often divided in a separate directory
messages	From services as defined in /etc/syslog.conf
rpmpkgs	Lists currently installed RPM packages
secure	Lists login and access messages
wtmp	Lists logins, in binary format; can be read by the **utmpdump** command

The SUSE definition of log management varies from the norm defined by the other selected distributions (Red Hat/Fedora, Mandriva, Turbolinux) and is defined by the /etc/syslog-ng/syslog-ng.conf configuration file. In addition, the standard Apache Web server on SUSE stores log files in the /var/log/apache2 directory.

Log Rotation

Logs can easily become very large and difficult to read. By default, there's a **logrotate** cron job that creates new log files on a weekly basis. Review it for yourself in the /etc/cron.daily directory. Read it, and observe how it calls settings in the /etc/logrotate.conf configuration file. The common directives are straightforward. For example, the **weekly** directive means logs are rotated on a weekly basis.

The **rotate 4** directive means that there are four weeks of back logs; for example, on my Red Hat system, I have cron, cron.1, cron.2, cron.3, and cron.4 log files. Next week, the contents of the current cron.4 file will be deleted, the contents of cron.3 will be moved to cron.4, the contents of cron.2 will be moved to cron.3, and so on. The following directive creates a new empty cron file (along with appropriate empty versions of any other log files):

```
create
```

If the **compress** directive is active, log files are compressed in GZIP format. While compressed log files have a .gz extension, they're still readable with *some* text readers such as **less** and **more**.

Specialized information for log rotation may be stored in separate files located in the /etc/logrotate.d directory, and are included in the configuration with the following directive:

```
include /etc/logrotate.d
```

Variations are possible; for example, the following stanza rotates /var/log/wtmp on a monthly basis, created with 664 permissions, owned by the root user and the utmp group. The **rotate 1** directive means only one log file is archived—in this case, login information from the previous month.

```
/var/log/wtmp {
    monthly
    create 0664 root utmp
    rotate 1
}
```

This stanza is typical of the directives found in the files in the /etc/logrotate.d directory. In other words, these are custom stanzas that fall outside the norm of /etc/syslog.conf.

Log files can easily fill partitions. As logs are rotated, older log files are easily identified by their extensions. A full /var directory can prevent users from logging in, keep certain services from starting, and more. If necessary, older log files can be moved to a different partition (or system) or even deleted.

Exam Tip

Unless you maintain /var, a full partition can result, which can result in new log files being truncated to a size of 0; in other words, once a /var partition is full, you'd get no new log data.

Set Up Remote Logging

If logs fill a dedicated partition such as /var, log files in that directory are truncated. Important data could be lost. A dedicated log server, remote to other systems on the local network, can help administrators manage log files.

The configuration of a remote logging server requires configuration changes on the client and server. Client logs are driven by individual /etc/syslog.conf files. Log messages can then be sent to remote systems. One option to log locally and remotely is adding /etc/syslog.conf directives such as:

```
authpriv.*      /var/log/secure
authpriv.*      @log.server
```

Of course, you can substitute the IP address for the domain name. Then to allow the log server to collect information from remote systems, look at the /etc/sysconfig/syslog configuration file. It includes switches applied to the **syslog** daemon when it's started. The -r switch activates access from remote systems.

 **Objective 6.07 Use Makefiles**

It isn't always possible to install RPM or other types of packages on a Linux system. For the latest software, RPM packages aren't always available. Generally packages are first made available in "tarball" format, as described in the Chapter 2 section "Installing from a Compressed Tarball."

Exam Tip

Learn to at least recognize the key commands associated with compiling source code.

Compiling Drivers and Other Packages

When packages include source code, they must be compiled before installation. That's where the Makefile comes in handy. If you see a file named Makefile, you may be able to compile the package with a command like **make** or variations such as **make config** or **make install**.

Equivalent options to Makefile may be available. For example, if the unarchived tarball includes a script file named config, navigate to that directory and run it with the **./config** command. Alternative names for the script file include configure and INSTALL. Other scripts may have less standard names, but can generally be identified by their permissions. If it's a script, it should have executable permissions, as revealed by the **ls -l** command.

More information on available **make** commands may be available in the Makefile, or a similar file such as config or configure, which should be in text format. For example, the following excerpt from the /etc/mail/Makefile file reveals more about what can be done to the sendmail e-mail server configuration files:

```
all: ${CFFILES} ${POSSIBLE} virtusertable.db access.db domaintable.db
mailertable.db
clean:
        rm -f *.db *~
start:
        service sendmail start
stop:
        service sendmail stop
restart:
        service sendmail restart
```

In other words, the **make all** command processes the noted database files, with the .db extensions. The **make clean** command removes the noted files with the .db extensions. The **make start** command starts the sendmail service; the command is equivalent to the **/etc/init.d/sendmail start** command, and so on for the stop and restart options.

Compiling a Kernel

One key skill for more advanced Linux administrators is knowing how to compile a Linux kernel. This skill enables administrators to create customized kernels. With a customized kernel, systems can run just the needed modules, without the overhead for unneeded hardware, filesystems, networks, and more.

The ability to compile a Linux kernel is beyond what is expected of a Linux+ Certification candidate. However, the Linux+ objectives do suggest that you need to know how to configure the system and perform basic changes to the Makefile to support compiling applications and drivers.

The Makefile associated with the Linux kernel source code is in some ways easy to understand. For example, the following excerpt from a Red Hat Enterprise Linux kernel Makefile lists the version number associated with a compiled kernel:

```
VERSION = 2
PATCHLEVEL = 6
SUBLEVEL = 18
EXTRAVERSION = -custom1
```

When compiled, this kernel will have version number 2.6.18-custom1. For more information on available **make** commands, run the **make help** command. Options, as shown in the output, include

```
clean - remove most generated files but keep the config
mrproper - remove all generated files + config + various
backup files
```

and

```
config - Update current config utilising a line-oriented program
menuconfig - Update current config utilising a menu based
program
```

Configure the X Window System

Unlike graphics on other operating systems, the X Window System for Linux is designed as a flexible and powerful client/server-based system. To configure the X Window interface, you need to understand the client/server nature of the X Window System.

As you might have guessed from the terms *client* and *server*, the X Window System is designed to work in a networked environment. The client and server can both exist on the local computer; or the client can be networked from remote computers on the network. In other words, you can run X Window applications not only on your system, but also on other computers on your network. The graphical displays from those remote applications are sent to the local monitor.

In fact, X Window applications handle this task so well that, providing the network is fast enough, you really can't tell from a performance point of view which applications are running locally and which applications are running remotely.

While the filenames and command names associated with the X server have changed, the basic configuration and command actions are still the same as they were when the Linux+ objectives were released.

The X Window Server, Old and New

When the Linux+ objectives were released, Linux distributions primarily used the X Server distributed by The XFree86 Project, Inc., available at www.xfree86.org. Due to licensing issues, many Linux distributions (including

Red Hat, SUSE, and Mandriva) now use the X.Org server, available from, believe it or not, X.Org.

With the exception of different filenames, there are very few differences in the configuration of the two servers. By and large, the same configuration and command-line options used for an XFree86 server also work for an X.Org server. So, except for the different file and command names, the techniques required to manage the X.Org server and the XFree86 server are essentially the same.

X clients exist for almost every basic application—word processing, spreadsheets, games, and more. GUI configuration tools were developed as X clients. There are even X client versions of popular utilities such as the emacs editor.

Different Meanings for Client and Server

Normally on a network, the local computer is the client and the remote computer acts as the server. X Window clients and servers work on a different paradigm. The X server controls local graphics and therefore always has to be located on the local computer. The X server draws images on your screen and takes input from *your* keyboard and mouse. In contrast, X clients are local or remote applications such as **xclock** that can be run on the local X server.

X clients can be run from local or remote systems. Local X clients run from the local workstation; remote X clients run on the local X server. When running a remote X Window client application, the program is started on a different computer and sends its output to use the X server on the local computer.

X Window Configuration Tools

There are a couple of now obsolete configuration tools that were still in active use when the Linux+ objectives were released: **xf86config** and **XF86Setup**. The **xf86config** tool is a console tool that asks configuration questions at the command line. While the **XF86Setup** tool has much of the same functionality, it did so in a low-level graphics format. Although the X.Org version of the **XF86Setup** tool is available, it normally isn't included in the selected distributions.

The X.Org version of the **xf86config** tool is **xorgconfig**, which works in the same way. One example is shown in Figure 6.5. It prompts for configuration of a mouse, keyboard, language, monitor, video card (including memory), and color depth. The X.Org version of the **XF86Setup** tool is **xorgsetup**.

There's even an **xf86cfg** tool usable in the GUI. The X.Org version of this tool is **xorgcfg**. When open, as shown in Figure 6.6, you can add or configure a mouse, keyboard, graphics card, and monitor. Click the associated button, and the tool provides a selection of available drivers.

```
First specify a mouse protocol type. Choose one from the following list:

    1.  Auto [Auto detect]
    2.  SysMouse [SysMouse]
    3.  MouseSystems [Mouse Systems (3-button protocol)]
    4.  PS/2 [PS/2 Mouse]
    5.  Microsoft [Microsoft compatible (2-button protocol)]
    6.  Busmouse [Bus Mouse]
    7.  IMPS/2 [IntelliMouse PS/2]
    8.  ExplorerPS/2 [Explorer PS/2]
    9.  GlidePointPS/2 [GlidePoint PS/2]
   10.  MouseManPlusPS/2 [MouseManPlus PS/2]
   11.  NetMousePS/2 [NetMouse PS/2]
   12.  NetScrollPS/2 [NetScroll PS/2]
   13.  ThinkingMousePS/2 [ThinkingMouse PS/2]
   14.  AceCad [AceCad]

The recommended protocol is Auto. If you have a very old mouse
or don't want OS support or auto detection, and you have a two-button
or three-button serial mouse, it is most likely of type Microsoft.

Enter a protocol number: █
```

FIGURE 6.5   Output from **xorgconfig**

Just about every major Linux distribution includes specific graphical configuration tools, such as SUSE's **SaX**, Red Hat's **system-config-display** Display
Manager, Mandriva's **XFdrake**, and Turbolinux's **turboxcfg**. Some distributions
use other tools during the installation process, such as Red Hat's **pyxf86config**
and Turbolinux's **xconfig**. But remember, the Linux+ objectives specifically ex-
clude distribution-specific utilities.

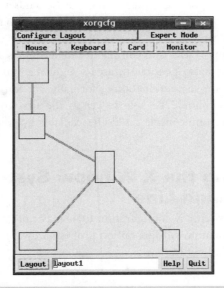

FIGURE 6.6   The **xorgcfg** tool

The X Window Configuration File

I don't expect that you have to know the X Window configuration file in minute detail for the Linux+ exam. It's not even a requirement for more advanced exams such as that for the Red Hat Certified Engineer (RHCE). But it can help you to know some of the basics. Depending on the distribution you're using, open the XF86Config or xorg.conf file in the /etc/X11 directory.

The comments at the start of the file identify the tool that created the file, which is normally distribution specific. As with other configuration files, the directives are organized into stanzas, not necessarily in a specific order. The titles of other stanzas are brought together in the section entitled

```
Section "ServerLayout"
```

The **Section "Files"** stanza normally cites **Fonts** or paths to font files. There are normally two **Section "InputDevice"** stanzas, one for a keyboard, and a second for a pointing device, usually a mouse or touchpad.

The **Section "Screen"** stanza usually consolidates the **Section "Monitor"** and **Section "Device"** stanzas, which configure the display or monitor and graphics hardware. Some configurations include a **Section "Module"** stanza for needed drivers or kernel modules.

X Window Management

There are some useful keystroke combinations associated with the X Window System. For example, pressing CTRL-ALT-BACKSPACE sends a termination signal to the X server. If you're in runlevel 5, this key combination restarts the default display login manager.

While GUIs support access to command-line terminals such as **konsole** or **gnome-terminal**, it's also possible to access regular command-line consoles with the right keystroke combinations. Normally, six consoles are available; from the GUI, you should be able to get to the first console by pressing CTRL-ALT-F1. The second console should be available by pressing CTRL-ALT-F2, and so on.

Configuring the X Window System from the Command Line

The distribution-specific X configuration tools may not always work. In that case, the following command-line option probes hardware and creates a local xorg.conf configuration file:

```
# Xorg -configure
```

> **Exam Tip**
>
> Know the console commands that create an X Window configuration file.

It's then best to back up the existing /etc/X11/xorg.conf file and copy the newly created xorg.conf file to that directory. As shown in the **Xorg** man page, there are a substantial number of options available; one useful option simulates the GUI start process:

```
# Xorg -probeonly
```

For older versions of Linux, specifically those which use the XFree86 server, the **XFree86 -configure** and **XFree86 -probeonly** commands work in the same way.

> **Travel Advisory**
>
> **Xorg -configure** may not work for all hardware configurations, such as RHEL 5 within VMware.

CHECKPOINT

✔**Objective 6.01: Set Up Environment Variables**   Environment variables set the defaults for the home directory, the GUI display, the shell, directory paths, and much more. The **env** command lists current environment variables.

✔**Objective 6.02: Configure Mounted Directories**   Mounted directories can be configured to start when Linux boots in /etc/fstab. These directories can be local or shared NFS/Samba directories from remote systems. Currently mounted directories are documented in /etc/mtab.

✔**Objective 6.03: Work Client Network Settings**   Network clients can be configured on regular and NIS domains; these settings are documented in files such as /etc/sysconfig/network.

✔**Objective 6.04: Manage a Network Card**   The **ifconfig** command can configure network cards statically, to use different hardware addresses, as well as to modify the card to listen to all traffic promiscuously. Individual network card configuration files have names like *ifcfg-eth0* for the first Ethernet card. Dynamic network card configuration depends on commands such as **dhclient**, **dhcpcd**, and **pump**.

✔**Objective 6.05: Implement Name Resolution**   The static name resolution database is /etc/hosts. The standard database is DNS. The search order between these databases depends on /etc/host.conf or /etc/nsswitch.conf. Remote DNS server addresses are listed in /etc/resolv.conf. DNS servers can be tested with the **dig, host,** and **nslookup** commands.

✔**Objective 6.06: Work with Log Files**   Log files are generally configured in /etc/syslog.conf or the configuration files associated with individual services. Remote logging can also be configured in this file. Log files are normally stored in the /var/log directory or subdirectories, and are rotated per /etc/logrotate.conf.

✔**Objective 6.07: Use Makefiles**   Source code packages often must be compiled before they can be used. The command that compiles those packages may have a name like **make, make install,** or **./configure.** The process can often be customized in the Makefile.

✔**Objective 6.08: Configure the X Window System**   Linux has transitioned from the XFree86 server to the X.Org server. The contents of the configuration file are the same for the purpose of the Linux+ exam. While commands such as **XFree86 -configure** essentially have been replaced by commands such as **xorg -configure**, the command options for configuring the X Window have not changed. CTRL key combinations can help restart the X Window or access text consoles.

REVIEW QUESTIONS

Before leaving for the next chapter, take a few minutes to go through these questions. While doing so, take in both the content and the question format. Understanding what to expect on the exam can increase your chances for success.

1. You want to run the /usr/sbin/apachectl command without typing in the full path. SUID permissions have been assigned. When you run **echo $PATH**, you see

```
/usr/kerberos/bin:/usr/local/bin:/bin:/usr/bin:/home/michael/bin
```

What do you need to do?

    A. Nothing.

    B. Just run **/usr/sbin/apachectl**.

    C. Run **PATH=$PATH:/usr/sbin**.

    D. Run **$PATH=$PATH:/usr/sbin**.

2. Which of the following commands controls network configuration on the first Ethernet adapter?

   A. ifconfig eth1

   B. ipconfig eth1

   C. ipconfig eth0

   D. ifconfig eth0

3. Which of the following configuration files is associated with a DNS server?

   A. /etc/dns.conf

   B. /etc/named.conf

   C. /etc/nameserver.conf

   D. /etc/domain.conf

4. If you've configured some custom FQDN/IP address combinations in /etc/hosts, where do you want to configure hosts before DNS?

   A. /etc/host.conf

   B. /etc/named.conf

   C. /etc/nsswitch.conf

   D. /etc/hosts

5. Which of the following log priority levels associated with the **syslog** daemon is most important?

   A. debug

   B. warn

   C. crit

   D. alert

6. If you've moved the local /var/log/secure log file for analysis to your home directory, it'll no longer exist in the /var/log directory. Which of the following commands re-creates the file in such a way that it is usable by the **syslog** service?

   A. touch syslog

   B. touch /var/log/secure

   C. /etc/init.d/secure restart

   D. /etc/init.d/syslog restart

7. If you configure a network card in promiscuous mode, what does it do?

   A. Sends all packets to all other systems on the local network

   B. Sends all packets as a broadcast to all systems on the local and connected networks

   C. Listens to all packets from all other computers on the local network

   D. Listens to all packets received from computers set to send in promiscuous mode

8. Which of the following directives in /etc/fstab configures a shared NFS directory named /inst from the computer named share on the local directory named /west during the boot process?

   A. *share:/inst   /west   rw,noauto,user 0 0*

   B. *west:/share   /inst rw,noauto,user 0 0*

   C. *west:/share   /inst rw,noauto,user 1 2*

   D. *inst:/share   /west rw,noauto,user 0 0*

9. If you've downloaded a tarball for a driver, and the instructions suggest that you need to compile the package, which of the following commands would definitely not help?

   A. make

   B. configure

   C. INSTALL

   D. install.exe

10. The system is in runlevel 5. If you're having trouble with the X Window and want to restart the X Server, what keys would you press?

    A. CTRL-ALT-BACKSPACE

    B. CTRL-ALT-F1

    C. CTRL-ALT-F7

    D. CTRL-ALT-DELETE

REVIEW ANSWERS

1. **C**   To add a directory to an environment variable, you need to set the value to the current value of the variable (**$PATH**), adding the desired directory at the end. Alternatively, you could just list all desired directories in the right side of the equation.

2. **D**   The command that controls network cards is **ifconfig**; the device file associated with the first Ethernet card is eth0.

3. **B**   The /etc/named.conf configuration file is associated with the default DNS server, the BIND service.

4. **C**   The /etc/nsswitch.conf file is where current Linux distributions specify name search order. Sometime before the Linux+ objectives were released, it was done in /etc/host.conf. Yes, the wording of the question is a bit awkward, but you need to be prepared for questions like this on the exam.

5. **D**   In increasing order of importance, the priority log messages associated with the **syslog** daemon are debug, info, notice, warn, err, crit, alert, and emerg.

6. **D**   The log file is /var/log/secure, which records login attempts, successful and otherwise. While it's easy to create the file directly with a command like **touch**, such a file isn't recognized by the associated service. The only way to get the service to recognize it is to restart the **syslog** service. For this purpose, the **service syslog restart** command will also work.

7. **C**   Promiscuous mode listens to and collects all packets transmitted by other computers on the network. Ethernet makes it possible to listen to all packets on a network, even those which aren't coming to or from the local system.

8. **A**   The NFS server is named share; the shared directory follows the name of the server. The mount point comes in the next column, and for NFS shares, the **noauto** option makes sure that the mount doesn't hang the system in case of network or server trouble.

9. **D**   Scripts with the .exe extension are associated with Microsoft Windows package installations.

10. **A**   The CTRL-ALT-BACKSPACE key combination exits from the X Window. If you're in runlevel 5, it restarts the graphical login manager. If you're in runlevel 3, it returns to the text console.

Basic Server Configuration

	NEWBIE	SOME EXPERIENCE	VETERAN
ETA	80+ hours	16 hours	4 hours

This chapter focuses on the configuration of Linux server systems. First, this chapter examines how Linux servers can be configured as routers, specifically ones that forward and masquerade IP addresses. Next, it examines basic commands associated with activating server services, such as the Domain Name Service (DNS), Dynamic Host Configuration Protocol (DHCP), and Squid. While there's no practical way to change and test a configuration during a multiple-choice exam, you should expect to see and recognize the functionality of typical command stanzas from Samba, Apache, and LPD/CUPS Printer services.

Objective 7.01 Implement Basic Routing and Subnetting

As of this writing, Wikipedia defines routing as "the process of selecting paths in a network along which to send data or physical traffic." In other words, routing supports the forwarding of data, and Linux systems are easy to configure as routers between networks.

IPv6 networking was not in common use when the Linux+ objectives were released, so the focus in this section is on forwarding on IPv4 networks.

Managing Routing Tables

When I review the routing table on my desktop, I run the **route** command. As described in the Chapter 5 section "Understand Network Troubleshooting," the output is actually the same as that for the **netstat -r** command:

```
192.168.1.0    *              255.255.255.0  U   0   0   0 eth0
192.168.0.0    *              255.255.255.0  U   0   0   0 eth1
169.254.0.0    *              255.255.0.0    U   0   0   0 eth1
```

The routing table includes connections to three different networks, as defined by network addresses 192.168.0.0, 169.254.0.0, and 192.168.1.0. The 169.254.0.0 network address can be ignored, unless you're using Zero Configuration Networking on all systems on the local network.

Travel Advisory

Zero Configuration Networking is known in the Linux world as Zeroconf, and in the Microsoft world as Automatic Private IP Addressing (APIPA). It's associated with the 169.254.0.0/255.255.255.0 Class B network.

But wait a second—there's no connection to other IP addresses, such as those on the Internet. The **route** command can also help here. For example, if the gateway address of your LAN is 192.168.0.1, you can add that route to the local system with the following command:

```
# route add default gw 192.168.0.1 dev eth1
```

Review the result by running the **route** command again. You should see the following line at the end of the output:

```
default  192.168.0.1  0.0.0.0  UG  0  0   0 eth1
```

A default network mask is assumed; since 192.168.0.0 is a Class C network, that would be 255.255.255.0. If you're using a nonstandard network mask, add that to the **route** command. For example, if the network mask is 255.255.254.0, the command would be

```
# route add default netmask 255.255.254.0 gw 192.168.0.1 dev eth1
```

If you needed to add a route to a different network, such as 192.168.2.0, say with a network mask of 255.255.255.128, the command would be

```
# route add 192.168.2.0 netmask 255.255.254.0 gw 192.168.0.1 dev eth1
```

After adding a route to the table, review the result. You can do so with either the **route** or the **route -n** command. The difference is that the **route -n** command does not look for a DNS server, which can help if the DNS server is down.

Return to the routing table noted earlier in this section. Note the connections to the 192.168.0.0 and 192.168.1.0 networks through different cards. This system clearly has access to both networks. But to configure routing between these networks, you still need to implement IP forwarding. In addition, IP masquerading hides the address of the network client to the remote network.

Exam Tip
Know how to use the **route** command to add routes to specific networks.

IP Forwarding

If the local Linux system has connections to two different networks, IP forwarding must be enabled for communication to work between the networks. There are two ways to configure IP forwarding on a local Linux system. First, to confirm the current forwarding status of the local system, run the following command:

```
# cat /proc/sys/net/ipv4/ip_forward
```

This is a binary setting associated with the kernel. If it's 0, IP forwarding is disabled. If it's 1, IP forwarding is enabled. Therefore, you can activate IP forwarding with the following command:

```
# echo 1 > /proc/sys/net/ipv4/ip_forward
```

To confirm, run the **cat /proc/sys/net/ipv4/ip_forward** command. But this change isn't permanent unless you add the following directive in the /etc/sysctl.conf file:

```
net.ipv4.ip_forward = 1
```

Exam Tip
Know the command and configuration file directive that configures IP forwarding.

IP Masquerading

IP masquerading is a form of Network Address Translation (NAT). It hides the IP address of the computers on a local network as they make a connection to external networks such as the Internet. NAT replaces the source address with the IP address of the router. The source address is cached on the router, so the router knows which computer made the request.

When the router receives data such as a webpage, the process is reversed. As the packets pass through the router, the originating computer is identified in the cache. The header of each packet is modified accordingly before the packets are sent back to the client.

This approach is useful for several reasons. Disguising internal IP addresses makes it harder for someone to break into your network. NAT allows you to connect computers to the Internet without needing to have an official IP address for each computer. This allows you to use the private IP addresses discussed in the Chapter 2 section "Identify Network Configuration Issues" on an internal LAN.

Connecting multiple systems to the Internet using IP masquerading is a fairly straightforward process. The router needs two (or more) network cards: one connected to the local LAN, and a second card for external networks such as the Internet. To help you configure a connection from a private network to the Internet, you should know how to

- Assign an official IP address to the network card on the router directly connected to the Internet
- Configure a private IP address class (and appropriate IP addresses) to the computers on the local LAN

- Add a private IP address for the second network card on the router connected to the LAN
- Use **iptables** to set up IP masquerading
- Configure IP forwarding
- Use the **route** command on other computers to navigate to the Internet through the router

While a full understanding of the **iptables** command is beyond the scope of the Linux+ objectives, review the following command. It configures masquerading of the private IP addresses on the LAN, using the network card associated with the eth1 device (remember, eth1 is the *second* Ethernet card on a system). In this case, the private network address and subnet mask for the local LAN are 192.168.0.0 and 255.255.255.0, respectively.

```
# iptables -t nat -A POSTROUTING -s 192.168.0.0/24 \
-o eth1 -j MASQUERADE
```

Travel Advisory

On the command line, a backslash (\) escapes the meaning of the next character. For the **iptables** masquerading command described in this section, the backslash makes the bash shell read the entire command as if it were on a single line.

To translate, the **iptables** command is set to configure a NAT table (**-t nat**). The **POSTROUTING** option modifies outgoing data. The source (**-s**) addresses are listed as those on the 192.168.0.0 network, with the 255.255.255.0 subnet mask (as signified by the **/24**). The backslash "escapes" the next character; in other words, the entire code shown here is read as one command. Outgoing data (**-o**) is sent through the eth1 network card. Finally, the **MASQUERADE** option adds the IP address of the router to outgoing data.

Travel Advisory

Classless Internet Domain Routing (CIDR) notation is used as shorthand for subnet or network masks. A network mask of 255.255.255.0 can be read as the number of bits associated with that mask, /24. A network mask of 255.255.0.0 is associated with a CIDR mask of /16. It could be helpful to know CIDR notation for other masks; for example, 255.255.254.0 corresponds to /23, and 255.255.255.128 corresponds to /25. As of this writing, the associated Wikipedia page provides an excellent detailed explanation: http://en.wikipedia.org/wiki/Classless_Inter-Domain_Routing.

Configure Basic Network Server Services

There are a number of different basic network server services available on Linux. Three are described in the Linux+ objectives: DNS, DHCP, and Squid. Corresponding DNS and DHCP clients were described in the Chapter 6 sections "Implement Name Resolution" and "Manage a Network Card."

Domain Name Service

To review, DNS is short for the Domain Name Service. As a server, it provides a distributed database of hostnames or fully qualified domain names (FQDN) and IP addresses. There are four basic types of DNS servers available:

- A forwarding-only DNS server, which refers all requests to other DNS servers.
- A caching-only DNS server, which stores recent requests like a proxy server. It otherwise refers to other DNS servers.
- A slave DNS server, which relies on a master DNS server for data.
- A master DNS server, which stores authoritative records for the local domain.

Dynamic DNS services were not generally used when the Linux+ objectives were released, and are therefore beyond the scope of the exam. Depending on whether the so-called "chroot jail" is used, DNS configuration files may be stored in the /etc/ and /var/named directories, or in dedicated distribution-specific directories.

Local Lingo

Chroot jail   A dedicated directory which, when properly configured, prevents crackers who log in to the associated service from exiting the directory; the top-level root directory is thereby protected. Thus, a chroot jail can improve security of a service. In this case, if a cracker logs into a DNS service where a chroot jail is enabled, access to the computer with the DNS service is limited to the associated DNS files.

The main DNS configuration file is named.conf and is normally stored in the /etc/ directory. It cites data files in /var/named or associated chroot jail directories. After customizing /etc/named.conf, activate the DNS start script, **named**, in the /etc/init.d directory.

In any DNS server, there are typically two types of databases. The regular DNS database translates hostnames or FQDNs, such as www.mcgraw-hill.com, to IP addresses. The reverse DNS database translates IP addresses, such as 10.11.12.13, to hostnames or FQDNs. The following sections describe available types of DNS servers in order of increasing complexity.

Exam Tip

Know the name of the basic DNS configuration file (/etc/named.conf) and the **named** start script, associated with the BIND service. These don't change regardless of whether you're configuring a forwarding, caching-only, slave, or master DNS server.

Forwarding DNS Server

The simplest type of DNS server forwards requests to another DNS server. The following entry in /etc/named.conf forwards requests to the DNS servers at IP addresses 192.168.0.1 and 192.168.0.2:

```
options {
     directory "/var/named";
     forward only;
     forwarders {
          192.168.0.1;
          192.168.0.2;
     };
};
```

With a forwarding DNS server, no database files are stored locally. This is a common option for many home routers.

Caching-only DNS Server

Three of the selected distributions (Red Hat, SUSE, and Turbolinux) include a caching nameserver configuration file. When configuring a caching-only name server, look at the associated configuration file. It may already be configured on the default /etc/named.conf file, or a sample configuration file might have a slightly different name, such as /etc/named.caching-nameserver.conf (which you can then modify and save to /etc/named.conf). The following is an excerpt from a simplified version of this file:

```
options {
     directory "/var/named";
```

The **options** directive encompasses a **directory** directive, which tells the DNS server where to look for data files. Of course, for a caching DNS server to work, a cache file is required, and may be listed with a **dump-file** directive.

```
dump-file "/var/named/data/cache_dump.db;
```

If you have an older hardware firewall, it might expect DNS communication on TCP/IP port 53. In that case, activate the **query-source address * port 53** directive by removing the two forward slashes.

```
//query-source address * port 53;
```

Another way to fix the TCP/IP port is by activating a command such as

```
//listen-on port 53 {127.0.0.1};
```

While some sample files have more information (and can be further customized), slave DNS servers require two stanzas. The first stanza, shown next, starts with the root zone, as signified by the dot (.), which stands atop the Internet database. The reference to named.ca refers to the root DNS servers for the Internet. If they don't have the information you require, they can refer to other DNS servers.

```
zone "." {
     type hint;
     file "named.ca";
};
```

The second stanza creates a reverse zone file for the local system. Because it's the only computer listed in the named.local file, it is the *master* reverse zone file.

```
zone "0.0.127.in-addr.arpa" {
     type master;
     file "named.local";
};
```

Slave Name Server

Conceptually, a slave DNS server refers to other DNS servers like a forwarding DNS server. It also caches requested information like a caching DNS server. The following entry in /etc/named.conf first checks the current database file in the file named example.org; if the requested data isn't there, requests are forwarded to the DNS server at IP address 192.168.10.1:

```
zone "example.org" IN {
     type slave;
     file "slaves/example.org";
     masters {
             192.168.10.1
                };
};
```

Reverse lookups rely on the DNS server labeled with the **masters** directive. Note the difference from the **master** directive, which specifies a zone file as the master database for the domain.

Master DNS Server

A master DNS server is the authoritative server for your local domain, often a private domain. The example.com, example.net, and example.org domains have been explicitly reserved for documentation; nothing keeps you from using these domains on your private networks or CompTIA from using them on its exams.

The key stanzas refer to local files. The first key stanza refers to the local zone database for hostnames (or FQDN) to IP addresses:

```
zone "example.org" IN {
    type master;
    file "example.net.zone";
};
```

The following stanza defines the file with the reverse database; when given an IP address, the database generally returns either a hostname or an FQDN:

```
zone "0.168.192.in-addr.arpa" IN {
    type master;
    file "example.net.rr.zone";
};
```

Travel Advisory

If you ever need to create a DNS server of any type, there are examples available in a /usr/share/doc subdirectory. In some cases, there's a separate bind-doc RPM package with these examples.

DNS Data Files

As described earlier, there are DNS data files that return IP addresses when given a hostname or FQDN, and there are other DNS data files that provide reverse records. Here's an excerpt from my personal DNS data file:

```
$TTL    86400
@       IN      SOA  Kub.example.net. root.Kub.example.net. (
                            2008011301; Serial
                            28800      ; Refresh
                            14400      ; Retry
                            3600000    ; Expire
                            86400 )    ; Minimum
        IN      NS      Kub
        IN      MX      Kub
Ent5    IN      A       192.168.0.2
Sus2    IN      A       192.168.0.3
Man3    IN      A       192.168.0.4
```

```
Tur4    IN    A       192.168.0.5
FC6     IN    A       192.168.0.6
Kub     IN    A       192.168.0.7
Test    IN    CNAME   Sus2
```

Ent5, Sus2, Man3, Tur4, FC6, and Kub are hostnames for systems on my network; for example, the FQDN for my DNS server system is Kub.example.net. Significant options from the data file are listed in Table 7.1.

Exam Tip

Understand the relationship between the serial number in a master DNS server and updates on a slave DNS server.

If you change the database, remember to update the serial number. The current serial number shown in the preceding DNS data file is 2008011301, which refers to the first database created on January 13, 2008. If you update the database, change the serial number to a higher number, such as 2008011302. Otherwise, slave name servers won't check the master DNS database for updates.

Dynamic Host Configuration Protocol

A DHCP server assigns IP addresses dynamically. Through a DHCP server, administrators can configure a range of IP addresses, assign a subnet mask, and reserve a specific IP address for the hardware address associated with a client's network card. In addition, they can assign information such as the hostname and the gateway IP address, as well as applicable DNS IP addresses.

TABLE 7.1	Items Associated with a DNS Data File
DNS Data Item	**Description**
$TTL	Time to live; by default, specified in seconds; **86400** is equivalent to **24h** (24 hours) or **1d** (one day).
@	Refers to the local domain; in this case, example.net. is the local domain. (It doesn't work without the trailing dot.)
SOA	Start of authority record; in this case, the name server is Kub.example.net. and the administrator can be reached at root@Kub.example.net.
NS	Name server; hostname of the DNS server.
MX	Mail server.
CNAME	Canonical name; can substitute for a hostname.

DHCP servers can simplify and centralize network administration. They're well suited for networks with more than a few systems. They're especially convenient for networks with a significant number of mobile users.

If you're configuring a DHCP server on a remote network, the BOOTP procotol can be used to support access through any gateway to that remote network.

Besides IP addresses, DHCP servers can assign several kinds of information to individual systems, including:

- IP address for the gateway system (for routing to outside networks)
- NIS domain name
- Network domain name
- Time offset and (Network Time Protocol) IP address for the NTP server
- IP address for the NetBIOS name server
- Hostname

Here are three more key points to keep in mind:

- The script associated with activating the DHCP server is **dhcpd**, in the /etc/init.d directory. Don't confuse the name of the service (**dhcpd**) with the associated clients (**dhcpcd, pump, dhclient**) discussed in the Chapter 6 section "Manage a Network Card."
- If the DHCP server is used for other networks, a BOOTP protocol service is required. When the Linux+ objectives were released, the **zebra** daemon was commonly used for this purpose. As of this writing, the BOOTP protocol is enabled through the **dhcrelay** service.
- The governing configuration file is /etc/dhcpd.conf. Sample versions of this file are available for each of the selected distributions, either in the default version of this file or, in Red Hat's case, in a dhcpd.conf.sample file in the /usr/share/doc/dhcp* directory.

Exam Tip
Know what a DHCP server can assign to a client; it can assign so much more than just IP addresses.

Squid   *PROXY SERVER*

Squid is a high-performance caching proxy server, also known as a Web proxy cache. As it stores data from frequently used webpages and files, it can often give users the data they need without their even having to look to the Internet. Users' access to the data is faster, and the load on the corporate Internet connection is reduced.

Not all requests for webpages should go through a proxy server. For example, time-sensitive requests, such as stock quotes, and teleconferences should not be routed through a proxy server. Squid includes settings that can bypass the cache for certain kinds of data.

In addition, Squid can log access requests, providing data on where your users navigate outside your network. With the right settings, Squid can even block specific sites, or URLs associated with a specific pattern, such as xxx.

Detailed settings for the Squid Proxy Server are documented in the Squid configuration file, squid.conf, in the /etc/squid directory. Even though it's several thousand lines long, most of the file consists of comments that explain the options. Details are beyond the scope of the Linux+ objectives.

Exam Tip

The configuration script for Squid is /etc/init.d/squid. The configuration file is /etc/squid/squid.conf (or in some cases, /etc/squid.conf). Squid can act as a filter, tracking and blocking access by users to various sites on external networks such as the Internet.

Objective 7.03   Configure Samba

Microsoft networking is based on the Common Internet File System (CIFS), which was developed from the Server Message Block (SMB) protocol. Samba was developed as a freely available SMB server for all Unix-related operating systems, including Linux, and has been upgraded to support CIFS. While the Linux+ objectives were developed before this upgrade, what is done to configure Samba remains almost identical, at least for the purpose of the exam.

Samba configuration is easier than that for many other services such as DNS, DHCP, and Squid. In other words, more of the Samba configuration process is within the capabilities of the Linux+ exam candidate. This objective examines the basics of the Samba configuration file, smb.conf in the /etc/samba directory, some individual stanzas, and, finally, some Samba-related commands.

There are three basic daemons associated with the Samba service. The **smbd** daemon is the basic Samba daemon. The **nmbd** daemon provides NetBIOS over IP naming services for Microsoft-style NetBIOS hostnames. The **winbindd** daemon runs a Windows Internet Name Service (WINS), which maps the same NetBIOS names to IP addresses.

While Samba now can work as a member of an Active Directory (AD) network and, with the release of Samba 4, should support configuration as an AD domain controller, such capabilities post-date—and thus are beyond the scope of—the Linux+ objectives.

The Basic Configuration File

The Samba configuration file is divided into two sections. The first section, "Global Settings," applies to all parts of the Samba configuration. The second section, "Share Definitions," applies to individual shares, including user home directories, printers, and other shared directories.

Several critical Global Settings are described in Table 7.2.

Options for the **security** directive require additional explanation. The security associated with peer-to-peer networks on older Microsoft Windows 9x/Me systems did not require usernames, and could be enabled on Samba with

```
security = share
```

To configure a server as a member on a pre-AD domain, which points to another server for the login database, set

```
security = domain
```

This requires a directive that points to the server with the login database; you can also specify the hostname or IP address:

```
password server = *
```

TABLE 7.2	Samba Global Settings
Global Setting	**Description**
workgroup	Specifies the name of the workgroup or domain
security	Assigns the server type
printcap name	Set to the file with shared printers, normally /etc/printcap
printing	Associated with the print service, normally *cups* or *lprng*
local master	A factor in master browser elections
os level	Sets priority in master browser elections
wins server	Set to the IP address of a WINS server; requires **wins support = yes**

To configure a server as a Primary Domain Controller (PDC), which is associated primarily with Windows NT 4–style domains, set

```
security = user
```

In this configuration, clients can point to this system as the authentication server; usernames and passwords are stored in the /etc/samba/smbpasswd file, and must also exist as regular users in /etc/passwd. AD configurations post-date the Linux+ objectives, so they are beyond the scope of the exam.

> **Exam Tip**
>
> Recognize the directives that configure Samba as a master browser, as a member server that transmits authentication requests, and as a PDC on a Microsoft domain.

Printer-related directives are described later in this chapter, in the "Set Up Linux Print Services" section.

Stanzas and Directives

This section examines some typical stanzas in the Samba configuration file. One common stanza is the standard [**homes**] share, which shares the home directory of the logged-in user:

```
[homes]
    comment = Home Directories
    browseable = no
    writable = yes
```

To interpret, user home directories are writable, but other users are unable to browse said directories.

The following is another common stanza, which specifies how the /tmp directory is commonly used as a writable share for a network:

> **Travel Advisory**
>
> Several Samba directives have more than one acceptable spelling. For example, **writable** is the same as **writeable**, and **browsable** is the same as **browseable**, even though the latter of each option is misspelled in standard English.

```
[tmp]
    comment = Temporary file space
    path = /tmp
    read only = no
    public = yes
```

You could limit access to specific users with a directive such as **valid users**. With this directive, individuals can be specified by their usernames, and groups can be specified with the at symbol (@). For example, the following directive allows access to the users named donna and michael as well as the group named bank:

```
valid users = donna michael @bank
```

Conversely, the **invalid users** directive can prohibit access to specified users and groups. In addition, if a stanza includes a **read only** = **yes** directive, the following provides write access to users tim and the group named publisher:

```
write list = tim @publisher
```

Samba Configuration Commands

There are several important Samba configuration commands, which can work as clients, print to shared Microsoft printers, configure passwords on Microsoft networks, and more. The first one in my toolbox is **testparm**, which checks the syntax of the Samba configuration file. Several other basic Samba configuration commands are listed and described in Table 7.3.

TABLE 7.3   Samba Configuration Commands

Command	Description
smbcacls	Manages access control lists (ACLs) on shared Samba/CIFS files and directories.
smbclient	Provides FTP and Network Neighborhood–style client access to shared Samba/CIFS files and directories.
smbcontrol	Supports messages to **smbd**, **nmbd**, and **winbindd**; the **smbcontrol** command, when run without switches, results in output with messages that can be sent to each daemon.
smbcquotas	Allows management of quotas for shared directories formatted to the NTFS 5 filesystem.
smbget	Supports downloads from shared Samba directories; similar to **wget**.
smbpasswd	Configures a Samba password for users already in the local Linux database.
smbprint	Provides a print filter; used for LPD and LPRng configuration in /etc/printcap.
smbspool	Sends an already filtered print file to a shared Samba printer.
smbstatus	Provides a status for current Samba/CIFS connections.
smbtar	Allows archiving of Samba/CIFS shares.
smbtree	Displays a browse list of shared systems and directories.

Travel Advisory

Access Control Lists (ACLs) are one area where Microsoft operating systems provide more finer-grained control of files and directories. The current ACLs associated with Linux files and directories are not listed in the Linux+ objectives.

To get a general view of systems connected to a Microsoft network, run the **smbtree** command. As shown in Figure 7.1, the Poohbear, Kubmike, and Enterprise5hp systems are on the workgroup named Workgroup, with the shared directories and printers as listed.

Another way to view shares is by system; for the workgroup shown in Figure 7.1, the following command would list all shares on the Kubmike system:

```
# smbclient -L kubmike
```

If there are shares limited to a specific user, the -U *username* option can help. In this case, to find the shares limited to user michael on kubmike, I run the following command:

```
# smbclient -L kubmike -U michael
```

```
[michael@enterprise5fc6d ~]$ smbtree
Password:
WORKGROUP
        \\POOHBEAR                          Donna's laptop
                \\POOHBEAR\Shared Docs
                \\POOHBEAR\print$                   Printer Drivers
                \\POOHBEAR\IPC$                      Remote IPC
                \\POOHBEAR\hppsc120                  hp psc 1200 series
                \\POOHBEAR\DonnaPooh
        \\KUBMIKE                           Samba 3.0.22
                \\KUBMIKE\cupsLaserJet-4L            cupsLaserJet-4L
                \\KUBMIKE\HP1200                     Color Printer Downstairs
                \\KUBMIKE\HPLaserJet4                HPLaserJet4
                \\KUBMIKE\HPLaserJet4b               The other HP Laser Jet Printer
                \\KUBMIKE\HPLaserJonHP               in the Office
                \\KUBMIKE\LaserJet-4L                Laser Jet
                \\KUBMIKE\PSC-1210                   PSC-1210
                \\KUBMIKE\ADMIN$                     IPC Service (Samba 3.0.22)
                \\KUBMIKE\IPC$                       IPC Service (Samba 3.0.22)
                \\KUBMIKE\print$                     Printer Drivers
        \\ENTERPRISE5HP                     Samba Server
                \\ENTERPRISE5HP\HP1200               Color Printer Downstairs
                \\ENTERPRISE5HP\HPLaserJet4          in the office
                \\ENTERPRISE5HP\HPLaserJet4@enterprise5fc6d      Printer in the Office
                \\ENTERPRISE5HP\HPLaserJet4b         The other HP Laser Jet Printer
                \\ENTERPRISE5HP\LaserJonHP           On the HP Laptop
                \\ENTERPRISE5HP\OneMore              on the HP
                \\ENTERPRISE5HP\PrintRoom            A group of printers
                \\ENTERPRISE5HP\IPC$                 IPC Service (Samba Server)
                \\ENTERPRISE5HP\PublicShare          public share
[michael@enterprise5fc6d ~]$
```

FIGURE 7.1   The **smbtree** command lists shares.

The **smbclient** command can also be used as an FTP-style client. To browse and access files in user michael's home directory on the same server, I run the following command:

```
# smbclient //kubmike/michael -U michael
```

The Samba password database is different though related to the standard Linux password database. In other words, all Samba users must already have accounts on the Linux system, but the passwords can be different. To set a Samba password for user donna, run the following command:

```
# smbpasswd -a donna
```

Older versions of Samba, including the version available when the Linux+ objectives were released, included a **smbadduser** command. But CompTIA has been excellent in the way it has managed the questions on the exam; I therefore don't expect questions on this now obsolete command on the exam.

However, there's still an smbusers file in the /etc/samba directory, which correlates users on the Linux system with their Microsoft usernames. In other words, users with the same account on Linux and Microsoft systems can have different usernames, such as the Linux root and Microsoft administrator user.

 **Objective 7.04** **Configure Apache**   *WEB SERVER*

Currently, Apache is the most popular Web server on the Internet. According to the latest Netcraft (www.netcraft.com) survey, which tracks the Web servers associated with just about every site on the Internet, Apache is currently used by more Internet websites than all other Web servers combined. Apache is included with and is the default Web server for the selected Linux distributions.

Based on the HTTP daemon (**httpd**), Apache provides simple and secure access to all types of content using the regular HTTP protocol as well as its secure cousin, HTTPS.

Although Apache 2.x was available when the Linux+ objectives were released, Apache 1.3.x was (and in some areas still is) in popular use. Because many 2.x features have been "backported," there are few substantive differences between the latest releases of Apache 1.3.x and 2.x.

The Structure of Apache Directories

There are two sets of Apache directories: the directories in /etc/httpd (/etc/apache2 in SUSE Linux) contain regular and secure configuration files, and the directories in /var/www include various website components, which range from icons to scripts. Run the **ls -l /etc/httpd** command. You'll probably see links to subdirectories of /var/www, similar to what's shown in Figure 7.2.

While there are often more subdirectories configured, the basic /etc/httpd subdirectories are conf/ and conf.d/. They contain the main configuration file, normally httpd.conf. That configuration file includes directives that incorporate the contents of files in the conf.d/ subdirectory.

Now examine the Apache data directories commonly found in /var/www, as shown in Table 7.4. SUSE Linux includes Apache data directories in /srv/www, which some suggest follows the Filesystem Hierarchy Standard (FHS), described in the Chapter 4 section "Manage Storage Devices and Filesystems" more closely. The directories shown in Table 7.4 are subdirectories.

Depending on your distribution, directory names may be different from those in Table 7.4 and additional directories may be used. But remember, distribution-specific issues are not covered on the Linux+ exam.

Associated Configuration Files

There are two key configuration files for the Apache Web server: httpd.conf, in the /etc/httpd/conf directory, and ssl.conf, most commonly in the /etc/httpd/conf.d directory. The default versions of these files create a generic Web server service that you can further customize and optimize, as desired. This section examines just a few of the directives in httpd.conf; most nitty-gritty details of Apache configuration are beyond the scope of the Linux+ exam.

Some of the basic Apache configuration files are described in Table 7.5. The actual locations of these files varies widely, even among the selected distributions.

Even the names of these configuration files may vary by distribution. For example, several Apache configuration files in SUSE include the httpd- prefix.

Older versions of Apache, namely those in the 1.3.x series, separated the contents of httpd.conf into three files. The httpd.conf file retained the main configuration directives. There was also an access.conf file for access restriction directives, and an srm.conf file for resource management directives.

```
[root@enterprise5fc6d ~]# \ls -l /etc/httpd/
total 28
drwxr-xr-x 2 root root 4096 2007-08-07 15:09 conf
drwxr-xr-x 2 root root 4096 2007-08-07 15:04 conf.d
lrwxrwxrwx 1 root root   19 2007-06-13 10:13 logs -> ../../var/log/httpd
lrwxrwxrwx 1 root root   29 2007-06-13 10:13 modules -> ../../usr/lib64/httpd/mo
dules
lrwxrwxrwx 1 root root   13 2007-06-13 10:13 run -> ../../var/run
[root@enterprise5fc6d ~]#
```

FIGURE 7.2   /etc/httpd subdirectories, including links

TABLE 7.4	Typical Apache Data Directories /VAR/WWW
Apache Data Directory	**Description**
cgi-bin	Storage for CGI (Common Gateway Interface) scripts; often used for Perl and PHP scripts.
error	Pages with various HTTP-based error messages; for example, a 404 error (page not found) is commonly associated with the HTTP_NOT_FOUND.html.var file, which returns 404 errors in different languages.
html	Main directory for Apache webpages.
icons	Standard icons for Apache webpages.
manual	Apache manual associated with the installed version.

Other configuration files are incorporated into the httpd.conf file with the **Include** directive. For example, the following directive includes the directives from all *.conf files in the conf.d/ subdirectory:

```
Include conf.d/*.conf
```

There are three major sections in most standard Apache configuration files, "Global Environment," "Main Server Configuration," and "Virtual Hosts." They may not be explicitly listed, as in the ssl.conf file. Secure *virtual hosts* may be configured separately in ssl.conf.

Global Environment

The "Global Environment" section configures the overall operation of the Apache Web server. The **ServerRoot** directive points to the default directory; other directories in the configuration file are subdirectories.

```
ServerRoot "/etc/httpd"
```

TABLE 7.5	Sample Apache Configuration Files
Apache Configuration File	**Description**
httpd.conf	Main Apache configuration file
perl.conf	Includes modules for the Perl language interpreter
php.conf	Adds modules for the PHP language interpreter
python.conf	Includes the Python language interpreter
ssl.conf	Adds settings for secure websites
webalizer.conf	Incorporates the Webalizer log analysis tool

The **Listen** directive specifies the local IP address and TCP/IP port to which the Apache server should listen for requests for webpages. If the IP address is missing, the Apache server listens for requests through all network cards on the local system.

```
Listen 10.11.12.13:80
```

There may be many **LoadModule** directives, which incorporate all kinds of website functionality. Finally, the aforementioned **Include** directive is also part of the "Global Environment" section.

Main Server Configuration

The "Main Server Configuration" section sets up the default server not otherwise configured as a virtual host. The **ServerAdmin** directive sets up the website administrator, at least the one commonly seen in error pages. Other directives add languages, headers, links to error pages, responses to different browsers, and even proxy directives.

One advantage of this section is that it sets up defaults for any virtual hosts that website administrators need to configure, including log files. Two standard log files in Apache are associated with access requests and errors, as suggested by the following directives:

```
ErrorLog logs/error_log
CustomLog logs/access_log common
```

When coupled with the aforementioned **ServerRoot** directive (in the "Global Environment" section), this suggests that the log files for this Apache server can be found in the /etc/httpd/logs directory. But try the **ls -l /etc/httpd** command, as shown earlier in Figure 7.2. Generally, you'll see the following output, which documents a soft link to a more standard log directory, /var/log/httpd/:

```
lrwxrwxrwx 1 root root 19 Aug 7 09:01 logs -> ../../var/log/httpd
```

Of course, when configuring a *virtual host*, you can configure log files in different locations in the appropriate stanzas.

Local Lingo

Containers Another name for stanzas in Apache. Each container starts with a directive like **<Directory />** and ends with a directive like **</Directory>**.

Virtual Hosts

The "Virtual Hosts" section supports configuration of individual websites within the active Apache server. Any website configured in this section appears

completely separate from any other website. When a Web provider sells shared hosting, it is usually selling a *virtual host* configuration.

Remember, any configuration directives not included in a "Virtual Hosts" stanza default to those cited in the "Main Server Configuration" section.

Control Through .htaccess

Apache directories, including individual virtual hosts, are controlled through their individual subdirectories, as defined by <**Directory**> containers. If necessary, one way to override inherited permissions in any subdirectory involves .htaccess files.

If you choose to use .htaccess files, add the following command to the associated <**Directory**> container.

```
AllowOverride Options
```

For example, .htaccess files can help create more fine-grained security control. Full access can be provided to a public website, while .htaccess in the right <**Directory**> stanza can limit access to an Intranet site to certain employees.

Apache Command Controls

As with other services, it's important to know at least a few of the control commands. The **httpd** service is also a command that can be used to control and even add configuration options when starting the service. Table 7.6 lists and describes some of the **/usr/sbin/httpd** daemon options.

Of course, you need to know how to control the Apache daemon. It can be controlled in the same way that other services are controlled. For example, Apache can be restarted directly from the service script in the /etc/init.d directory:

```
# /etc/init.d/httpd restart
```

Apache can also be started with the **service** script:

```
# service httpd start
```

TABLE 7.6   Some Important **/usr/sbin/httpd** Daemon Switches

httpd Command Switch	Description
-d *serverroot*	*serverroot* specifies the root directory for other Apache configuration files.
-e *loglevel*	Sets the log level, as defined in the Chapter 6 section "Work with Log Files."
-M	Lists standard and shared Apache modules.
-S	Notes configured *virtual hosts*.
-t	Checks configuration file syntax.

Apache can also be controlled with the **apachectl** script. For example, the following command provides a current status:

```
# apachectl status
```

> ## Exam Tip
> Understand the different ways to control the Apache service, including major command switches associated with the **httpd** command.

Objective 7.05 Set Up Linux Print Services

As noted in the Chapter 5 section "Configure Printer Systems," there were two major printer systems in use when the Linux+ objectives were released: the Line Printer Daemon (LPD, as implemented with the LPRng daemon) and the Common Unix Printing System (CUPS). The focus in that chapter was on print clients; the focus in this chapter is on print servers. But since Linux clients commonly are configured as print servers, there is some overlap between these chapters.

Just remember, if you install packages for both print services, they can't both be active simultaneously. For example, if you want to run LPD and not CUPS, run the following commands:

```
# service cups stop
# service lpd start
```

The Line Printer, Next Generation Service

The LPD service, along with its Linux cousin, Line Printer, next generation (LPRng) service, is more familiar to Unix users. Linux is a clone of Unix. Because Linux has cost advantages over Unix, many administrators who convert from Unix-based networks may be more familiar with LPRng. As LPRng is derived from LPD, references to LPD in the Linux+ objectives in reality refer to both services as a single topic.

> ## Travel Advisory
> For selected distributions other than SUSE, LPRng is available for current Linux distributions only from third parties. One option is the software from the associated SourceForge project, available online from http://sourceforge.net/projects/lprng/.

As noted in the Chapter 5 section "Configure Printer Systems," the LPRng service is configured in /etc/lpd.conf and /etc/lpd.perms, and LPRng filters are configured in /etc/printcap. Although the LPD and LPRng services are not in common use on current Linux distributions, CUPS includes a number of commands based on those earlier services.

> **Exam Tip**
>
> CompTIA does an excellent job of keeping the Linux+ exam up to date, but the LPRng service was an important part of Linux, so expect to at least know that **lpd** is the LPRng print daemon, as well as the names of configuration files.

The Common Unix Printing System

As noted in Chapter 5, CUPS is the standard on the selected distributions. It can connect to and control printers configured with a variety of different services, from Microsoft to Internet Print Protocol (IPP) and even LPD printers, as described in Table 7.7.

Some of these queue connections require that you know the Universal Resource Identifier (URI) address for the printer. The URI is a superset of a URL, with a similar format. For example, a URL corresponds to an address like http://www.example.org, while the URI corresponds to a similar format, such as socket://printer.example.org:9100. This URI connects to a printer on the printer.example.org FQDN, using the socket protocol, on port 9100.

One key advantage of CUPS is the ability to configure a group of printers into a class. A print class can be shared like any regular printer. Jobs sent to a print class are sent to the first available printer in that class.

| **TABLE 7.7** | CUPS Configuration Queues |

CUPS Queues	**Description**
Local	CUPS can handle printers attached to standard local ports.
Networked CUPS	CUPS can connect to printers shared with CUPS servers from remote systems; networked CUPS is associated with IPP.
Remote LPD	CUPS can connect to shared LPD.
HP JetDirect Servers	HP JetDirect Servers use the JetDirect protocol associated with TCP/IP port 9100; access to such servers are based on a URI which starts with **socket:**.
Other URIs	In general, systems that can be shared through a URI can be shared with a CUPS server.

The following sections take a brief look at the variety of available CUPS configuration files, as well as some of the control commands for this service.

CUPS Configuration Files

There are a number of printer configuration files in the /etc/cups directory. Each of these files includes a substantial number of commands and comments. Table 7.8 describes some of these files. As before, not all of these files may be used; some of these files may be in different directories on different distributions.

While it's generally best to edit configuration files directly, CUPS directives can be difficult to learn. Several of the files in /etc/cups don't include the same quality of comments as seen for other services. And, in my opinion, the Web-based (as well as the distribution-specific) configuration tool provides excellent levels of functionality. But the functionality is not complete; fortunately, user and IP address limits are easy to add to configured printers, as you'll see later in the chapter, in the "Apply Basic Printer Permissions" section.

The cupsd.conf Configuration File

The main CUPS configuration file is cupsd.conf in the /etc/cups directory. While not even the RHCE exam requires detailed knowledge of CUPS configuration files, it can be helpful to understand a few key directives. For example, the following directive makes shared printers visible to CUPS clients:

```
Browsing On
```

TABLE 7.8   CUPS Configuration Files

CUPS Configuration File	Description
/etc/cups/classes.conf	Configures groups of printers in a class
/etc/cups/client.conf	Sets the default CUPS server for this computer; it can be local or another remote print server
/etc/cups/cupsd.conf	The main CUPS configuration file
/etc/cups/mime.convs	Includes file format filters, such as images and documents
/etc/cups/mime.types	Sets file types that can be processed through CUPS printers
/etc/cups/printers.conf	Documents printers configured by the CUPS Web-based tool
/etc/cups/pstoraster.convs	Includes a conversion filter that supports PostScript printers
/etc/printcap	Adds a list of printers for sharing; used by Samba
/etc/cups/ppd/	Includes a directory with customized printer settings
/etc/cups/ssl/	Sets a directory with SSL certificates
/etc/cups/interfaces/	Organizes interface scripts, such as filters

Log files are normally stored in the /var/log/cups directory, and these directives specify their types and locations:

```
ErrorLog /var/log/cups/error_log
AccessLog /var/log/cups/access_log
PageLog /var/log/cups/page_log
```

As these directives are defaults, they do not need to be included in cupsd.conf. The names are almost self-explanatory: errors are logged in error_log, print server messages are stored in access_log, and print requests from local and remote systems are logged in page_log. Shared printers are stored as documented with the **Printcap** directive.

```
Printcap /etc/printcap
```

The **ServerRoot** directive should look familiar from the "Configure Apache" section earlier in this chapter:

```
ServerRoot /etc/cups
```

It's also possible to configure dedicated print administrators. The following directive limits administrative access to members of the sys and root groups. Of course, you can add the groups of your choice to the directive, or just add selected printer administrators to the sys group in /etc/group.

```
SystemGroup sys root
```

The following stanza documents administrative access in encrypted format. This level appears to be beyond the scope described in the Linux+ objectives, so I just present it for your review.

```
<Location /admin>
  Encryption Required
  AuthType BasicDigest
  AuthClass Group
  AuthGroupName Admins
  # Allow remote administration...
  Order allow,deny
  Allow @LOCAL
</Location>
```

Once the digest AuthType is configured, the **lppasswd** command can create Print Administrative accounts. For example, the following command by the root user makes user elizabeth an administrator:

```
# lppasswd -a elizabeth
```

User elizabeth can then change her passwords from her own account with the **lppaswd** command. Of course, this command works only if user elizabeth has a regular account on the local CUPS print server, and has an account in the sys or root group, as documented in /etc/group.

CUPS Service Control Commands

The CUPS Web-based interface is essentially a front-end to the **lpadmin** command. It's a rich command, as shown by the options listed and described in Table 7.9.

The same switches listed in Table 7.9 also work with the **lpoptions** command. But **lpoptions** can also control print options such as cover pages, notifications, configurability in classes, and more. More options are available that can limit access to specific users and groups, as described shortly in the "Apply Basic Printer Permissions" section.

Once configured, printers can be controlled with the **cupsenable** and **cupsdisable** commands. If a printer is stuck, these commands can give the printer a necessary jolt. These commands are straightforward; for example, I can disable a configured HPLaserJet4 printer connected to my office laptop with the following command:

```
# cupsdisable HPLaserJet4
```

Of course, the effect of the command can be reversed:

```
# cupsenable HPLaserJet4
```

These two commands have several switches, as described in Table 7.10. As described a bit earlier, these switches also apply for other printer-related commands such as **lpoptions** and **lpadmin**.

Sharing Printers with Samba

Linux administrators need to know how to share with Microsoft-based networks. That includes sharing printers via Samba. To see how this is done, review a standard printer share stanza in the smb.conf configuration file:

```
[printers]
   comment   = All Printers
   path = /var/spool/samba
   browseable = yes
   public = yes
   guest ok = yes
   writable = no
   printable = yes
```

This stanza stores spool files in /var/spool/samba, makes shared printers browsable by all, and makes printers accessible to the public and runnable by guest users. Unless you're limiting printer access to specific users, it's important to include the **guest ok = yes** directive.

> **Travel Advisory**
>
> Until recently, the default Red Hat version of the Samba configuration file had **path=/usr/spool/stanza**, which is an error.

TABLE 7.9   **lpadmin** Command Switches

lpadmin Switches	Description
-E	Forces encryption; useful over a network
-U *username*	Specifies the username of the print administrator
-h *server:port*	Points to the CUPS server (or IP address); include the port if it's not the default (631)
-d *printer*	Specifies the default destination as the printer named *printer*
-p *printer*	Sends a job to the printer named *printer*
-x *printer*	Deletes a configured printer named *printer*
-c *class*	Adds the specified printer to the noted print *class*

But these are details, and it's important to keep the big picture in mind. Configuring shared printers in the Samba configuration file requires appropriate settings for the **printing** and **printcap name** directives. Depending on whether the local system uses CUPS or LPRng, the printing directive should be set to one of the following:

```
printing = cups
printing = lprng
```

Normally, the **printcap name** is set to the list of shared printers. For both the LPRng and CUPS services, that file is /etc/printcap. So expect to see the following directive:

```
printcap name = /etc/printcap
```

TABLE 7.10   Switches for **cupsenable** and **cupsdisable**

Switch	Description
-E *server*	Enables encryption when administering a remote CUPS printer
-U *username*	Specifies a username, if required for administering remotely
-c *printer*	Cancels active print jobs on the noted printer
-h *server:port*	Administers a printer on a remote server, on a specified TCP/IP port

Apply Basic Printer Permissions

In larger organizations, there is a hierarchy. Bosses want priority permissions to certain printers. Production groups may also need higher priority to printers. These permissions can be implemented by address and/or user, or on a wider scale by network and/or group.

Limiting Access by Address

Print access can be limited in the stanza associated with the printer, which may be configured in either cupsd.conf or printers.conf in the /etc/cups directory. For example, the following directive starts the configuration stanza for the default printer in my office:

```
<DefaultPrinter HPLaserJet4>
```

Within the stanza, the **Allow from** directive can limit access to a specific IP address or network; for example, the following directives limit access to users on the 192.168.0.22 system and the 10.22.33.* network:

```
Allow from 192.168.0.22
Allow from 10.22.33.*
```

In contrast, the following directive denies access to a different network:

```
Deny from 10.22.34.*
```

CUPS supports the use of CIDR notation, as well as regular expressions of subnet masks. In other words, two other ways to write the preceding directive are

```
Deny from 10.22.34.0/24
Deny from 10.22.34.0/255.255.255.0
```

CUPS also allows the use of FQDNs with asterisks, such as *.example.org.

Limiting Access by User

Print access can be limited by user and/or group in the stanza associated with the printer, which may be configured in either cupsd.conf or printers.conf in the /etc/cups directory. The associated directive is similar to that which limits by IP address; the following directives limit access to user michael and group supervisors:

```
AllowUser michael
AllowUser @supervisors
```

Note how @ is associated with a group of users, just as was done in the smb.conf file described earlier in the "Configure Samba" section. Similarly, the following directives deny access to user cracker and group badguys:

```
DenyUser cracker
DenyUser badguys
```

Access can also be limited by other means. For example, the following stanza from the Samba configuration file, smb.conf, limits access to the user named fred:

```
[fredsprn]
    comment = Fred's Printer
    valid users = fred
    path = /homes/fred
    printer = freds_printer
    public = no
    writable = no
    printable = yes
```

Naturally, the **valid users** directive shown limits access to the user fred. Similar rules apply to groups; for example, **valid users = @mechanics** would limit access to members of the mechanics group. Conversely, users and groups can be stopped with the **invalid users** directive.

CHECKPOINT

✔**Objective 7.01: Implement Basic Routing and Subnetting**   Because Linux is built for networking, Linux administrators need to understand how to add routes to new networks, configure forwarding to turn a Linux system into a gateway, and, at least, the principles of how IP masquerading hides the private network address of a client computer that asks for information online.

✔**Objective 7.02: Configure Basic Network Server Services**   Three basic network server services are DNS, DHCP, and Squid. The four different kinds of DNS servers are forwarding, caching, slave, and, of course, the regular DNS server. A DHCP server is primarily used to lease IP addresses. It can also be used to provide the IP addresses of the gateway and DNS server(s); it can even allocate hostnames. Squid provides Web proxy services that can also log where users browse online.

✔**Objective 7.03: Configure Samba**   Samba configures a Linux system as a client, a server, or even a PDC on a Microsoft-based network. The Samba configuration file, /etc/samba/smb.conf, can connect to printers, set preferences for browser elections, and customize access to shared directories and printers. Various Samba commands can browse remote shares, configure authentication, and more.

✔**Objective 7.04: Configure Apache** Apache is the most popular Web server on the Internet. There are separate directories for secure websites, scripts, images, and more. Key configuration files are httpd.conf in /etc/httpd/conf and ssl.conf in /etc/httpd/conf.d. Apache can be controlled with standard service scripts or the **apachectl** command.

✔**Objective 7.05: Set Up Linux Print Services** When the Linux+ objectives were released, there were two major print services associated with Linux: CUPS and LPD (or LPRng). CUPS is now the Linux standard print service, in part because of its Web-based tool, accessible via http://127.0.0.1:631. CUPS printers can be controlled with several LPD-based commands as well as commands like **cupsenable** and **cupsdisable**.

✔**Objective 7.06: Apply Basic Printer Permissions** Access to printers can be limited in the stanzas that configure specific printers. Users can be regulated by **AllowUser** and **DenyUser** directives; systems can be regulated by IP addresses or domain names with **Allow from** and **Deny from** directives. Access to printers shared through Samba can be regulated in a similar fashion.

REVIEW QUESTIONS

Before leaving for the next chapter, take a few minutes to go through these questions. While doing so, take in both the content and the question format. Understanding what to expect on the exam can increase your chances for success.

1. Which of the following commands adds a gateway to the 192.168.0.0/16 network through the second Ethernet card?

   A. route add 192.168.0.0 gw 10.11.12.13 dev eth1

   B. route add 192.168.0.0 netmask 255.0.0.0 gw 10.11.12.13 dev eth1

   C. route add 192.168.0.0 netmask 255.255.0.0 gw 10.11.12.13 dev eth1

   D. route add 192.168.0.0 netmask 255.255.255.0 gw 10.11.12.13 dev eth1

2. Which of the following configuration files would you use to set up a caching DNS server?

   A. /etc/named.caching-nameserver.conf

   B. /etc/named.caching.conf

   C. /etc/caching.conf

   D. /etc/named.conf

3. Which of the following items absolutely is not shared with network clients by a DHCP server?

   A. NIS Domain

   B. NFS shared directories

   C. Time server

   D. Hostname

4. What service would you configure if you want to track the websites visited by your employees?

   A. Squid

   B. Apache

   C. Samba

   D. Syslog

5. Which of the following commands does not restart the Apache Web server? Assume the service script is httpd.

   A. /etc/httpd restart

   B. /etc/init.d/httpd restart

   C. service httpd restart

   D. apachectl restart

6. Which of the following directories normally contains the basic Apache webpages? Assume default settings for a distribution other than SUSE Linux.

   A. /etc/httpd/html

   B. /var/httpd/html

   C. /etc/www/html

   D. /var/www/html

7. Which of the following files is normally used to configure IP forwarding when Linux is booted?

   A. /etc/syslog.conf

   B. /proc/sys/net/ipv4/ip_forward

   C. /etc/sysctl.conf

   D. /etc/rc.local

8. Based on the following stanza in the Samba configuration file

```
[backups]
    comment = Network Backups
    path = /backups
    read only = no
```

which of the following directives, when added, would limit access to the group named backup?

A. allowed users = @backup

B. valid users = @backup

C. allowed groups = backup

D. valid groups = backup

9. Several users have different account names on Microsoft and Linux systems on your network. Samba supports a database that matches these usernames in which of the following files?

A. /etc/samba/sambausers

B. /etc/samba/smbpasswd

C. /etc/samba/samba

D. /etc/samba/smbusers

10. Which of the following directives prohibits the use of a printer from a user named enemy?

A. Deny from enemy

B. DenyUser enemy

C. Deny enemy

D. Deny user enemy

REVIEW ANSWERS

1. **C** The **route add** command adds a route to an external network. The network address is 192.168.0.0. Because the default network mask for this Class C network address is 255.255.255.0, only answer C (which specifies a Class B subnet) meets the requirements described.

2. **D** No matter what kind of DNS server you're planning to configure, the associated configuration file is /etc/named.conf.

3. **B** NIS Domains, time servers (NTP), and hostnames can all be allocated by a DHCP server. While none of these options are required, they illustrate what a DHCP server can do. NFS shared directories are controlled in the NFS server's /etc/exports configuration file.

4. **A** Squid is the Web proxy service that can also log websites visited, through its caching service.

5. **A** The service script in the /etc/init.d directory can also be controlled by the **service** command. The **apachectl** command works as well. There is no /etc/httpd script, at least on the selected distributions.

6. **D** The default directory for a website, normally associated with directives in the "Main Server Configuration" section, is /var/www/html. Incidentally, it's /srv/www if you're running SUSE Linux. Of course, you can configure any directory in each *virtual hosts* container.

7. **C** While changing the contents of /proc/sys/net/ipv4/ip_forward enables IP forwarding when Linux is running, the change will not survive a reboot. The standard configuration for setting up IP forwarding upon boot is /etc/sysctl.conf.

8. **B** The **valid users** directive regulates users and groups allowed to access any Samba share. The @ is associated with group names. The other directives listed as options do not exist.

9. **D** The default /etc/samba/smbusers file should already show at least one directive correlating the Linux root user with the Microsoft administrator and admin users.

10. **A** The directive which prohibits access by users in CUPS is **Deny from** *username*.

PART

IV

Securing Accounts and Services

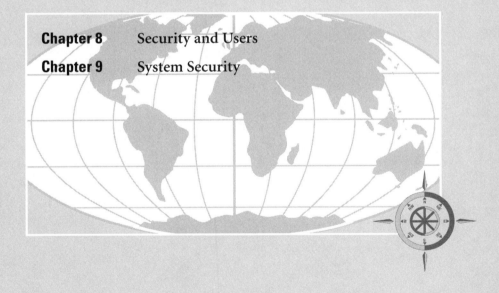

Security and Users

	NEWBIE	SOME EXPERIENCE	VETERAN
ETA	80+ hours	16 hours	8 hours

217

Security in any service starts with the user. Account management can be challenging when users move within or leave the organization. Account management gets trickier when others need partial or full administrative privileges. When needed, it's easy to temporarily deactivate all but the root account. You can even deactivate login access to the root account, but that's a feature of Ubuntu Linux, not covered on the Linux+ exam.

A variety of security files are available to regulate administrative and remote access. Service-specific configuration options and Pluggable Authentication Modules (PAM) can help. Specialized permissions can help regulate user access to key files and directories. Appropriate password and login policies can help keep individual accounts even more secure.

Objective 8.01 Manage User Accounts

One basic responsibility of a Linux administrator is the management of user accounts. As described in the Chapter 5 section "Manage User Accounts," commands such as **useradd**, **usermod**, **userdel**, and **chage** can help an administrator manage how accounts are created, deleted, and otherwise used.

Two security-related skills associated with these commands are deactivating accounts and deleting accounts while managing the data. The selected Linux distributions enable the Shadow Password Suite by default, so this section assumes that the associated /etc/shadow and /etc/gshadow configuration files are installed. For more information on the Shadow Password Suite, see the "Configure Password Policies" section later in this chapter.

Deactivating Accounts

In many organizations, people leave temporarily for various reasons: extended vacations, additional schooling, medical convalescence, and so on. For such users, you need to know how to temporarily deactivate their accounts. There are three basic ways to perform this task.

One option is to deactivate the password for the account. Assuming /etc/shadow exists, the simplest method is to open /etc/passwd in a text editor, navigate to the line associated with the account, and replace the x in the password field with an asterisk (*), as shown here:

```
michael:*:500:500::/home/michael:/bin/bash
```

When someone tries to log in with that account at the console, even with the correct password (which still exists in the /etc/shadow file), that user gets the following message:

```
Login incorrect
```

The second way to deactivate an account is to replace the login shell with a null shell. One standard null shell is **/sbin/nologin**; the following example replaces /bin/bash in /etc/passwd.

```
michael:x:500:500::/home/michael:/sbin/nologin
```

In that event, if user michael tries to log in, he may see the following message flash too quickly on the screen. The message sometimes is stable if the user tries to log in a few times.

```
login: no shell: No such file or directory.
```

The third way to deactivate an account is with the **chage** command. Specifically, the **chage** command can be used to set the expiration date for the account to yesterday (or some other previous date). As described in the Chapter 5 section "Manage User Accounts," it can be done with the **chage -E** *date* command, where the date can be in YYYY-MM-DD format. For example, the following **chage** command sets an expiration date of August 8, 2007:

```
# chage -E 2007-08-08 michael
```

Travel Advisory

The dates associated with user accounts can also be specified in the number of days since January 1, 1970 (the Unix epoch). In fact, if you use YYYY-MM-DD format, Linux translates it to the number of days since that date in the /etc/shadow configuration file.

After trying to log in three times, that user will see the following message the next time he logs in:

```
Your account has expired; please contact your system administrator
```

There's another command that does the same thing as **chage -E** *date*; for more information, see the **usermod** command, as described later in this chapter in the "Promote User-level Security" section. Once configured, the deactivated user who tries to log in sees the same "Your account has expired" message.

For more information on failed logins, see the associated log file. This file varies even among the selected distributions; typical log files associated with failed logins include /var/log/secure, /var/log/auth.log, and /var/log/messages. Login attempts can also be read with the following command:

```
# utmpdump /var/log/wtmp
```

The right way to temporarily deactivate accounts depends on the policies of your organization. But you now know the options and the messages presented to users, and should be able to recognize these messages on the exam.

Travel Advisory

When deactivating accounts, even temporarily, administrators might
need to change more than just the user account. They may also need to
deactivate e-mail, IRC accounts, membership in shared groups, and more.

Deleting Accounts While Keeping the Data

By default, the **userdel** *username* command by itself does not change the
/home/*username* directory. (In contrast, the **userdel -r** *username* command
does delete the /home/*username* directory.) All files in that directory are not
changed, though the UID and GID numbers replace the deleted user and
group names as file owners. For example, this is what I see when I run the
ls -l /home/test1 command after running the **userdel test1** command:

```
-rw-rw-r-- 1 502 502  0 Apr 17 06:20 abcd
-rw-rw-r-- 1 502 502 29 Apr 17 06:20 test.txt
```

In this case, the number 502 is in place of the now deleted *user* and *group* owners. At this point, no user other than the administrator has access to these files.
Even administrators are supposed to access regular files from regular accounts. If
there's an immediate replacement for the user, the administrator could just
change the username in the appropriate authentication files or databases.

But that may not be enough. The now deleted user may have saved files in
other directories. Fortunately, as described in the Chapter 3 section "Work with
Files and Directories," it's easy to identify all files owned by a specific UID. For
example, the following **find** command searches through the directory tree for all
files owned by UID 502:

```
# find / -uid 502
```

If the new user comes before the files can be reassigned, you can run the
useradd command with the UID of the old user. For example, the following
command assigns UID 502 to the new user named replacement:

```
# useradd -u 502 replacement
```

And the following command would assign GID 502 to the new group named replacement, but you'd find that it already exists, courtesy of the previous **useradd**
command.

```
# groupadd -g 502 replacement
```

You can then copy the files from the old user's home directory to that of the
new user. The following command copies only regular (not hidden) files:

```
# cp -ar /home/test1/* /home/replacement
```

You may want to take a different action on hidden files such as test1's **.evolution/** subdirectory, which contains that user's e-mail files, assuming the Evolution e-mail client is used. Because even work e-mails may contain private information, what you do may depend on the privacy policies of your organization and applicable governmental regulations.

If you're reassigning files from the old user to someone else, it's not enough to just copy the contents of that user's home directory. First, you need to make sure you're not overwriting any important file or directory in the target user's home directory. You'll also need to change user and group ownership of the files being moved. As described in the Chapter 3 section "Modify Ownership and Permissions," this is easy to accomplish with commands such as **chown** and **chgrp**. For example, the following command changes both the user and group owner of all files and subdirectories in /home/test1 recursively:

```
# chown -R replacement.replacement /home/test1/
```

Exam Tip

There are two ways to change both the user and group owner of a file simultaneously: you can divide the user and group with either a dot (.) or a colon (:). In other words, **chown -R replacement.replacement /home/test1** is functionally identical to **chown -R replacement:replacement /home/test1**.

In this case, the user named replacement now has access to the /home/test1 directory, as well as ownership of all files and subdirectories therein, and is now free to manage those files as he manages those in his own home directory.

Deactivating Regular Accounts

It's easy to deactivate all regular accounts at once. Just create an /etc/nologin file. If you do, it disallows logins from all regular users. It works even if the file is blank. If desired, you can add a text message to that file, such as "The server will be down until I get my ice cream." But that message will be seen only by users who log in remotely.

Just remember to delete the /etc/nologin file when you're ready to accept regular users again.

Changing Groups

When users are promoted or moved to different departments, the administrative task may be as simple as changing the group memberships associated with those users. For most of the selected distributions (except SUSE), users are by default members of their own private groups. As can be verified in /etc/passwd, the UID and GID of regular users are identical.

However, in real life, users are also made members of special groups, such as supervisors, accountants, and mechanics. When people are promoted, you may need to change their group memberships.

There are two ways to change the membership of a user in a group: directly through the configuration files, or with the **usermod** command.

If your system is running the Shadow Password Suite, you could open the /etc/group and /etc/gshadow files in a text editor. As noted in the Chapter 3 section "Manage Text Files," the **vigr** command automatically opens /etc/group in the vi editor. For example, if user donna were promoted, it's easy to move user donna from the accountants group to the supervisors group, as shown here:

```
accountants:x:5000:donna
supervisors:x:6000:
```

Just use the commands associated with your text editor to move user donna. The advantage of the **vigr** command is that when you're finished editing /etc/group, it prompts you to edit /etc/gshadow, where you can (and should) make the same change.

Alternatively, you could just run the **usermod -G** *newgroup username* command, which changes the group memberships for the *username*. To change user donna's group membership from accountants to supervisors, the following command works:

```
# usermod -G supervisors donna
```

The command is straightforward: because the group named accountants was not included in the group list after the **-G**, user donna is removed from membership in that group.

Objective 8.02 Control Administrative Accounts

There are regular users and administrative users. Users with UIDs between 1 and 99 are typically configured as users dedicated to specific services such as the FTP and Apache servers. It's also possible to configure accounts for users named guest and nobody with minimal privileges. The focus in the Linux+ objectives is on the difference between regular and administrative users, and on how regular users can be given partial or full administrative privileges.

In general, even administrators should have a regular account. When they need access to administrative interfaces, they can use the **su** and **sudo** command front-ends described in this section. However, it may be appropriate to log in as the root user during periods of heavy administrative activity, or to access files and accounts (such as the root e-mail account and cron jobs) accessible only to the root user. For example, many log files are configured by default to e-mail reports to the root account, so administrators may want to check the root e-mail account at least once in a while.

Travel Advisory

If you're running an e-mail service such as sendmail or Postfix, it's possible to forward root e-mail to a real e-mail address. Just modify /etc/aliases with the mapping, save, and run the **newaliases** command.

When I've taken the Red Hat Certified Engineer (RHCE) exam, I've logged in as the root user because just about every command that needs to be run during that exam is administrative in nature.

This section does not cover the administrative privileges that can be configured for a few services. For example, it's possible to set up dedicated print administrators on CUPS, as described in the Chapter 7 section "Set Up Linux Print Services."

Regular and Administrative Accounts

Users with regular accounts have access to their own home directories and to any directories shared either globally or specifically. The /tmp directory is shared generally with all regular users. As described later in this chapter in the "Work with Special File Permissions" section, the so-called "sticky bit" allows all users to write files to /tmp, sharing them with other users.

There are two ways for regular users to get administrative access.

- Users who have the administrative password can use the **su** command.
- Users who are properly authorized in /etc/sudoers can use the **sudo** command and confirm administrative commands with their own regular user passwords. Such users do not need to know the administrative root password.

Temporary Administrative Access with su

The **su** command, which normally requires that you know the root password, can be used in three basic ways. By itself, it supports access to the administrative account, without changing directories. When run with a space and a dash (**su -**), it logs into the root account as the root user, with the same rights, privileges, settings, and risks. It's just as if you logged directly into the administrative account.

Travel Advisory

Incidentally, the **su – *username*** command can log into the account of your choice, as long as you know that user's password. For example, if I know user donna's password, I could run the **su – donna** command, enter her password when prompted, and access her account with all her privileges and permissions. Don't forget a space on either side of the dash in these commands.

Finally, the **su** command can be used to run an individual administrative command without logging into the root account. For example, I could run the following command from my regular account to change user nancy's password:

```
# su -c "passwd nancy"
```

This command first prompts for the administrative password, followed by prompts for the password that I want to give to user nancy. Once the command is complete, I'm returned to my regular account.

Administrative Privileges with sudo

You can also provide administrative privileges to selected users in /etc/sudoers. Such users have access to administrative commands with the **sudo** command with their own regular account password. You don't need to give out the administrative password to everyone who thinks he knows as much as you do about Linux.

Just to illustrate what regular users can do with the **sudo** command, see what happens when user dickens uses it to change the runlevel to 3:

```
$ sudo /sbin/init 3
```

The first time user dickens runs the **sudo** command, she sees the following message:

```
We trust you have received the usual lecture from the local System
Administrator. It usually boils down to three things:

    #1) Respect the privacy of others
    #2) Think before you type
    #3) With great power comes great responsibility

Password:
```

If user dickens is properly enabled in /etc/sudoers, she can enter her own regular password to run the administrative **/sbin/init 3** command. She doesn't need to know the administrative root password. See the next section for more information on editing /etc/sudoers.

Objective 8.03 Set Up Security Environment Files

There are several files that can help you configure and promote security on Linux systems:

- The /etc/sudoers file can give regular users limited or full administrative privileges, without having to give away the administrative password.
- Remote access through the Secure Shell (SSH) service can be regulated through appropriate directives in the /etc/ssh/sshd_config configuration file.
- Access to individual system configuration tools can be regulated using Pluggable Authentication Module (PAM) files in the /etc/pam.d directory.
- Access to FTP servers can be regulated through files such as /etc/ftpusers.
- Access to a variety of network services can be limited with appropriate directives in the /etc/hosts.allow and /etc/hosts.deny configuration files.

The following sections describe the configuration of each of these security configuration files.

Users as Administrators in /etc/sudoers

Regular users can be given administrative privileges when so configured in the /etc/sudoers configuration file. To access /etc/sudoers in the vi editor, run the **visudo** command. From the following directive, the root user is allowed full access to administrative commands:

```
root    ALL=(ALL) ALL
```

This directive provides a pattern that can help you configure regular users as administrators. For example, if you want to allow user randy full administrative access, add the following directive to /etc/sudoers:

```
randy    ALL=(ALL) ALL
```

In this case, all user randy needs to do to run an administrative command, such as starting the vsFTPd service from his regular account, is to run the following command, entering his own user password (once so configured, user randy does not need the administrative password):

```
$ sudo /sbin/service vsftpd start
Password:
```

It's possible even to allow special users administrative access without a password. As suggested by the comments, the following directive in /etc/sudoers would allow all users in the wheel group (the % in front of wheel labels it as a group in /etc/sudoers) to run administrative commands without a password:

```
%wheel   ALL=(ALL)   NOPASSWD: ALL
```

Of course, this action is fraught with risk; regular users with less administrative experience may make more mistakes. But you don't have to allow full administrative access. Privileges can be limited to specific commands. For example, to allow members of the users group to shut down the local system, include the following directive:

```
%users  localhost=/sbin/shutdown -h now
```

The % in front of users indicates that it is a group in the syntax associated with the /etc/sudoers file.

But there's one more risk—users so enabled, such as randy, are allowed to use the **sudo** command to log in with full root privileges with the following command:

```
# sudo su
```

To limit these risks, you can also limit access to the **su** command described earlier in the "Control Administrative Accounts" section. For example, the following directive disables access to **su** with the "bang" (the !), which in this case supports access to anything but the **su** command:

```
randy   ALL=(ALL)   !/bin/su
```

Later, the "Pluggable Authentication Module User Limits" section examines another method for limiting access to the **su** command.

Secure Shell Limits

Once the SSH server package is installed, you don't have to do much to configure it for basic operation. As long as the service script is active (**/etc/init.d/sshd**) and the service isn't blocked by a firewall or TCP wrappers and services like Security-Enhanced Linux (SELinux) or AppArmor, SSH should be accessible over the network. Then all you need to configure is host- and/or user-based security for the service.

Local Lingo

SELinux   The system developed in part by Red Hat for mandatory access control, which provides a different layer of security for Linux services. It was originally developed by the U.S. National Security Agency.

AppArmor   An alternative system used by SUSE for mandatory access control.

The SSH server configuration file is /etc/ssh/sshd_config. The first directive (**Protocol 2**) configures SSH version 2. While a full analysis of this file is beyond the scope of the Linux+ exam, there are a few key directives. For example, the following directive authorizes password authentication, based on local user passwords:

```
PasswordAuthentication = yes
```

The following directive is important for anyone who needs remote access to a GUI tool:

```
X11Forwarding yes
```

For example, when I'm writing outside, on my front deck, I can connect to and open GUI tools from remote systems in my office when I use SSH to connect with the following command:

```
# ssh -X michael@mandrival
```

The **ssh -Y** command also enables remote access to GUI tools, equivalent to the **ForwardX11Trusted yes** directive in the sshd_config file. Its use is discouraged due to security issues beyond the scope of the Linux+ exam.

The final directive supports the use of SSH encryption for secure FTP file transfers:

```
Subsystem   sftp   /usr/libexec/openssh/sftp-server
```

Exam Tip

In the same way that SSH provides encrypted connections, the **sftp** client also provides encrypted secure connections. Know how to limit root access to an SSH server, and where public client keys are stored.

I normally change my systems with two directives that promote security by user and host. For example, logins by the root user are normally allowed on SSH. By adding the following directive,

```
PermitRootLogin no
```

I keep administrative users from logging in with SSH. They can still use the **su** or **sudo** command (as described in the previous section) to access administrative account privileges once connected. This reduces the risk of crackers identifying the administrative password at the beginning of an SSH session.

Exam Tip

Once an SSH connection is made, all communication over that connection is encrypted. That makes SSH the most secure way to administer a remote system.

I also like to limit the users allowed to access a system via SSH. The key is the **AllowUsers** directive. You can limit by user with a directive such as:

```
AllowUsers randy nancy
```

It's possible to make the limitation more specific. For example, the following directive limits access by each user to certain hosts:

```
AllowUsers michael@kubmike donna@poohbear
```

In other words, this limits SSH access to user michael from the computer with hostname kubmike, and user donna from the computer named poohbear. No other users are allowed login access to the SSH server.

But even when encrypted, the act of sending passwords over a network can be a risk. Crackers who can identify the packet with the password can eventually decrypt that password. For that reason, the **ssh-keygen** command on the SSH server creates a public/private pair of keys, based on a passphrase. The public key, once copied to client user home directories, allows the passphrase to be used for logins. The passphrase is authenticated against the local public key. Communication is confirmed with the private key on the server.

The public key for SSH clients is stored in each user's home directory, in the .ssh/authorized_keys file. Older SSH clients stored the public key in the .ssh/authorized_keys2 file. In either case, these files should be protected with 600 permissions (read/write only for the file owner).

Exam Tip

Know how to limit user access to SSH services, as well as the command and file associated with passphrases for private/public key authentication. Remember the command that securely accesses remote FTP servers.

Pluggable Authentication Module User Limits

Linux uses the Pluggable Authentication Modules (PAM) system to check for authorized users. PAM includes a group of dynamically loadable library modules that govern how individual applications verify their users. First, review various files in the /etc/pam.d directory. Note the four separate tasks, as listed here:

- **Authentication management (auth)**   Establishes the identity of a user. For example, a PAM **auth** command decides whether to prompt for a username and/or a password.
- **Account management (account)**   Allows or denies access according to the account policies. For example, a PAM **account** command may deny access according to time, password expiration, or a specific list of restricted users.
- **Password management (password)**   Manages password policies. For example, a PAM **password** command may limit the number of times a user can try to log in before a console is reset.
- **Session management (session)**   Applies settings for an application. For example, the PAM **session** command may set default settings for a login console.

PAM was developed to standardize the user authentication process. For example, the /etc/pam.d/su configuration file uses PAM to authenticate users who use the **su** command to access administrative commands. For more information, open the /etc/pam.d/su file. Examine the first line from this file:

```
auth       sufficient  pam_rootok.so
```

This line means that if the root user runs the **su** command, the authorization is **sufficient**, in which case PAM doesn't even read the other directives in the file. The next two **auth** directives, if active, limit su access to users in the wheel group, based on the conditions noted in the comments:

```
# Uncomment the following line to implicitly trust users in
# the "wheel" group.
#auth     sufficient  pam_wheel.so trust use_uid
# Uncomment the following line to require a user to be
# in the "wheel" group.
#auth     required     pam_wheel.so use_uid
```

Several directives refer to the **system-auth** file; in fact, the **include** directive includes associated directives from the /etc/pam.d/system-auth configuration file. Individual directives are required to incorporate **auth**, **account**, **password**, and **session** directives from the system-auth file:

```
auth            include      system-auth
account         include      system-auth
password        include      system-auth
session         include      system-auth
```

> **Travel Advisory**
>
> The directives normally in the system-auth file are separated into task-specific files in SUSE Linux. Remember, because distribution-specific items are explicitly excluded from the Linux+ exam, examine SUSE's /etc/pam.d/su file yourself for more information.

For those PAM configuration files which use the pam_access.so module, it's possible to further customize PAM security through the /etc/security/access.conf configuration file. This file supports configuration directives in the following format:

```
permission : users : origins
```

The **permission** directive can be set to either + or -, which enables or disables access, respectively. Users are separated by spaces; groups can be specified with @. Origins are clients, which can be represented by their IP addresses or FQDNs. A subdomain of FQDNs can be specified with a leading dot; for example, the following directive in /etc/security/access.conf,

```
+ : michael donna @goodguys : .mommabears.com
```

allows both users michael and donna and members of the goodguys group to access the local system from all remote systems on the mommabears.com network.

FTP Access with ftpusers

There are a number of ways to limit access to FTP servers. While there are a variety of FTP servers available for the selected distributions, the file associated with FTP server security in the Linux+ objectives is /etc/ftpusers.

The /etc/ftpusers file can be configured with users who are not allowed to log into the local FTP server. It works for the vsFTP, WU-FTP, and ProFTP services (assuming they're properly configured). And you don't want service users (or the root user) to log in with their accounts, as their privileges can lead to security problems through the FTP server.

> **Travel Advisory**
>
> Some distributions put the ftpusers file in a slightly different directory; for example, the latest Red Hat distributions put it in the /etc/vsftpd/ directory.

Server Limits with /etc/hosts.allow and /etc/hosts.deny

The best way to secure any service is to remove it completely from your Linux system. But that's not possible for every service. So we do our best to secure the services needed by our users. Standard security includes firewalls and other security services such as SELinux and AppArmor. In addition, it's possible to block access to suspect users, computers, or even networks by configuring the hosts.allow and hosts.deny files in the /etc directory.

When a system receives a network request for a service, it passes the request on to a system known as TCP Wrappers. This system logs the request and then checks configured rules in /etc/hosts.allow and /etc/hosts.deny. The sequence is fairly straightforward: users and clients listed in hosts.allow are allowed access; users and clients listed in hosts.deny are denied access.

Exam Tip

The TCP Wrappers system checks /etc/hosts.allow, and then checks /etc/hosts.deny. If a service is specifically allowed in /etc/hosts.allow, then it doesn't matter if it's limited in /etc/hosts.deny; access is allowed to that service.

The basic format for commands in both /etc/hosts.allow and /etc/hosts.deny is as follows:

```
daemon_list : client_list
```

The simplest directive which follows this format is as follows:

```
ALL : ALL
```

In this directive, the first **ALL** specifies all services; the second **ALL** makes the rule applicable to all hosts on all IP addresses. If this line is in /etc/hosts.deny, access is prohibited to all services.

It's possible to configure very fine-grained filters. For example, the following directive in /etc/hosts.allow allows Telnet access from a client with an IP address of 10.11.12.13 (**in.telnetd** is the daemon for the non-Kerberos version of the Telnet server, in the /usr/sbin directory):

```
in.telnetd : 10.11.12.13
```

The same line in /etc/hosts.deny would prevent the computer with that IP address from using Telnet to connect to your system. Several other ways to configure clients in these files are listed and described in Table 8.1.

TABLE 8.1	Sample Client Descriptions in /etc/hosts.allow and /etc/hosts.deny
Client	**Description**
.example.org	Domain name. Since this domain name begins with a dot, it specifies all clients in the example.org domain, such as client1.example.org.
192.168.	IP address. Since this address ends with a dot, it specifies all clients with an IP address of 192.168.*x.y.*
192.16.72.0/255.255.240.0	IP network address with subnet mask. (TCP Wrappers do not recognize CIDR notation.)
ALL	All clients or services.
user@linux1.example.org	Applies to the specific *user* on the given computer.

As shown in Table 8.1, there are two different types of wildcards. **ALL** can be used to represent any client or service, and the dot (.) specifies all hosts associated with the specified domain name or IP network address.

Multiple services and addresses can be included on separate lines. Exceptions are easy to make with the **EXCEPT** directive, as shown in the following example from a /etc/hosts.allow file:

```
ALL : .example.net
rsync : 10.18.25.0/255.255.0.0 EXCEPT 10.18.25.73
sshd, telnetd : 10.18.1.10
```

The first line opens **ALL** services to all computers in the example.net domain. The following line opens the **rsync** service to all computers on the 10.18.25.0 network, except the one with an IP address of 10.18.25.73. In the third line, the SSH and Telnet services are made available to the computer with an IP address of 10.18.1.10. The same kind of code can be used in /etc/hosts.deny.

Objective 8.04 Work with Special File Permissions

There are three levels of specialized file permissions available: SUID, SGID, and the sticky bit. The basics of file permissions were described in the Chapter 3 section "Modify Ownership and Permissions." As described in that chapter, specialized file permissions can be a security risk, but can also minimize the need to provide administrative privileges to more users.

Because this chapter falls under the Linux+ objectives Security domain (Domain 4.0), I'll just show you how to identify files (and directories) with these permissions, and how to keep users from setting these bits on their own files.

Two other important tools described in this section are immutability, which prevents users (or even administrators) from accidentally deleting or changing key files, and specialized group directories, which can accommodate dedicated groups of users.

Identifying Files with Specialized Permissions

The **find** command can identify files with specialized permissions. Its ability to detect these permissions takes advantage of the octal format. As noted in Table 8.2, these permissions take advantage of the first digit in the octal representation, where xyz is the octal representation of read, write, and execute permissions assigned to the user owner, group owner, and everyone else on the system.

Fortunately, you don't need to know the current read, write, or execute permissions to identify files with specialized permissions. Without using scripts, the simplest way to identify files with the SUID bit is with the following **find** command:

```
# find / -perm +4000
```

Naturally, finding files with the SGID and sticky bits is just as simple:

```
# find / -perm +2000
# find / -perm +1000
```

As with other octal permissions, these numbers and what they search for are additive. For example, the following command searches for all files with *either* the SUID or sticky bit:

```
# find / -perm +5000
```

Preventing Specialized Permissions

Specialized permissions present a security risk, so you may want to prohibit their use on certain filesystems. For example, if the /home directory were mounted on a dedicated partition, you could prevent the use of SUID and SGID scripts in this directory by adding a couple of settings to /etc/fstab. For example, my office system has the following /etc/fstab entry for the /home directory (bold indicates what I've added to my /etc/fstab):

```
/dev/sda5    /home    ext3    defaults,nosuid,nosgid  1 2
```

TABLE 8.2 Octal Representation of Specialized Permissions

Specialized Permission	Octal Representation
SUID	4xyz
SGID	2xyz
Sticky bit	1xyz

Then, the following commands unmount and remount the /home directory with the new settings (yes, the **umount** command is properly spelled):

```
# umount /home
# mount /home
```

Then, when I check the result in /etc/mtab, I see the following entry associated with the /home directory partition:

```
/dev/sda5 /home ext3 rw,nosuid,nosgid 0 0
```

While no such option exists to prevent the use of the sticky bit, the associated shared directories aren't as big of a security issue.

Immutability Protects Files

Filesystem attributes can help you control what anyone can do with different files. One attribute which protects a file from deletion, even by the root user, is immutability. For example, you could protect /etc/inittab from tinkering by other administrators with the following command:

```
# chattr +i /etc/inittab
```

Then, when the root user tries to delete the file, he or she gets the following message:

```
# rm /etc/inittab
rm: remove write-protected regular file '/etc/inittab'? y
rm: cannot remove '/etc/inittab': Operation not permitted
```

Of course, as an administrator, that user could remove the immutable attribute with the following command:

```
# chattr -i /etc/inittab
```

But immutability requires an administrator to think twice before tinkering with the file, thus helping to prevent careless mistakes.

From the following **lsattr** command, see how the aforementioned **chattr** command added the immutable (**i**) attribute to /etc/inittab:

```
# lsattr /etc/inittab
----i-------- /etc/inittab
```

As you only need to understand what makes a file immutable, Table 8.3 summarizes just three of the attributes that can be controlled with the **chattr** command. For your information, the **c** (compressed), **s** (secure deletion), and **u** (undeletable) attributes don't currently work for files in the ext2 and ext3 filesystems.

TABLE 8.3	File Attributes

Attribute	Description
append only (**a**)	Prevents deletion, but allows appending to a file. For example, if you've run **chatter +a tester**, **cat /etc/fstab >> tester** would add the contents of /etc/fstab to the end of the tester file.
no dump (**d**)	Does not allow backups of the configured file with the **dump** command.
immutable (**i**)	Prevents deletion or any other kind of change to a file.

Special Group Directories

Most people work in groups. They may share files. They may also want to limit access to their work to those who "need to know." The standard way to set up this kind of configuration is with a shared directory for a group. First, it's important to set up a dedicated group, such as supervisors, and then add the users to that group through the /etc/group configuration file.

Set the group ID bit (SGID) on the dedicated directory. Then, any file created in this directory inherits the group ID. If you have set appropriate permissions, all members of this group can then access files in that directory. When I set up a supervisors group on my system, I set up a dedicated /home/supervisors directory. As shown in the output to **ls -l /home**,

```
rwxrws--- 2 manager supervisors 4096 Apr 17 06:24 supervisors
```

the permissions include read, write, and execute permissions for both the user owner and group owner, as well as SGID permissions. The manager owns the directory, and all members of the supervisors group also can read to, write from, and execute scripts in /home/supervisors.

Travel Advisory

The group execute and SGID bits occupy the same position in the permissions column. If the supervisors directory shown in the preceding example did not have execute permissions set for group members, the SGID bit shown would be an uppercase *S*.

If necessary, you can set up such ownership and permissions with the following commands:

```
# chown manager.supervisors /home/supervisors
# chmod 2770 /home/supervisors
```

Configure Password Policies

S tandard password policies on the selected distributions include the Shadow Password Suite, which encrypts passwords in more secure files. The files associated with the Shadow Password Suite also support sophisticated aging. These password policies go hand in hand with the strength checkers associated with PAM.

> **Exam Tip**
>
> Understand that shadow passwords are in effect only when /etc/shadow exists and there's an "x" in the password column for regular users in /etc/passwd.

The Shadow Password Suite

Historically, all that was needed to manage Linux users and groups was the information included in the /etc/passwd and /etc/group files. This section assumes that there are group passwords, which in reality is rarely the case. These files at one time included (and can still include) passwords and are by default readable by all users.

The Shadow Password Suite was created to provide an additional layer of protection. It is used to encrypt user and group passwords in shadow files (/etc/shadow and /etc/gshadow) that are readable only by users with root privileges. Encryption uses Message-Digest algorithm 5, more popularly known by its acronym, MD5.

The Shadow Password Suite is now enabled by default on the selected Linux distributions. Standard commands for creating new users and groups automatically set up encrypted passwords in the Shadow Password Suite files. When the Shadow Password Suite is in effect, passwords are not stored in /etc/passwd and /etc/group.

But if you're restoring a system, you may not have access to these special commands. The old way of creating new users and groups is by editing the /etc/passwd and /etc/group files directly. Four commands support password conversion and movement to and from the /etc/shadow and /etc/gshadow files:

- **pwconv** Converts and moves passwords from /etc/passwd to /etc/shadow. This command works even if some of the passwords are already encrypted in /etc/shadow. Creates /etc/shadow if it doesn't already exist. Enables the Shadow Password Suite.

- **pwunconv** Opposite of **pwconv**. Disables the Shadow Password Suite. Removes /etc/shadow if it currently exists.

- **grpconv** Converts passwords from /etc/group to /etc/gshadow. This command works even if some of the passwords are already encrypted in /etc/gshadow. Creates /etc/gshadow if it doesn't already exist. Enables the Shadow Password Suite.

- **grpunconv** Opposite of **grpconv**. Disables the Shadow Password Suite. Removes /etc/gshadow if it currently exists.

Exam Tip

Recognize the commands that enable and disable the Shadow Password Suite, as well as the associated files. To enable the Shadow Password Suite, you have to run both the **pwconv** and **grpconv** commands.

Password Aging

Password aging can help manage the security of user passwords. In other words, if users have to change their passwords periodically, crackers will have a more difficult time breaking into a system.

The **chage** command can be used to manage the expiration date of a password. Password aging information is stored in the /etc/shadow file. In order, the columns in /etc/shadow are listed and described in Table 8.4. If the **chage** command can modify the setting, the associated switch is shown in the description. For example, if you wanted to require that user elizabeth keep a password for at least two days, use the **chage elizabeth -m 2** command.

Account Aging

While it's possible to make a password expire with the **chage** command using switches described in Table 8.4, the simplest way to do this is with the **usermod -e** *date username* command. For example, if I want to deactivate the madman account, I set an expiration date sometime before today, using a date in YYYY-MM-DD format—the following command sets an expiration date of July 7, 2007 for the madman account:

```
# usermod -e 2007-07-07
```

TABLE 8.4	Password Aging Information in /etc/shadow	

Column	Field	Description
1	Username	Username
2	Password	Encrypted password; assumes there's an *x* in the second column of /etc/passwd
3	Password history	Date of the last password change, in number of days after January 1, 1970; can be cited by **chage** in YYYY-MM-DD format
4	mindays	Minimum number of days that you must keep a password (**-m**)
5	maxdays	Maximum number of days after which a password must be changed (**-M**)
6	warndays	Number of days before password expiration when a warning is given (**-W**)
7	inactive	Number of days after password expiration when an account is made inactive (**-I**)
8	account disable	Number of days after password expiration when an account is disabled (**-E**)

Exam Tip

The **usermod -c "Comment"** *username* command can add more information to the fifth column for the *username* in /etc/passwd. It's commonly used for full names, phone numbers, and more.

PAM and Password Complexity

The complexity of a password for the selected distributions is defined by PAM, specifically the /etc/pam.d/login and /etc/pam.d/passwd configuration files. While editing these files is beyond the scope of any multiple-choice exam, you should recognize the complexity required by specific directives in the noted files.

For the selected distributions, both of these files transfer password checks to the system-auth (for SUSE Linux, common-passwd) configuration file, also in the /etc/pam.d directory.

For more information on the /etc/pam.d/login password directives, you'll need to refer to the three **password** directives in /etc/pam.d/system-auth:

```
password requisite    pam_cracklib.so try_first_pass retry=3
password sufficient   pam_unix.so md5 shadow nullok try_first_pass \
use_authok
password required     pam_deny.so
```

The first directive from this list allows the use of a previously successful password entry from a previous auth module (try_first_pass) and then sets a maximum of three retries. But more importantly, the pam_cracklib.so module uses the libCrack password-strength libraries. We'll come back to this module in a moment.

The next directive encrypts passwords using the MD5 algorithm, supports the Shadow Password Suite described earlier in this section, allows the use of zero-length (nullok) passwords, allows the use of a previously success-ful password (try_first_pass), and prompts the user for a password (use_authok). If you've configured NIS, you'll see **nis** in this list as well. The **password required pam_deny.so** directive is trivial; as mentioned in README.pam_deny in the /usr/share/doc/pam-*versionlevel*/txt directory, that module always fails.

Now return to the pam_cracklib.so module. Normally, if you try a password either based on a dictionary word or as short as six alphanumeric characters, you'll see one of the following messages:

```
BAD PASSWORD: it is based on a dictionary word
BAD PASSWORD: it is too short
```

However, these are just warnings; in other words, if you repeat the same bad password, the **passwd** command accepts it. Other options can require complex passwords. For example, the **minlen=8** option requires a minimum password length of eight alphanumeric characters.

Objective 8.06 Promote User-level Security

In the context of the Linux+ objectives, user-level security is related to login limits and other memory and process limits. Login limits can help regulate the number of times a user logs into a system. Memory and process limits can help regulate the resources taken by individual users.

Login Limits

It's possible to limit root logins in the /etc/securetty configuration file. The de-fault version of this file supports access by the root user to several virtual con-soles. Before making any changes, back up this file.

Now for the test. To limit root logins to the sixth virtual console, limit the tty entries to tty6; delete the entries for tty1 through tty5.

From a regular console, press ALT-F6. From a GUI, press CTRL-ALT-F6. You should be able to log in as the root user from this console. Log out, and then press ALT-F5. If you've properly modified the /etc/securetty file, any attempt to log in as the root user is denied.

Control by /etc/securetty of root logins is available through the /etc/pam.d/ login file. Take a look at the first line:

```
auth [user_unknown=ignore success=ok ignore=ignore default=bad] \
pam_securetty.so
```

This line means that root users can log in only from secure terminals as defined in the /etc/securetty file, and unknown users are ignored. Restore your system by restoring the original version of /etc/securetty.

Travel Advisory

A backslash in a command line "escapes" the meaning of the next character; in the preceding command, **pam_securetty.so** is added to the end of the previous command line. Due to limits in the format of this series, I've had to change the spacing of some lines and add backslashes to others.

A *virtual console* is a command line where you can log into and control Linux. Since Linux is a multiterminal operating system, you can log in even with the same user ID, several times.

It's easy to open a new virtual console. Just use the appropriate ALT-*function key* combination. For example, pressing ALT-F2 brings you to the second virtual console. You can switch between adjacent virtual consoles by pressing ALT-RIGHT ARROW or ALT-LEFT ARROW. For example, to move from virtual console 2 to virtual console 3, press ALT-RIGHT ARROW.

Virtual consoles are configured in /etc/inittab. By default, the selected distributions are configured with six virtual consoles. You can configure up to 12 virtual consoles in /etc/inittab. Here are the default /etc/inittab entries for the first six virtual consoles:

```
1:2345:respawn:/sbin/mingetty tty1
2:2345:respawn:/sbin/mingetty tty2
3:2345:respawn:/sbin/mingetty tty3
4:2345:respawn:/sbin/mingetty tty4
5:2345:respawn:/sbin/mingetty tty5
6:2345:respawn:/sbin/mingetty tty6
```

Virtual consoles really bring the multiuser capabilities of Linux to life. You can be viewing a man page on one console, compiling a program in another, and editing a document in a third virtual console. Other users who are connected through a network can do the same thing at the same time.

To see how this works for yourself, first, back up /etc/inittab. Then comment out one or more of the virtual consoles. For example, to deactivate virtual console 6, deactivate it by adding a comment character in front. The standard comment character in /etc/inittab (as well as most Linux scripts) is the hash mark (#), also known as the pound sign:

```
#6:2345:respawn:/sbin/mingetty tty6
```

Don't forget to restore /etc/inittab to the original configuration.

Memory Usage and Process Limits with ulimit

Part of the concept of user-level security is limits on the resources taken by individual users. Current memory and process limits can be displayed with the **ulimit -a** command, shown in Figure 8.1. The administrative user can set limits for all users; individuals can further regulate their own usage, within the administrative limits.

Some of the limits shown in Figure 8.1 are described in more detail in Table 8.5. Those not described are beyond the scope of the Linux+ exam.

To change any of these parameters on a more permanent basis, include the appropriate **ulimit** command in /etc/profile or /etc/security/limits.conf. That ensures that desired settings are active the next time Linux is booted.

```
[root@enterprise5hp ~]# ulimit -a
core file size          (blocks, -c) 0
data seg size           (kbytes, -d) unlimited
max nice                        (-e) 0
file size               (blocks, -f) unlimited
pending signals                 (-i) 14225
max locked memory       (kbytes, -l) 32
max memory size         (kbytes, -m) unlimited
open files                      (-n) 1024
pipe size            (512 bytes, -p) 8
POSIX message queues     (bytes, -q) 819200
max rt priority                 (-r) 0
stack size              (kbytes, -s) 10240
cpu time               (seconds, -t) unlimited
max user processes              (-u) 14225
virtual memory          (kbytes, -v) unlimited
file locks                      (-x) unlimited
[root@enterprise5hp ~]#
```

FIGURE 8.1   Current memory and process limits

TABLE 8.5	Process and Memory Limits as Defined by **ulimit -a**
Limit	**Description**
core file size	Core dumps are disabled by default; users may need them for debugging; for example, **ulimit -c unlimited** enables core dumps by regular users.
max nice	Limits the **nice** and **renice** commands, as described in the Chapter 4 section "Learn Process Management."
file size	Limits the maximum file size; for example, **ulimit -f 10000** limits the maximum size of a file to 10,000 blocks.
max locked memory	Limits the amount of locked memory per process. Some distributions require that you run **ulimit -l unlimited** before running a writable DVD program.
max memory size	Limits the amount of real memory per process.
max user processes	Sets a maximum number of processes per user.
virtual memory	Sets the maximum amount of memory available to a shell.

CHECKPOINT

✔**Objective 8.01: Manage User Accounts**   To keep up with users who move, take longer vacations, or leave the organization, Linux administrators can deactivate accounts, change group memberships, and identify and move the files associated with users who have left the organization.

✔**Objective 8.02: Control Administrative Accounts**   Administrators need to be able to run administrative commands from regular accounts. The **su** command can run administrative commands on a one-time basis; the **sudo** command can run administrative commands as enabled in /etc/sudoers.

✔**Objective 8.03: Set Up Security Environment Files**   Systems can be made more secure; /etc/sudoers can be customized to provide partial administrative privileges. Secure Shell services can be limited by the right directives in /etc/ssh/sshd_config. The PAM system can limit logins and more. FTP login access can be limited by /etc/ftpusers. Servers can be regulated in /etc/hosts.allow and /etc/hosts.deny.

✔**Objective 8.04: Work with Special File Permissions**   Specialized permissions provide SUID, SGID, and sticky bit access to other users. Immutability prevents accidental deletion. Special group directories can accommodate the needs of groups who need security while sharing data freely.

✔**Objective 8.05: Configure Password Policies**   The   Shadow   Password Suite encrypts passwords based on the MD5 algorithm in more secure files. Password aging means users have to change passwords periodically. PAM requires a customizable level of password complexity.

✔**Objective 8.06: Promote User-level Security**   The   number   of   allowed logins can be limited at the console. Memory usage can also be limited by user.

REVIEW QUESTIONS

Before leaving for the next chapter, take a few minutes to go through these questions. While doing so, take in both the content and the question format. Understanding what to expect on the exam can increase your chances for success.

1.   As an administrator for the local Linux system, when should you log in as the root user?

   A.   All the time; a power unused atrophies

   B.   When accessing the root e-mail account for system logs

   C.   Whenever you have to run administrative commands

   D.   To create new users

2.   If you activate the following directive in /etc/sudoers, what users are allowed to access the noted administrative commands?

   `%users  ALL=/sbin/mount /mnt/cdrom, /sbin/umount /mnt/cdrom`

   A.   users

   B.   All regular users

   C.   Members of the users group

   D.   nobody

3.   To prevent remote access by users to the local FTP server, to what file would you add their usernames? The local FTP server is running the ProFTP service.

   A.   /etc/pam.d/ftp

   B.   /etc/ftpusers

   C.   /etc/nologin

   D.   /etc/vsftpd.conf

4. Which of the following commands searches from your root directory for all files with the sticky bit?

  A. find / -perm +4000

  B. find / -perm +2000

  C. find / -perm +6000

  D. find / -perm +1000

5. If you have the administrative password and don't want to log into the administrative account, which of the following commands can you use to run the **useradd randy** command?

  A. sudo /usr/sbin/useradd randy

  B. su -c /usr/sbin/useradd\ randy

  C. su - /usr/sbin/useradd randy

  D. sudo /usr/sbin/useradd

6. Which of the following directives in /etc/ssh/sshd_config prevents direct network logins from the root user?

  A. PermitRoot yes

  B. PermitRoot no

  C. PermitRootLogin yes

  D. PermitRootLogin no

7. To create a private and public key for SSH logins, using passphrases, what command would you use?

  A. ssh-keyscan

  B. ssh-keygen

  C. ssh-key

  D. ssh-agent

8. Based on the following excerpt from /etc/passwd, are there any limitations to logging into either of the following accounts? This system is configured to the Shadow Password Suite.

```
michael:*:500:500::/home/michael:/bin/bash
donna:x:501:501::/home/donna:/bin/bash
```

  A. No restrictions apply.

  B. User michael can log into his account; user donna cannot.

  C. User donna can log into her account; user michael cannot.

  D. Neither user can log into their account.

9. If you want to prevent even the root user from accidentally deleting the secret file in the current directory, what command can help?

A. chmod +i secret

B. chattr +i secret

C. chattr -i secret

D. lsattr +i secret

10. Which of the following commands creates a secure connection to a remote FTP server?

A. ssh

B. scp

C. sftp

D. vsftpd

REVIEW ANSWERS

1. **B**   Access to the root e-mail account is just about the only reason to log in as the root user. The other commands listed can be run from regular accounts with the **su** command or with the **sudo** command if privileges are properly granted in the /etc/sudoers configuration file.

2. **C**   Per the noted directive, users have to specifically be made members of the users group to have access to the noted commands. Among the selected distributions, only SUSE Linux automatically makes all regular users members of the users group.

3. **B**   The /etc/ftpusers file is the standard file that lists restricted users for various FTP services, including ProFTP, vsFTP, and WU-FTP.

4. **D**   The octal permission associated with the sticky bit is 1000. Just watch out, as octal permissions are additive. Commands such as **find / -perms +3000** and **find / -perms +5000** would also do the job.

5. **B**   Multiword commands have to be passed to the **su** command with the -c switch. The backslash escapes the meaning of the space between the **useradd** command and the new username randy. While the **sudo** command also can work, it does not require knowledge of the administrative password.

6. **D**   The directive associated with root logins for the SSH server is **PermitRootLogin**.

7. **B**   The command that actually generates private and public keys based on a passphrase is **ssh-keygen**. The other commands listed are related to gathering private and public keys on SSH clients and servers.

8. **C**   The asterisk (*) in the password column means that the account is inactive.

9. **B**   The **chattr** command can change attributes associated with a file. The **+i** switch sets the immutable attribute, which can even stop an attempt by the root user to run the **rm** command on that file. Of course, the root user can run the **chattr -i secret** command to remove the immutable attribute before deleting the file, but immutability can help prevent accidental deletion.

10. **C**   The **sftp** command is a secure client. Because it is based on the SSH client, it encrypts connections to FTP servers.

System Security

	NEWBIE	SOME EXPERIENCE	VETERAN
ETA	60+ hours	12 hours	8 hours

Understanding Linux security means understanding the options for encryption as well as the basic files and tools administrators can configure to record attempts to break into Linux systems. Additional security options not covered elsewhere are associated with the Internet Super Server, configured by service in the /etc/xinetd.d/ directory.

It's important to also have a basic understanding of the **iptables** firewall tool, along with ports that can be blocked by a firewall. Auditing key security files and logs on a periodic basis can help you detect problems based on intrusions that may have otherwise gone undetected. Part of the auditing process means identifying file corruption with tools such as the **rpm -V** command and the Tripwire tool.

 **Objective 9.01** # Configure Encryption

I t's far too easy to break into most computer systems. Many users still insist on connecting to remote systems using unencrypted services. As shown in Figure 9.1, unencrypted passwords are sent (and can be read) over networks in clear text; in this case, the figure shows the first letter of a Telnet password. Every other alphanumeric character in the password follows in subsequent packets.

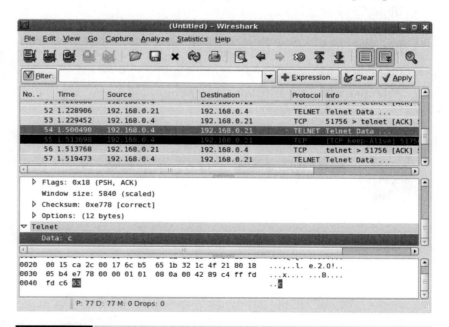

FIGURE 9.1 It's too easy to find unencrypted passwords.

Encryption can help Linux systems protect passwords, files, partitions, and even entire hard disks. You need to at least know the names of several encryption schemes for the Linux+ exam.

Exam Tip

Know about programs, such as Crack, that can detect weak passwords and common encryption schemes for passwords, networks, and more.

Shadow Passwords

The Shadow Password Suite described in the Chapter 8 section "Configure Password Policies" encrypts passwords in files available only to the administrative root user. As defined by PAM (Pluggable Authentication Modules), passwords are hidden using the MD5 (Message-Digest algorithm 5) encryption scheme. It uses a 128-bit hash value; in other words, passwords are processed into a 128-bit number, which corresponds to the second column shown in this excerpt from /etc/shadow:

```
donna:$1$o1w6g9zo$DH1yvuuIUlHgRvX7QGebk/:13741:0:99999:7:::
```

Travel Advisory

It's an oversimplification to refer to MD5 as an encryption mode. Strictly speaking, MD5 is a cryptographic hash function.

The Linux password encryption scheme is controlled in /etc/pam.d/passwd, which in the selected Linux distributions (except SUSE) refers to the following directive from the /etc/pam.d/system-auth file. The settings in bold highlight the use of MD5 encryption and the Shadow Password Suite.

```
password  sufficient  pam_unix.so md5 shadow nullok try_first_pass \
use_authtok
```

One other encryption scheme is available when using PAM for passwords, as described in the documentation for the associated module, pam_unix.so. The **bigcrypt** scheme uses the DEC C2 extension to the crypt algorithm, developed by the former Digital Equipment Corporation (now a part of HP).

Older distributions configured MD5 encryption in the /etc/login.defs file with the following directive:

```
MD5_CRYPT_ENAB=yes
```

Password Strength

Password encryption helps only if the passwords are sufficiently complex. Stronger passwords depend on users avoiding dictionary words and other simple alphanumeric patterns. As described in the Chapter 8 section "Configure Password Policies," the "Crack" libraries (short for libCrack) are often used to evaluate the strength of user passwords. While the default configuration objects to passwords that may be too short or are based on dictionary words, it does not prohibit them.

Because weak passwords may violate organizational policies, many Unix and Linux administrators often use the *Crack* password-cracking program to identify users with such passwords.

Travel Advisory

We do not endorse the use of programs like Crack, Cain, John the Ripper, or LC5 to break into user accounts. But as an administrator, you already have access to regular user accounts. So when you use such programs as an administrator, these programs can help you learn if your users are creating sufficiently strong passwords.

Disk Encryption

Files, partitions, and hard disks on a Linux system can be encrypted. As described in the Disk Encryption HOWTO (http://tldp.org/HOWTO/Disk-Encryption-HOWTO/), a 128-bit version of the Advanced Encryption Standard (AES128) is the current standard for this purpose.

AES128 is the successor to the Data Encryption Standard (DES), which is faster than the 3DES (also known as Triple DES) standard, which is still in use. It's often used with a separate key embedded in a bootable CD or USB drive. When properly configured, data on protected systems isn't readable and therefore is protected without that key.

Other Encryption Schemes

There are several other encryption schemes commonly used on Linux systems. Perhaps the most common is used for secure Web communications, based on the secure HTTP protocol (HTTPS), which normally uses TCP/IP port 443. The old standard for this protocol used the Secure Sockets Layer (SSL). Today, most Web servers encrypt HTTPS communications using the Transport Layer Security (TLS) protocol, which was being introduced when the Linux+ objectives were released.

There's also encryption for e-mail. Conceptually similar to SSH private and public keys (as discussed in the Chapter 8 section "Set Up Security Environment Files"), GPG encryption is often used to secure e-mail communications.

Local Lingo

GNU Privacy Guard (GPG) The Linux implementation of the Pretty Good Privacy (PGP) encryption program. Private/public encryption key pairs in Linux are often known as GPG/PGP keys.

SSH private/public key pairs can be created using either the RSA or DSA encryption algorithms. The RSA algorithm is named after its developers, Rivest, Shamir, and Adelman. DSA is the acronym of the Digital Signature Algorithm, which was developed by the U.S. government and made publicly available on a royalty-free basis. Either key pair can be generated with the **ssh-keygen** command. (The RSA algorithm is the default with **ssh-keygen**; if you prefer the DSA algorithm, it can be generated with the -**t dsa** switch.)

Virtual Private Networks (VPNs) in Linux are implemented through Crypto IP Encapsulation (CIPE), which can be configured to use a variety of algorithms, including Blowfish, 3DES, AES128, or IDEA (which is short for the International Data Encryption Algorithm).

The password associated with the GRUB bootloader described in the Chapter 2 section "Understand and Reinstall a Boot Manager" is normally encrypted to the MD5 standard. You can create a GRUB password from the command line with the **grub-md5-crypt** command. After typing and confirming a password, the command returns an MD5 hash similar to

```
$1$Ekcy5$rFZE7/bEJUxXfuPvnw/5N.
```

which can then be associated with the **password --md5** directive in the GRUB configuration file, as shown here:

```
password --md5 $1$Ekcy5$rFZE7/bEJUxXfuPvnw/5N.
```

You may have noticed that the Samba passwords created by the **smbpasswd** command in /etc/samba/smbpasswd are encrypted. While the hash in this file is similar to the MD5 encryption algorithm associated with the Shadow Password Suite, the encryption actually conforms to Microsoft NT–series encryption. Because it uses the MD4 encryption algorithm, it's incompatible with current Linux passwords.

> **Travel Advisory**
>
> Microsoft clients can't use an unadulterated Linux password database.

Objective 9.02

Detect Intrusion Attempts

There are several files and commands that can help Linux administrators detect attempts by crackers to break into their system. Local and remote logins are normally reported in /var/log/secure. Depending on configuration, other log files, such as /var/log/auth.log, /var/log/messages, and /var/log/wtmp, are also frequently used to document local and remote logins. There are also commands that list logged-in users, including those who log in from remote locations.

One useful tool for monitoring these log files is the **tail -f** *logfile* command. For example, I could use the following command to monitor the latest changes to /var/log/messages:

```
# tail -f /var/log/messages
```

This command locks the screen on the last few lines of /var/log/messages; as new messages are logged in this file, you can watch as they're added. (You need to press CTRL-C to return to the command line.)

Logging Logins

There are several files in the /var/log directory that document how and when users log into a Linux system, normally associated with the **auth** and **authpriv** directives in the /etc/syslog.conf configuration file, as described in the Chapter 6 section "Work with Log Files."

The most common option for these directives is /var/log/secure. On Red Hat/Fedora systems, this file documents all local and remote logins. For example, this excerpt documents a remote login:

```
Aug 15 19:08:32 enterprise5hp login: LOGIN ON pts/1 BY michael FROM
192.168.0.4
```

This documents the date and time of a login to my system named enterprise5hp from a remote client, with IP address 192.168.0.4. But /var/log/secure isn't configured on all Linux distributions. In several cases, including SUSE, Mandriva, and Turbolinux, remote logins are documented in /var/log/messages. If you believe an attack is in progress, it might make sense to watch /var/log/messages with the **tail -f** command described in the introduction to this section. For example, I saw the following ominous looking items when I monitored my /var/log/messages file (192.168.0.50 is the IP address of one of my other home systems):

```
Aug 16 13:08:18 enterprise5hp sshd[7743]: pam_unix(sshd:auth):
 authentication failure; logname= uid=0 euid=0 tty=ssh
ruser=rhost=192.168.0.50  user=root

Aug 16 13:08:20 enterprise5hp sshd[7743]: Failed password for
root from 192.168.0.50 port 54711 ssh2

Aug 16 13:08:32 enterprise5hp last message repeated 2 times

Aug 16 13:08:32 enterprise5hp sshd[7744]: Connection closed
by 192.168.0.50
```

The default Mandriva configuration includes login messages in /var/log/auth.log. The actual file depends on the configuration in the /etc/syslog.conf file. The applicable Mandriva directive is

```
auth,authpriv.*    /var/log/auth.log
```

whereas the applicable directive for Turbolinux and Red Hat in /etc/syslog.conf is

```
authpriv.*    /var/log/secure
```

Other Log Files

Services such as Apache and CUPS also maintain logs of access attempts. Thus, any cracker who tries to break into a Linux system through these services may be logged through their log files.

By default, both Apache and CUPS maintain access logs in the access_log file in the /var/log/cups and /var/log/httpd directory, respectively. (Substitute /var/log/apache2 for /var/log/httpd if you're running SUSE Linux.) The location is as documented in the configuration files for each service.

The w and who Commands

A couple of commands can also help you check for crackers who may be currently logged into the local Linux system. For example, the following output from the **who** command suggests that I've logged in both locally and from a remote system:

```
michael  tty1  2007-08-15 10:53
michael  pts/0 2007-08-14 (10.11.12.13)
```

If I know that I haven't logged in remotely from a system with the noted IP address, I should worry that someone may have cracked my account and is currently logged in from the noted address.

As strange as it may sound, you can get more information with the **w** command. One example output is shown in Figure 9.2, which illustrates how user michael is now logged in from more IP addresses. Just be aware that the programs being run may just be a cover for what a cracker is really doing to your system.

One more option is the **top** command, which is examined in the Chapter 10 section "Document a System Performance Baseline." The user column in the output to this command documents the user who is running specific processes.

Checking Up on Users with last and utmpdump

The **last** *username* command searches through the /var/log/wtmp database for user logins. It's possible to read through the whole database with the **utmpdump /var/log/wtmp** command. But the output is long, and is mixed with reboot and shutdown events, as shown in Figure 9.3.

Alternatively, the **last** *username* command can help the Linux administrator investigate potential security breaches on suspect accounts. For example, the following output illustrates logins from the root account into the first (tty1) and second (tty2) local terminals as well as remote logins from IP address 192.168.0.30:

```
$ last root
root tty1                        Mon Aug  6 19:59 - crash (8+23:17)
root pts/1  192.168.0.30         Mon Aug  6 19:43 - crash (8+23:34)
root pts/1  192.168.0.30         Mon Aug  6 19:42 - 19:43  (00:00)
root tty2                        Sun Aug  5 06:29 - crash (10+12:48)

wtmp begins Wed Aug  1 20:49:24 2007
```

While it's certainly possible to "spoof" logins from a different IP address, a login to the root account from an unknown IP address certainly suggests reason for concern.

```
[michael@enterprise5hp ~]$ w
 15:14:53 up 1 day,  3:07,  5 users,  load average: 0.14, 0.05, 0.01
USER     TTY      FROM          LOGIN@   IDLE   JCPU   PCPU WHAT
michael  pts/0    192.168.0.4   Wed18    7.00s  1.15s  0.45s gnome-terminal
michael  tty2     -             15:05    9:10   0.03s  0.03s -bash
michael  pts/1    192.168.0.50  15:11    2:11   0.55s  0.49s top
michael  pts/2    192.168.0.60  15:13    1:17   0.10s  0.18s sshd: michael [
michael  pts/3    localhost:10.0 15:14   0.00s  0.09s  0.01s w
[michael@enterprise5hp ~]$ █
```

FIGURE 9.2   **w** command output

```
[5] [03285] [4   ] [        ] [          ] [2.6.20-2925.9.fc7xen] [0.0.0.0       ] [Wed Aug 15 19:18:01 2007 PDT]
[5] [03286] [5   ] [        ] [          ] [2.6.20-2925.9.fc7xen] [0.0.0.0       ] [Wed Aug 15 19:18:01 2007 PDT]
[5] [03287] [6   ] [        ] [          ] [2.6.20-2925.9.fc7xen] [0.0.0.0       ] [Wed Aug 15 19:18:01 2007 PDT]
[6] [03282] [1   ] [LOGIN   ] [tty1      ] [          ] [0.0.0.0       ] [Wed Aug 15 19:18:01 2007 PDT]
[6] [03283] [2   ] [LOGIN   ] [tty2      ] [          ] [0.0.0.0       ] [Wed Aug 15 19:18:01 2007 PDT]
[6] [03284] [3   ] [LOGIN   ] [tty3      ] [          ] [0.0.0.0       ] [Wed Aug 15 19:18:01 2007 PDT]
[6] [03285] [4   ] [LOGIN   ] [tty4      ] [          ] [0.0.0.0       ] [Wed Aug 15 19:18:01 2007 PDT]
[6] [03286] [5   ] [LOGIN   ] [tty5      ] [          ] [0.0.0.0       ] [Wed Aug 15 19:18:01 2007 PDT]
[6] [03287] [6   ] [LOGIN   ] [tty6      ] [          ] [0.0.0.0       ] [Wed Aug 15 19:18:01 2007 PDT]
[7] [03318] [ts/0] [michael ] [pts/0     ] [192.168.0.4 ] [192.168.0.4   ] [Wed Aug 15 19:18:12 2007 PDT]
[7] [07209] [ts/1] [michael ] [pts/1     ] [192.168.0.4 ] [192.168.0.4   ] [Wed Aug 15 22:20:06 2007 PDT]
[7] [11039] [2   ] [michael ] [pts/2     ] [localhost   ] [127.0.0.1     ] [Thu Aug 16 01:54:12 2007 PDT]
[8] [11038] [    ] [        ] [pts/2     ] [          ] [0.0.0.0       ] [Thu Aug 16 01:54:13 2007 PDT]
[7] [14339] [2   ] [michael ] [pts/2     ] [localhost   ] [127.0.0.1     ] [Thu Aug 16 20:01:28 2007 PDT]
[8] [14338] [    ] [        ] [pts/2     ] [          ] [0.0.0.0       ] [Thu Aug 16 20:01:30 2007 PDT]
[8] [03318] [    ] [        ] [pts/0     ] [          ] [0.0.0.0       ] [Fri Aug 17 01:48:07 2007 PDT]
[8] [07209] [    ] [        ] [pts/1     ] [          ] [0.0.0.0       ] [Fri Aug 17 01:48:08 2007 PDT]
[7] [17674] [ts/0] [michael ] [pts/0     ] [192.168.0.4 ] [192.168.0.4   ] [Fri Aug 17 14:23:20 2007 PDT]
[8] [17674] [    ] [        ] [pts/0     ] [          ] [0.0.0.0       ] [Fri Aug 17 16:00:14 2007 PDT]
[7] [09320] [ts/0] [michael ] [pts/0     ] [192.168.0.4 ] [192.168.0.4   ] [Sun Aug 19 04:25:14 2007 PDT]
[8] [09320] [    ] [        ] [pts/0     ] [          ] [0.0.0.0       ] [Sun Aug 19 06:19:59 2007 PDT]
[7] [01285] [ts/0] [michael ] [pts/0     ] [192.168.0.4 ] [192.168.0.4   ] [Mon Aug 20 03:12:12 2007 PDT]
[7] [04582] [ts/1] [michael ] [pts/1     ] [192.168.0.30] [192.168.0.30  ] [Mon Aug 20 20:08:33 2007 PDT]
[michael@enterprise5fc6d ~]$ █
```

FIGURE 9.3   **utmpdump /var/log/wtmp** command output

Objective 9.03 # Understand Intrusion Detection Systems

Two Intrusion Detection Systems (IDSs) are listed in the Linux+ objectives: Snort and PortSentry. Both IDS applications can capture and analyze packets on a network. While these systems are not *currently* packaged by the companies behind the selected distributions, you need to know that these tools are available. However, even the basic operation of these tools is beyond the scope of this book.

Exam Tip

Although you don't need to know how to use either Snort or PortSentry for the exam, you do need to understand the basic functionality of each of these tools.

While the Simple WATCHer (SWATCH) and the Linux Intrusion Detection System (LIDS) are also often cited as IDSs, they are focused on protecting configuration files and other files. Other tools in this chapter that also technically qualify as IDSs are Tripwire and the **rpm -V** command. This section also takes a look at the **tcpdump** and **netstat -a** commands, which are used to monitor the network at the command-line interface (CLI).

> **Travel Advisory**
>
> Some countries regulate the use of IDSs, because the port scans associated with IDSs such as PortSentry and Snort often precede attempts to break into computer systems.

Snort

The Snort IDS can analyze network packets against known security issues, also known as *exploits*. You can download and install this program from the Snort website at www.snort.org. It's available as a "tarball"; guidelines for installation are provided in the Chapter 2 section "Perform Post-Installation Package Management."

As described on the Snort website, "Snort is the most widely deployed intrusion detection and prevention technology worldwide and has become the de facto standard for the industry."

In essence, Snort can be used to detect attacks such as the following:

- Stealth TCP/IP network port scans
- Buffer overflows (where a program goes beyond allocated memory)
- CGI-based attacks

> **Travel Advisory**
>
> The related airsnort package can recover forgotten encryption keys. It can detect Wireless Encryption Protocol (WEP) keys associated with wireless networks. While we do not endorse the unauthorized use of the airsnort package to break into encrypted wireless networks, you should be aware of this security weakness in wireless networking.

PortSentry

PortSentry is one of three sentry host-level security service tools in the TriSentry suite. Third parties have repackaged and customized it in RPM format for some distributions. The latest version of the PortSentry package can be downloaded in tarball format from http://sourceforge.net/projects/sentrytools/. Guidelines for installation from a tarball are discussed in the Chapter 2 section "Perform Post-Installation Package Management."

PortSentry is intended to monitor various TCP/IP ports for a wide variety of network scans associated with both the TCP and UDP protocols. Such scans can be used to gather information on network weaknesses, which a cracker can use to attack systems on your network.

Local Lingo

Transmission Control Protocol (TCP)   A connection-oriented protocol that tells the client if a connection is made.
User Datagram Protocol (UDP)   A connectionless protocol that does not wait for network acknowledgment before sending the message. TCP and UDP are mutually exclusive alternative protocols for different ports as defined in /etc/services.

Command-line Monitoring

There are two major tools associated with monitoring the network at the command-line interface: **tcpdump** and **netstat -a**. The **tcpdump** command by itself displays the headers of all network packets that can be read from available network interfaces. The command by itself scrolls information on the screen at high speed, with time, source, destination, and packet type.

While it's possible to send the output to files or search through the output with filters like the **grep** command, front-ends such as Wireshark, shown earlier in Figure 9.1, can help classify what's captured by the **tcpdump** command.

Travel Advisory

Wireshark is the successor to Ethereal, which is a protocol analyzer, more popularly known as a "sniffer."

The **netstat -a** command can help administrators identify open network connections, which may help them to detect forgotten TCP/IP ports in use by crackers. The output in Figure 9.4 shows connections from systems with names like enterprise5hp, as well as IP addresses like 192.168.0.30. It also shows connections from remote systems such as ns1.centos.org and rhlx01.hs-esslingen.de. It's worth some investigation. CentOS.org is the URL for the group behind the most popular rebuild of Red Hat Enterprise Linux 5; rhlx01.hs-esslingen.de is the URL for a Linux users group in Germany, which administers some mirrors of major Linux repositories.

```
Active Internet connections (servers and established)
Proto Recv-Q Send-Q Local Address           Foreign Address           State
tcp       0      0 enterprise5hp:2208       *:*                       LISTEN
tcp       0      0 *:nfs                    *:*                       LISTEN
tcp       0      0 *:shell                  *:*                       LISTEN
tcp       0      0 *:netbios-ssn            *:*                       LISTEN
tcp       0      0 *:sunrpc                 *:*                       LISTEN
tcp       0      0 *:telnet                 *:*                       LISTEN
tcp       0      0 192.168.0.30:ipp         *:*                       LISTEN
tcp       0      0 enterprise5hp:smtp       *:*                       LISTEN
tcp       0      0 enterprise5h:x11-ssh-offset *:*                    LISTEN
tcp       0      0 enterprise5hp:6011       *:*                       LISTEN
tcp       0      0 enterprise5hp:6012       *:*                       LISTEN
tcp       0      0 *:rquotad                *:*                       LISTEN
tcp       0      0 *:microsoft-ds           *:*                       LISTEN
tcp       0      0 *:32765                  *:*                       LISTEN
tcp       0      0 *:32766                  *:*                       LISTEN
tcp       0      0 *:32767                  *:*                       LISTEN
tcp       0      0 enterprise5hp:2207       *:*                       LISTEN
tcp       1      0 192.168.0.30:34015       ns1.centos.org:http       CLOSE_WAIT
tcp       1      0 192.168.0.30:34009       ns1.centos.org:http       CLOSE_WAIT
tcp       1      0 192.168.0.30:34017       ns1.centos.org:http       CLOSE_WAIT
tcp       0     32 enterprise5h:x11-ssh-offset enterprise5hp:55629    ESTABLISHED
tcp       1      0 192.168.0.30:52647       75.174.92.64.static.re:http CLOSE_WAIT
tcp       1      0 192.168.0.30:35991       rhlx01.hs-esslingen.de:http CLOSE_WAIT
tcp       1      0 192.168.0.30:36002       rhlx01.hs-esslingen.de:http CLOSE_WAIT
tcp       0      0 enterprise5hp:55629      enterprise5h:x11-ssh-offset ESTABLISHED
--More--
```

FIGURE 9.4   **netstat -a** command output

Objective 9.04 — # Decipher Basic Firewall Configurations

Firewalls are intended to regulate traffic in three directions. Normally configured on a router or gateway computer, a firewall can regulate the traffic that goes into the gateway, traffic that originates from the gateway, and traffic that is forwarded through that gateway system. Most of the configuration on the firewall is designed to regulate through the gateway, to help protect users and computers on a LAN behind the gateway.

Firewalls on Linux are configured with the **iptables** command. For the selected distributions, the configuration is normally saved in /etc/sysconfig/iptables and is controlled by the /etc/init.d/iptables script. (As usual, SUSE Linux is different; while it's not necessary to know for the Linux+ exam, substitute SuSEfirewall2 and SuSEfirewall2_init, respectively, for the aforementioned files.)

While it's possible to create firewall rules based on factors such as IP addresses and packet types, you need to be aware of the TCP/IP ports that should be blocked or kept open.

The **iptables** command is not the only way to protect a system. The TCP Wrappers system described in the Chapter 8 section "Set Up Security Environment Files" can also protect network services. PAM, AppArmor, and SELinux can also help protect network services. But firewalls in Linux normally refer to **iptables**.

This assumes you have activated IP forwarding, which configures a Linux system as a router, per the discussion in the Chapter 7 section "Implement Basic Routing and Subnetting."

Travel Advisory

Firewalls with **iptables** are sometimes known as netfiltering. The **iptables** command can also be used for the IP masquerading described in the Chapter 7 section "Implement Basic Routing and Subnetting."

Common Ports

Common ports on a Linux system are configured in /etc/services. While you don't need to memorize the services associated with all 65,000 TCP/IP ports, it can be helpful to know some of the more common ports, as listed and described in Table 9.1. When you read this file, note how many ports are configured for both TCP and UDP packets. Be aware that these are just default ports. Services can be configured on nonstandard ports. For example, Apache can be (and often is) configured to serve webpages on port 8080.

If a TCP/IP port such as 23 is open, or is otherwise not protected by a firewall such as that based on **iptables**, then it is a vulnerability that could be exploited. If there's also an active service that serves that port, such as Telnet, then your system is at risk.

Exam Tip

Know the TCP/IP port numbers associated with common protocols such as FTP, Telnet, SSH, POP, and IMAP. Because Telnet is considered insecure, an open port 23 is often considered a sign of an insecure system. Recognize the basic functionality of various **iptables** commands.

One common firewall configuration blocks all standard TCP/IP ports, between 1 and 1023, with custom rules that open ports such as 80 for Web access and 22 for SSH access.

Travel Advisory

Some services, such as the **rpc.mountd** service associated with NFS, do not normally work on fixed ports. The ports for these services can be fixed in /etc/services (and in this case, /etc/sysconfig/nfs), which can enable firewalls that allow the use of services such as NFS.

TABLE 9.1	More Important TCP/IP Ports, per /etc/services

Port Number	Description
20	FTP data (actual data is sent through port 20)
21	FTP connections
22	SSH (Secure Shell)
23	Telnet
25	SMTP, the Simple Mail Transfer Protocol, for outgoing e-mail; common for sendmail and Postfix
53	DNS, the Domain Name Service, the standard for name resolution
69	TFTP, the Trivial File Transfer Protocol, commonly used for terminal servers
80	HTTP, the well-known protocol for webpages
110	POP3, the current version of the Post Office Protocol, for receiving e-mail
111	Portmapper service, required for NIS and NFS connections
123	Network Time Protocol (NTP), for connections to time servers
139	NetBIOS Session Service, for sharing connections over Microsoft networks
143	IMAP, associated with the Internet Message Access Protocol version 4, for incoming e-mail
443	HTTPS, for secure, encrypted Web connections
631	IPP, associated with the Internet Printing Protocol, for CUPS, the Common Unix Printing System

Configuring iptables

The way **iptables** works is based on a "chain" of rules. Each rule is implemented by an **iptables** command. The rules, chained together, are applied to each network packet. Each rule does two things: specifies a pattern that **iptables** uses to see if a packet qualifies for firewalling, and specifies what **iptables** is supposed to do if the packet matches.

Because the Linux+ objectives were developed before IPv6 came into common use on Linux, I don't expect any reference to the **ip6tables** command. But, except for IPv6 addressing, the **ip6tables** command isn't all that different from **iptables**.

To take full advantage of the **iptables** command, you need to understand its basic command format of switches and options:

```
iptables -t tabletype <action direction> <packet pattern> -j <what to do>
```

Let's analyze the switches and options, one by one. The first setting is based on the -t *tabletype* switch. There are two basic *tabletype* options available, the choice of which drives settings in the rest of the command:

- **-t filter**   Supports configuring a pattern for matching packets
- **-t nat**   Sets up Network Address Translation, also known as IP masquerading, discussed in the Chapter 7 section "Implement Basic Routing and Subnetting"

The default is **-t filter**; if you don't specify a **-t** *tabletype*, the **iptables** command assumes that you're trying to create a rule for filtering.

The next setting is the <*action direction*>. There are four settings available for **iptables** filtering rules:

- **-A (--append)**   Adds another rule to the end of a chain
- **-D (--delete)**   Deletes a rule from a chain
- **-L (--list)**   Lists the currently configured rules in the chain
- **-F (--flush)**   Flushes all the rules in the current set of **iptables** chains

If you're appending to (**-A**) or deleting from (**-D**) a chain, you'll want to apply it to network data traveling in one of three directions:

- **INPUT**   Packets that come into the network are checked against the rules in this chain.
- **OUTPUT**   Packets that are going out from this computer through the firewall are checked against the rules in this chain.
- **FORWARD**   All packets being sent through the firewall from a computer on the local network to a remote computer are checked against the rules in this chain.

Next, the **iptables** command needs to see a <*packet pattern*>. The firewall checks every packet against this pattern. The simplest pattern is by IP address:

- **-s** *ip_address*   All packets are checked for a specific source IP address.
- **-d** *ip_address*   All packets are checked for a specific destination IP address.

The *ip_address* can be associated with a network. IP addresses in **iptables** rules can handle CIDR notation, so you can specify addresses such as that from a private 192.168.0.0/24 network.

Packet patterns can be more complex. In TCP/IP, packets travel over a network using the TCP, UDP, or ICMP protocol. The protocol can be specified with the **-p** switch, followed by the destination port (**--dport**). For example, the **-p tcp --dport 21** extension affects users outside your network who are trying to connect to an FTP server on your network.

Once the **iptables** command finds a packet pattern match, it needs to know what to do with that packet, which leads to the last part of the command, **-j** *<what to do>*. There are three basic options:

- **DROP** The packet is dropped. No message is sent to the requesting computer. Attempts to connect to the associated service may be locked.
- **REJECT** The packet is dropped. An error message is sent to the requesting computer, which can help users help you diagnose problems.
- **ACCEPT** The packet is allowed to proceed through the firewall.

Let's examine how you can use **iptables** commands to configure a firewall. The first step is always to see what is currently configured; the following command lists active firewall rules:

```
# iptables -L
```

If **iptables** is properly configured, the output will display rules in at least three different categories: **INPUT**, **FORWARD**, and **OUTPUT**.

Normally, **iptables** returns output with hostnames. For this purpose, the system requires a reliable connection to a DNS server, and real host and domain names. As many crackers may use fake domain names, Linux administrators sometimes add the -n switch, which keeps the output in the numeric format associated with IP addresses. One example which lists all active rules is

```
# iptables -n -L
```

Travel Advisory

The **-n** switch is a common command option that specifies the use of IP addresses, disabling searches for host files and sometimes problematic DNS servers. It can work with commands such as **route**, **arp**, **netstat**, and more.

Run both the **iptables -L** and **iptables -n -L** commands. Observe the differences. For example, here's the firewall rule, as listed in the output to **iptables -L**, which allows SSH connections:

```
ACCEPT  tcp  --  anywhere  anywhere  state NEW tcp dpt:ssh
```

Now here's the same rule, as listed in the output to the **iptables -n -L** command:

```
ACCEPT  tcp  --  0.0.0.0/0  0.0.0.0/0  state NEW tcp dpt:22
```

Note the difference: **anywhere** is associated with the default IP address, 0.0.0.0, and **ssh** is translated to its standard TCP/IP port number, 22, as listed in /etc/services.

Now let's go a bit further. The following command defines a rule that rejects all traffic from the 10.18.75.0 subnet, and it sends a "destination unreachable" error message back to any client that tried to connect:

```
# iptables -A INPUT -s 10.18.75.0/24 -j REJECT
```

The next rule stops users from the computer with an IP address of 192.168.88.212 from "pinging" your system. This **iptables** command has that effect because the **ping** command uses the ICMP protocol.

```
# iptables -A INPUT -s 192.168.88.212 -p icmp -j DROP
```

The following command guards against TCP SYN "packet flood" attacks from outside the local network. Assume that your network IP address is 192.168.10.0. The "bang," as expressed by the exclamation point (!), inverts the meaning; in this case, the command applies to all IP addresses except those with a 192.168.10.0 network address (and a 255.255.255.0 subnet mask, which translates in CIDR notation to /24).

```
# iptables -A INPUT -s !192.168.10.0/24 -p tcp -j DROP
```

Then, if you want to delete the rule related to the **ping** command in this list, use the following command:

```
# iptables -D INPUT -s 192.168.88.212 -p icmp -j DROP
```

The default rule for **INPUT, OUTPUT,** and **FORWARD** is to **ACCEPT** all packets. One way to stop packet forwarding is to add the following rule:

```
# iptables -A FORWARD -j DROP
```

Any changes made to a firewall don't survive a reboot unless they're saved to the appropriate configuration file. While in most cases, the file is /etc/sysconfig/iptables, that's not the case for all of the selected distributions. For that reason, once you've made any desired changes, run the following command to save the new firewall to the appropriate configuration file:

```
# iptables-save > configfile
```

On the other hand, **iptables** rules are complex. Mistakes are far too easy to make. When it makes sense to start over, the following command can restore the original firewall:

```
# iptables-restore < configfile
```

One common option for the *configfile* is /etc/sysconfig/iptables.

 **Objective 9.05** **Audit Key Security Files**

There are a wide variety of security files on any Linux system. Some were described earlier; for example, firewall commands associated with **iptables** are normally saved in the /etc/sysconfig/iptables configuration file. Most security files are configured somewhere in the /etc/ directory tree.

> **Exam Tip**
>
> Recognize standard security log files. Know how they're monitored. Understand the security risk associated with a dot (.) and related hidden directories in the **PATH** variable.

Security-related /etc/ Configuration Files

Most security configuration settings are included in configuration files based in the /etc/ directory. Key files include /etc/passwd, /etc/group, /etc/shadow, /etc/gshadow, /etc/hosts.allow, /etc/hosts.deny, /etc/securetty, /etc/sudoers, /etc/fstab, and more. Others, such as those for **iptables**, are configured in the /etc/sysconfig directory. Details are described throughout the book. Just be aware that most services can promote security within their base configuration files.

The Internet Super Server

The Extended Internet Services Daemon (**xinetd**) is also known as the "Internet Super Server." The **xinetd** script can start a number of server daemons configured in the /etc/xinetd.d directory simultaneously. The generic configuration file for **xinetd** services is /etc/xinetd.conf. The files in the /etc/xinetd.d directory are service specific.

> **Exam Tip**
>
> Recognize common services associated with the Extended Internet Services Daemon (**xinetd**), including Telnet, rsync, and TFTP.

Examine the directives in /etc/xinetd.conf. They vary a bit between the selected distributions. The order of directives vary, but all enable default settings with the following command:

```
defaults
```

This allows services such as rsync to retain their default TCP/IP ports (873) within the **xinetd** service.

The next line,

```
instances =
```

limits the number of active services for a particular service. Depending on distribution, it may be **30, 50,** or **60.** In other words, no more than 30, 50, or 60 users can be logged into an **xinetd**-based Telnet server simultaneously. If other **xinetd** services are running, that reduces the number of **instances** available to Telnet.

This is often followed by

```
log_type SYSLOG
```

which specifies logging through the **syslog** daemon as configured in /etc/syslog.conf, described in more detail in the Chapter 6 section "Work with Log Files."

This is followed by two lines that specify logging information for success and failure through an **xinetd**-controlled service:

```
log_on_success PID HOST
log_on_failure HOST
```

Naturally, this specifies the hostname (or IP address) of the client host, as well as the Process Identifier (PID) of the connection. One option is to add **USERID** to the list, which lists the UID number associated with the login.

Other directives are distribution specific; a substantial number of options are available as defined in the man page for xinetd.conf. But remember, the Linux+ exam covers only common settings, so that information is beyond the scope of this book.

But there is one more common directive, which includes the contents of the configuration files in the /etc/xinetd.d directory:

```
includedir /etc/xinetd.d
```

Each file in the /etc/xinetd.d directory is normally associated with a specific service. Normally, scripts in this directory are disabled with the following directive:

```
disable = yes
```

You can enable any **xinetd** service by changing **disable = yes** to **disable = no** in its custom /etc/xinetd.d/ configuration file.

Examine the options in Table 9.2. Note the **only_from** and **no_access** directives, as they can help configure security by hostname or IP address.

There are two basic ways to activate a service. First, you can edit a configuration file in the /etc/xinetd.d directory directly. Just open it in a text editor and

TABLE 9.2	Standard Parameters for xinetd Configuration Files
Field	**Description of Field Entry**
user	Specifies the server user account.
group	Specifies the server group account.
server	Notes the full path to the server daemon.
only_from	Associates with the hostname or IP address allowed to use the server. CIDR notation (such as 192.168.0.0/24) is okay.
no_access	Works with the hostname or IP address not allowed to use the server. CIDR notation is okay.
log_on_success	Sets the information sent to a log file if there's a successful login attempt.
log_on_failure	Assigns the information sent to a log file if there's a failed login attempt.
disable	By default, set to **yes**, which disables the service.

change the **disable** directive from **no** to **yes**. The other way is to use the **chkconfig** command; for example, the **chkconfig telnet on** command automatically changes the **disable** directive in the /etc/xinetd.d/telnet configuration file.

Security Logs

Security logs can be general for the system, or specific based on services. They commonly include access and error logs. For example, the CUPS service includes access_log and error_log files in the /var/log/cups directory. Alternatively, Samba access logs are available by IP address or hostname in the /var/log/samba directory.

Details are customized in service-specific configuration files.

Other Security Configuration Issues

One key security configuration issue is related to the **PATH**. When logged in, review your own path with the **echo $PATH** command. If you see a dot in the path, such as in the following outputs,

```
.:/bin:/usr/bin:/sbin
```

```
/bin:/usr/sbin:/usr/.sbin:/sbin
```

there may be a security problem with your system. A cracker who has logged into an account with the first **PATH** is able to execute scripts from the current directory. A cracker who has logged into an account with the second **PATH** has access to scripts in the /usr/.sbin directory. As the dot (.) in front of a file or directory hides that object, an unobservant Linux administrator could miss a whole bunch of malicious scripts in that directory.

 **Objective 9.06** Identify File Corruption

File corruption is often a symptom of something worse. For example, a so-called rootkit appears to conceal malware in familiar commands. Such malware could open network ports to transmit data such as packets with passwords or keylogs with data such as your credit card numbers.

Two available tools for fighting malware are the **rpm -V** command and Tripwire. These tools can help the Linux administrator detect unauthorized changes to critical files. Options such as the **md5sum** and **sha1sum** commands are often also used to identify corruption in large downloads.

Verifying with rpm

One way to identify corruption in files or packages is to verify the integrity of the associated RPM package. When verifying an installed package, it compares information about that package with information from the local system RPM database. The **--verify** (or **-V**) switch compares the MD5 checksum, size, permissions, type, user owner, and group owner of each file in the package. For example, you can verify every file associated with every installed RPM package with the following command:

```
# rpm --verify -a
```

With the hundreds and even thousands of RPMs that may be installed, this process may take some time. As described in the RPM man page, you can substitute -V for the **--verify** option, and take the same action with the **rpm -Va** command.

Alternatively, a limited level of verification is possible against a downloaded RPM. For example, the following command verifies all files associated with the Samba RPM package, as installed from the home directory of the root user:

```
# rpm --verify -p /root/samba-3.*.rpm
```

Another option is to verify a specific file installed from an RPM. For example, the following command checks the integrity of the **mount** command:

```
# rpm --verify --file /bin/mount
```

If the integrity of the file is good—in other words, if there are no changes from the originally installed RPM package—there will be no output. If there's output, that means that there have been changes to files and/or packages.

If there are a few changes, there might not be a problem. For example, administrators do change configuration files. Users change files in their own home directories. So we need more information. When running **rpm --verify**, there are eight tests. Changes are associated with output of up to eight characters. Each active character is associated with a change.

Alternatively, a dot (.) in a column means that there is no change in that category. For example, the following command, which verifies the integrity of the /bin/vi file, shows an incorrect user ID assignment:

```
# rpm --verify --file /bin/vi
.....U..   /bin/vi
```

Table 9.3 lists and describes the meaning of failure codes shown in the output to the **rpm --verify** command.

Running Tripwire

There are open source and commercial versions of Tripwire. The open source version of Tripwire is designed to detect changes to files and associated system objects. Based on parameters set in a policy file, Tripwire takes a "snapshot" of the current state of a system.

As Tripwire is no longer included in the default versions of the selected Linux distributions, it must be installed separately. The commercial version is available from www.tripwire.com; the open source version is available from http://sourceforge.net/projects/tripwire/.

A standard Tripwire report provides a big-picture view of files that have been added, deleted, or otherwise changed. Objects or files that have been modified can be defined more closely.

Checking Download Integrity

When downloading large files, there is often a small file known as a checksum. The most common checksum is associated with the MD5 hash, and is normally stored in a text file in the same directory as the download. For example, after downloading the Snort RPM package for my system, I run the following command to verify the MD5 hash:

```
# md5sum snort-2.7.0.1-1.RHEL4.i386.rpm
1de7e5190c73ab3d3a6154a0a7748874  snort-2.7.0.1-1.RHEL4.i386.rpm
```

TABLE 9.3	rpm --verify Codes
Code	**Description**
5	MD5 checksum
S	File size
L	Symbolic link
T	File modification time
D	Device
U	User
G	Group
M	Mode

I should be able to verify the bolded long number in the left column against the MD5 hash available from the download server.

Sometimes, the Secure Hash Algorithm 1 (SHA1, developed by the U.S. National Security Agency) hash is used instead of MD5. For example, Red Hat makes a SHA1SUM file available with the ISO files associated with Fedora Linux downloads. Before burning a DVD or CD from a Fedora Linux download, I usually check its integrity with a command like:

```
# sha1sum F-7-x86_64-DVD.iso
7cdbd9e1bed9cc9ce2c7970abeaca4da08d2994a   F-7-x86_64-DVD.iso
```

I should be able to verify the SHA1 hash (shown in bold) against the SHA1SUM file available with the Fedora Linux 7 download.

CHECKPOINT

✔**Objective 9.01: Configure Encryption** Encryption in Linux starts with the Shadow Password Suite, which uses MD5 encryption. Files can also be encrypted. Communications can be encrypted using CIPE and SSH. To this end, a number of encryption schemes are available, including SSL/TLS for websites, GPG for e-mail, and RSA and DSA keys for SSH connections.

✔**Objective 9.02: Detect Intrusion Attempts** Intrusions can be detected through log files like /var/log/secure, as well as those customized per service. The **who, w,** and **last** commands can also help.

✔**Objective 9.03: Understand Intrusion Detection Systems** There are a number of third-party Intrusion Detection Systems available, including Snort, PortSentry, SWATCH, and LIDS. Excellent command-line IDS tools include **tcpdump** and **netstat -a.**

✔**Objective 9.04: Decipher Basic Firewall Configurations** To configure a firewall, you need to know at least the basic TCP/IP ports. Then you can use the **iptables** command to secure all but essential ports.

✔**Objective 9.05: Audit Key Security Files** Some security files are specific to the Internet Super Server in the /etc/xinetd.d directory. Others are service specific and are configured in the configuration file associated with the service.

✔**Objective 9.06: Identify File Corruption** The **rpm -V** and Tripwire tools can help the administrator detect files that may be altered by corruption or even crackers breaking into the local system.

REVIEW QUESTIONS

Before leaving for the next chapter, take a few minutes to go through these questions. While doing so, take in both the content and the question format. Understanding what to expect on the exam can increase your chances for success.

1. Which of the following encryption algorithms is standard for Linux Virtual Private Network connections?

   A. CIPE

   B. GPG

   C. Blowfish

   D. MD5

2. Which of the following applications is often used to check the integrity of a password?

   A. Crack

   B. pwcheck

   C. Snort

   D. PAM

3. You're checking the **PATH** of several users. Which of the following values of **PATH** is the highest security risk?

   A. /usr/local/sbin:/usr/local/bin:/usr/sbin

   B. /usr/kerberos/bin:/bin:/usr/bin:/home/michael/bin

   C. /usr/bin:/root/bin

   D. .:/bin:/usr/bin:/sbin

4. Which of the following Intrusion Detection Systems is not intended to help protect systems from network intrusions?

   A. Snort

   B. Tripwire

   C. PortSentry

   D. netstat

5. Which of the following TCP/IP ports is not associated with the FTP, SSH, or SMTP protocols?

   A. 21

   B. 22

   C. 23

   D. 25

6. Which of the following is the current standard for encryption of the Apache Web server?

   A. HTTPS

   B. SSL

   C. Virtual Hosts

   D. TLS

7. If you're running a Samba-based File server, which of the following TCP/IP ports should not be blocked by a firewall?

   A. 139

   B. 110

   C. 80

   D. 53

8. Which of the following commands displays the current firewall rules associated with **iptables**?

   A. iptables

   B. iptables -D

   C. iptables -A

   D. iptables -L

9. Which of the following files is normally edited in order to activate the Telnet service?

   A. /etc/telnet

   B. /etc/krb5-telnet

   C. /etc/xinetd.conf

   D. /etc/xinetd.d/telnet

10. Which of the following commands checks the integrity of all files and packages on the local system?

    A. rpm -V /var/log/rpmpkgs

    B. rpm -V

    C. rpm -A

    D. rpm -Va

REVIEW ANSWERS

1. **C**   Linux Virtual Private Networks, implemented through Cryptographic IP Encapsulation (CIPE), are frequently configured with the Blowfish encryption algorithm.

2. **A** The Crack software tries to decipher passwords using standard dictionary checks. It's intended to help administrators identify users who use passwords of inadequate strength.

3. **D** The dot (.) means that scripts in the local directory are run without the full path. Crackers may be able to run root-level scripts from the current directory, which can put at least the local system at risk. That is a more substantial risk than any specific directory, even any subdirectory of the root user.

4. **B** The Tripwire system is intended to detect unauthorized changes to files. Snort and PortSentry are commonly used to detect network intrusions. The **netstat** command, as suggested in the Chapter 5 section "Understand Network Troubleshooting," can display current network connectivity information.

5. **C** As shown in /etc/services, port 23 is associated with Telnet. Port 21 is associated with FTP, port 22 is associated with SSH, and port 25 is associated with SMTP.

6. **D** Transport Layer Security (TLS) is the successor to SSL, which provides encryption on client connections to the Apache Web server.

7. **A** TCP/IP port 139 is associated with the NetBIOS session service, which supports connections between Samba systems. Port 110 is associated with POP3 e-mail connections, port 80 is associated with Web connections, and port 53 is associated with DNS services.

8. **D** The **iptables -L** command lists all rules currently configured and active for the local system. The **iptables -D** command deletes a selected rule. The **iptables -A** command adds a selected rule. If you see a -n with it as well, don't let it confuse you. The -n just keeps rules associated with IP addresses.

9. **D** For the selected distributions, Telnet is an **xinetd** service, configured in individual files in the /etc/xinetd.d/ directory. There is a Kerberos-enabled version of Telnet available, configured in the krb5-telnet file, which is also in the /etc/xinetd.d directory. Otherwise, answer B would also be correct.

10. **D** The **rpm -Va** command verifies the integrity of files from all installed RPM packages. Any file which has been changed or is otherwise different from its status as originally installed is listed with labels associated with the type of change.

PART

V

An Overview of Linux Documentation

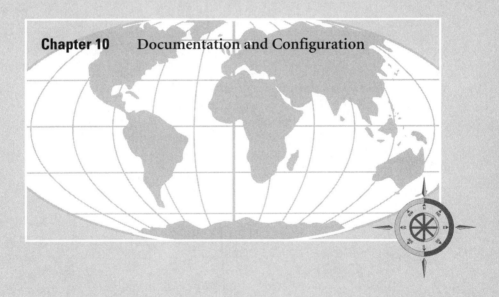

Documentation and Configuration

	NEWBIE	SOME EXPERIENCE	VETERAN
ETA	40+ hours	8 hours	4 hours

Linux administrators need to document what they do. With documentation, other competent administrators can keep systems and networks running even if something happens to you. To that end, it's important to document baseline performance with tools like **top**, **sar**, **vmstat**, and **pstree**.

If the system needs to be restored or replicated, you need to document how the system was installed, the current configuration files, a list of installed packages, a list of network settings, and more. Extensive general documentation is already available on just about every Linux service.

Security and maintenance procedures should be consistent with organizational policies. System logs can be used to verify compliance with many policies. Linux licensing is a part of this process.

Document a System Performance Baseline

The Linux+ objectives list four commands that can help create a system performance baseline:

- **top**   Displays currently running Linux tasks
- **sar**   Creates a system activity report
- **vmstat**   Reports virtual memory statistics
- **pstree**   Lists currently running processes with visual links

---

Exam Tip

Try variations of the commands described in this section (and throughout the book). Go beyond what you normally do when running Linux. Even if you're already familiar with these commands, you may see switches other than what you might normally use.

Display Linux Performance with top

As shown in Figure 10.1, the **top** command illustrates the current status of a running system, including the following details:

- Current uptime status, logged-in users, and system load
- Number of loaded and running tasks
- Load on the CPU
- Use of RAM memory and swap space
- Tasks as defined by the PID and user

```
top - 23:10:21 up 12 days,  4:01,  3 users,  load average: 0.05, 0.04, 0.01
Tasks: 137 total,   1 running, 136 sleeping,   0 stopped,   0 zombie
Cpu(s):  0.0%us,  0.0%sy,  0.0%ni,100.0%id,  0.0%wa,  0.0%hi,  0.0%si,  0.0%st
Mem:   1894208k total,  1784836k used,   109372k free,   145904k buffers
Swap:   987988k total,      76k used,   987912k free,  1281508k cached

  PID USER      PR  NI  VIRT  RES  SHR S %CPU %MEM    TIME+  COMMAND
  339 root      10  -5     0    0    0 S  0.7  0.0  0:00.60 kjournald
14596 root      15   0  283m  14m 8468 S  0.3  0.8  0:00.08 gnome-terminal
    1 root      15   0 10316  676  560 S  0.0  0.0  0:00.49 init
    2 root      RT   0     0    0    0 S  0.0  0.0  0:00.00 migration/0
    3 root      34  19     0    0    0 S  0.0  0.0  0:00.04 ksoftirqd/0
    4 root      RT   0     0    0    0 S  0.0  0.0  0:00.00 watchdog/0
    5 root      10  -5     0    0    0 S  0.0  0.0  0:00.00 events/0
    6 root      10  -5     0    0    0 S  0.0  0.0  0:00.00 khelper
    7 root      11  -5     0    0    0 S  0.0  0.0  0:00.00 kthread
    9 root      10  -5     0    0    0 S  0.0  0.0  0:00.00 xenwatch
   10 root      10  -5     0    0    0 S  0.0  0.0  0:00.00 xenbus
   48 root      10  -5     0    0    0 S  0.0  0.0  0:00.04 kblockd/0
   49 root      20  -5     0    0    0 S  0.0  0.0  0:00.00 kacpid
  151 root      20  -5     0    0    0 S  0.0  0.0  0:00.00 cqueue/0
  156 root      10  -5     0    0    0 S  0.0  0.0  0:00.00 khubd
  158 root      16  -5     0    0    0 S  0.0  0.0  0:00.00 kseriod
  180 root      15   0     0    0    0 S  0.0  0.0  0:00.00 pdflush
```

FIGURE 10.1   Output from the **top** command

More highly loaded processes are listed first to help you identify processes that are overloading the system.

By default, the information in the list is updated every three seconds. You could change the updates with the -d switch; for example, the following command changes the default to every second:

```
# top -d1
```

System Activity Reports with sar

The **sar** command can provide customized system activity reports. It requires the sysstat RPM package, which is not installed by default. Once sysstat is installed, **sar** reports are taken every ten minutes and are logged daily, as governed by the **cron** job in the /etc/cron.d/sysstat configuration file.

Available statistics provide a detailed analysis of CPU loading, kernel usage, and the amount of time waiting for input and output. Further details are beyond the scope of the Linux+ exam.

Reports are saved daily in the /var/log/sa directory. Because they're saved in sa*yx* files, where *yx* represents the day of the month, there's access only to a month's worth of system activity reports. Therefore, some administrators may choose to archive reports on a monthly basis.

The sar -A command lists all statistics for the current day. To get the report for a previous day, specify the log file. If it's from the past month, say from the 22nd of the month, you can do so with the following command:

```
# sar -f /var/log/sa/sa22
```

The **sar** command requires separate entries for multiple switches. For example, if you want to review a complete report for the 22nd from the logs, you'd run the following command:

```
# sar -A -f /var/log/sa/sa22
```

Memory Statistics with vmstat

The **vmstat** command provides a subset of what's available from the **top** command. As shown in Figure 10.2, the **vmstat** command lists free RAM, other memory allocated to buffers, memory cached from a swap partition, memory swapped in and out of the partition and block devices, system interrupts, and CPU usage.

More can be done with the **vmstat** command. For example, the following command monitors active and inactive memory (**-a**), with the headers listed only once (**-n**), every 60 seconds, ten times:

```
# vmstat -a -n 60 10
```

One more option lists reads and writes to specified partitions. For example, if you suspect a lot of activity on the /dev/sda1 partition, run the following command:

```
# vmstat -p /dev/sda1
```

Review the Process Tree with pstree

The **pstree** command lists currently running processes in a tree format, which can help administrators trace the heredity of processes. As described in the Chapter 4 section "Learn Process Management," processes have Process Identifiers (PIDs) as well as parents (PPIDs). When administrators have trouble killing a process, one option for them is to kill the parent process. However, this action could have unintended consequences, such as killing other processes.

Figure 10.3 illustrates an excerpt from **pstree** output, without switches. If I have trouble killing the process which governs the Adobe Acrobat application (**acroread**), I could kill the **kdeinit** process, but that would kill a whole bunch of other processes (those shown in the figure) that I might rather keep running.

```
[root@enterprise5fc6d ~]# vmstat
procs -----------memory---------- ---swap-- -----io---- --system-- -----cpu------
 r  b   swpd   free   buff  cache   si   so    bi    bo   in   cs us sy id wa st
 0  0     76 109312 145956 1281532    0    0    10     1   30   33  0  0 100  0  0
[root@enterprise5fc6d ~]#
```

FIGURE 10.2   Output from the **vmstat** command

```
      |-kdeinit-+-acroread
      |         |-evolution-2.6---6*[{evolution-2.6}]
      |         |-evolution-alarm---{evolution-alarm}
      |         |-firefox---run-mozilla.sh---firefox-bin-+-java_vm---14*[{java_vm
}]
      |         |                                        `-11*[{firefox-bin}]
      |         |-katapult
      |         |-kio_file
      |         |-klauncher
      |         |-konsole-+-3*[bash]
      |         |         |-bash---gnome-terminal-+-bash-+-bash
      |         |         |                       |      `-pstree
      |         |         |                       |-gnome-pty-helpe
      |         |         |                       `-{gnome-terminal}
      |         |         `-2*[bash---ssh]
      |         |-kwin
      |         |-soffice---soffice.bin---4*[{soffice.bin}]
      |         |-wrapper-gtk24.s-+-vmware---2*[vmware-remotemk]
      |         |                 `-wrapper-gtk24.s
      |         |-wrapper-gtk24.s-+-vmware---vmware-remotemk
      |         |                 `-wrapper-gtk24.s
      |         `-wrapper-gtk24.s-+-vmware---3*[vmware-remotemk]
      |                           `-wrapper-gtk24.s
:█
```

| **FIGURE 10.3** | Output from the **pstree** command |

Useful switches for the **pstree** command are listed and described in Table 10.1. As with all commands, if you want to examine additional switches, start with the man page.

One more example **pstree** command follows. With the -**a** and -**u** switches, the following identifies command-line arguments in the tree, as well as the users responsible for said commands:

```
# pstree -au
```

| **TABLE 10.1** | Switches for the **pstree** Command |

pstree Switch	Description
-a	Shows command-line arguments in the tree, which can help identify the command in the tree
-p	Identifies the PID of each process, which can be used to kill unwanted processes
-u	Identifies user-controlled processes in the tree

Create Installation, Configuration, and Security Management Procedures

Installations of many Linux distributions can often be replicated with tools such as Red Hat's Kickstart and SUSE's AutoYaST. In other words, with the right configuration file and access to the installation RPMs, you can automate the installation of another system with the same configuration. But that may not be enough. Administrators often customize configuration files and set up security procedures.

Document the Installation Configuration

Most modern Linux distributions include a configuration file that supports replication. While it's common to copy or "ghost" the contents from one system to another, it's often best to reinstall Linux, using the same basic settings. The reinstallation process allows the distribution to adapt to different networks, minor hardware differences, and other personal settings.

With the right configuration file, all you need is access to the installation repository, which is often available from a DVD copied to a network server. The actual techniques for automated reinstallation vary by distribution, and are therefore beyond the scope of the Linux+ exam.

Back Up Configuration Files

One disadvantage of Kickstart-style installations is the lack of customization support for individual configuration files. However, a Kickstart file can be set to copy configuration files from network servers. Of course, you could copy configuration files manually after installation is complete. In any case, it can be helpful to have a backup of configuration files you need from the /etc/ directory.

> **Travel Advisory**
>
> When backing up a system, you may not want to back up everything. For example, the /proc directory includes running kernel data, which can change from system to system.

Set Up Security Procedures

Security procedures can be created on two levels. Some security procedures, such as stronger passwords and encryption keys, have already been described in Chapters 8 and 9. Other procedures go beyond Linux, and include options such as the following:

- BIOS passwords, card keys, and biometric authentication
- Secure physical systems such as locked USB ports, CD/DVD drives, Secure Digital slots, and network ports
- Physical security measures such as locked rooms, closed circuit cameras, and so on

 **Objective 10.03**

Document the Installed Configuration

There are several important elements associated with any Linux installation that should be documented. First, any baseline documentation requires a list of installed packages. Any options associated with compiled source packages must be understood.

Consistent installations require an understanding of Linux hardware support. Consistent networking eases integration of new clients. Finally, the right maintenance procedures can help you, as an administrator, keep Linux systems running smoothly.

Perhaps the simplest but most important piece of documentation is the identity of the current kernel. Applications such as proprietary databases are certified to work only with specific kernels, and they can be identified with the following command:

```
# uname -r
```

Exam Tip
Know what the **uname** command (and switches) can identify.

Find the Package List

There are two places to find the list of installed packages. When Linux is installed on the selected distributions, the list of packages is normally stored in the install.log file in places such as the administrative home directory, /root. As systems evolve, more packages get installed, and the list of packages is updated periodically through a **cron** job in the /var/log/rpmpkgs file.

The most current list of installed packages can be found with the following **rpm** command, which literally queries for all installed packages. The list returned by this command is more up to date than the /var/log/rpmpkgs file.

```
# rpm -qa
```

With the latest hardware, it usually takes a few seconds for this command to create an updated list of installed RPM packages. With file filters like the **grep** command, it's easy to search through this database.

Even though all of the selected distributions use RPM packages, not all packages on Linux distributions are installed from an RPM. Frequently, the latest versions of many packages are available only in tarball format. Such packages do not show up as part of a database created by the **rpm -qa** command or any standard log file.

There are variations on the **rpm -qa** command. If you're checking whether a package is installed, such as samba, the **rpm -q** *packagename* command lists the version number of the package:

```
$ rpm -q samba
samba-3.0.23c-2.el5.2.0.2
```

If you don't know what files are associated with a package, the **rpm -ql** *packagename* command can help. For example, the following command lists all files installed from the bind-utils package:

```
# rpm -ql bind-utils
/usr/bin/dig
/usr/bin/host
/usr/bin/nslookup
/usr/bin/nsupdate
/usr/share/man/man1/dig.1.gz
/usr/share/man/man1/host.1.gz
/usr/share/man/man1/nslookup.1.gz
/usr/share/man/man8/nsupdate.8.gz
```

While you may already be familiar with these commands from the Chapter 6 section "Implement Name Resolution," you could also learn more with the **rpm -qi** *packagename* command. As shown in Figure 10.4, when applied to the bind-utils package, the output confirms that the package contains a collection of utilities for querying DNS servers.

Finally, to identify a package associated with a particular file, the **rpm -qf** */path/to/filename* command can help. For example, the following command identifies the RPM package from where the **smbpasswd** command was installed:

```
# rpm -qf /usr/bin/smbpasswd
samba-common-3.0.25-2.fc7
```

```
[root@enterprise5fc6d ~]# rpm -qi bind-utils
Name       : bind-utils              Relocations: (not relocatable)
Version    : 9.4.0                        Vendor: Red Hat, Inc.
Release    : 6.fc7                    Build Date: Mon 16 Apr 2007 07:52:48
 AM PDT
Install Date: Wed 13 Jun 2007 10:16:13 AM PDT    Build Host: hs20-bc2-2.build.
redhat.com
Group      : Applications/System     Source RPM: bind-9.4.0-6.fc7.src.rpm
Size       : 351822                      License: BSD-like
Signature  : DSA/SHA1, Fri 18 May 2007 10:06:46 AM PDT, Key ID b44269d04f2a6fd2
Packager   : Red Hat, Inc. <http://bugzilla.redhat.com/bugzilla>
URL        : http://www.isc.org/products/BIND/
Summary    : Utilities for querying DNS name servers.
Description :
Bind-utils contains a collection of utilities for querying DNS (Domain
Name System) name servers to find out information about Internet
hosts. These tools will provide you with the IP addresses for given
host names, as well as other information about registered domains and
network addresses.

You should install bind-utils if you need to get information from DNS name
servers.
[root@enterprise5fc6d ~]#
```

FIGURE 10.4 Getting information on an RPM package

And there's a straightforward bit of information available from an RPM package file. Check the list of RPMs on your installation CD/DVD. The following file identifies the CPU required on the system where you plan to install this package:

```
samba-common-3.0.25-2.fc7.x86_64.rpm
```

The x86_64 in the filename identifies this package as being built for AMD 64-bit CPU systems. Several other options are listed in Table 10.2. It's not a complete list, as it does not include more specialized hardware such as that associated with IBM servers.

TABLE 10.2 Hardware Identification in RPM Package Files

Option	Associated CPU
noarch	Does not depend on CPU architecture; can be installed on any system where Linux can be installed
i586	Intel 586 CPUs—may be in the i386 package tree
i686	Intel 686 CPUs—may be in the i386 package tree
ia64	Intel Itanium 64-bit CPU
ppc	Power PC CPU
ppc64	Power PC, 64-bit CPU
x86_64	AMD 64-bit systems

If you're not sure of the current hardware, run either the **uname -m** or **uname -p** command. The **uname -p** command is preferred for identifying appropriate RPM packages; however, it doesn't work on systems with Intel Core 2 Duo CPUs. In any case, such CPUs were released well after the date of the current Linux+ objectives.

> **Exam Tip**
>
> Know the various **rpm** commands associated with a current list of installed packages, how to list the files associated with a package, and how to identify the package associated with a particular file, as well as the basic information associated with a package. Be able to identify appropriate hardware for an RPM package based on its filename.

Document Compiled Package Options

As not all packages, even on the selected distributions, are installed with the **rpm** command, it's even more important to document those packages otherwise compiled. The details of customizing specific packages are beyond the scope of the Linux+ exam, so just remember to document the options used when compiling packages and kernels processed from source code.

Documented Hardware

With the relatively new Linux hardware abstraction layer (HAL) daemon, it's easier to document the hardware on current Linux systems. Unfortunately, HAL was adapted for the selected distributions after the current Linux+ objectives were released. The commands associated with HAL are too important to ignore; major HAL commands are summarized in Table 10.3.

Hardware is covered in more detail in Chapter 11.

TABLE 10.3   Hardware Abstraction Layer Commands

HAL Command	Description
lshal	Lists devices in the HAL database
lspci	Lists PCI devices; **lspci -v** and **lspci -vv** provide more information
lspcmcia	Lists current PC cards; related to the **cardctl** command
lsusb	Lists currently installed USB hubs and devices

Set Up Consistent Networking

When adding new clients to a local network, it's helpful if the new system is installed with network settings consistent with those of the other systems on the network. Specifically, you need to make sure required network services are installed, and that network addresses are consistent with the rest of the network.

In other words, when installing a new client, you need a list of network services to install, such as Samba, NFS, NIS, SSH, and so on, details on how each service is to be configured, as well as an IP address for the new client. Just make sure it's on the same network as other LAN clients.

Create Maintenance Procedures

Proper maintenance procedures include tools described throughout the book. For example, Chapter 3 covers the basic skills of managing files and directories, and Chapter 4 can help you maintain partitions and boot processes. Just remember, such procedures should be well documented in the scripts you create, the procedures you set up, and the policies you implement. These procedures should be understandable by any competent Linux administrator.

When to Update the Kernel

Kernel updates are usually easy, but can become tricky. The kernel can and often is automatically upgraded using the standard update tools for the selected distributions. But automatic updates can be a problem because important software such as database systems and hardware drivers may be certified or may only work for a certain kernel release. In those cases, a kernel update could invalidate support for the database system or inactivate the hardware driver. Therefore, it's important to know when key applications and drivers are tied to a specific version of the kernel.

However, kernel updates can and often do add new features, address security issues, fix hardware bugs, and more. Even when a custom distribution-specific kernel update is not available, the need for a new kernel makes it worth the trouble to recompile a kernel for a driver or update a database system or other application.

If available, it's best to update a kernel with a binary RPM customized by the developers of your distribution. If such an update is not available, you could download and compile a new kernel from www.kernel.org. However, such an update, if not carefully configured and installed, could negate special features configured by the developers of your distribution. When you do update a kernel, make sure to document any required changes to drivers or applications.

Troubleshoot System and Application Errors with Logs

Objective 10.04

L inux troubleshooting frequently involves working with system and application log files. As described in the Chapter 6 section "Work with Log Files," log file locations are driven by the /etc/syslog.conf configuration file and individual application configuration files. As the tools were also covered in Chapter 3, this section may seem repetitive. However, this is a documentation skill specifically listed in the Linux+ exam objectives, so the review is worthwhile.

Monitoring Logs with head and tail

Log files can go on for thousands of lines. Access logs for applications, such as those for Web servers, can reach into the gigabytes. Just opening a file of this size can take minutes or more. The **head** and **tail** commands enable you to look at only the start or end of a file. By default, **head** displays the first ten lines of a file and **tail** displays the last ten lines. If you need to review the last 100 lines of the current Apache access log, run the following command:

```
# tail -n100 /var/log/httpd/access.log
```

In contrast, to review the first 100 lines of the current Apache error log, run the following command:

```
# head -n100 /var/log/httpd/error.log
```

In older versions of the **head** and **tail** commands, a space between the **-n** and number (**-n 100**) led to a syntax error. While a space would be okay now, it's important to recognize commands where spaces are not required, as they may come up as trick questions on Linux exams.

The **tail** command is a bit more important. With the **tail -f** command, it's possible to monitor log files for information as it develops. For example, if you believe there's an active attempt to break into your system, you may want to monitor the security log with the following command:

```
# tail -f /var/log/secure
```

Searching Through Logs with grep

The **grep** command is another useful tool for searching through log files, especially when they're long. All you need is a keyword, such as root or sda. For example, the following command searches through the security log for issues with the root account:

```
# grep root /var/log/secure
```

Alternatively, if you suspect problems with the first SCSI hard drive, it can help to review hardware messages associated with the kernel ring buffer, as defined by either of these commands:

```
# grep sda /var/log/dmesg
# dmesg | grep sda
```

Access System Documentation

Objective 10.05

System documentation is available on all Linux systems, and online. It's available in command manuals and package documentation. Online documentation encompasses a wide variety of options, from more traditional HOWTOs to IRC channels.

Command Manuals

Two basic types of command manuals are available on Linux distributions: the man page and the info manual.

The man page is available for almost all commands and for many configuration files. For example, to read a man page for the Samba configuration file, run the following command:

```
# man smb.conf
```

To find a list of the man pages associated with a specific keyword, try the **man -k** *keyword* command. There's also the equivalent **apropos** command; for example, the following command lists all man pages associated with the term *passwd*:

```
# apropos passwd
```

But there are eight sections (also known as chapters) of man pages available. For example, consider the following excerpt from the **apropos passwd** command:

```
smbpasswd     (5)   - The Samba encrypted password file
smbpasswd     (8)   - change a user's SMB password
```

The **man smbpasswd** command may not be enough. On my Fedora system, it defaults to the command. If I want to read the man page for the encrypted password file, I have to add the section or chapter number:

```
# man 5 smbpasswd
```

If you want more information on a command, try prefacing it with **whereis**. Doing so locates the binary, source, and man page for the command. For example, when I run the following command:

```
# whereis smbpasswd
smbpasswd: /usr/bin/smbpasswd
/usr/share/man/man5/smbpasswd.5.gz
/usr/share/man/man8/smbpasswd.8.gz
```

I can identify the location of the binary executable smbpasswd file and both associated man pages. Note that the section number is embedded in each man page filename. Because I did not compile the Samba package from source code, the **whereis** command does not list the location of the associated source file.

If you just want a list of available man pages, run the **whatis** command:

```
# whatis smbpasswd
smbpasswd    (5) - The Samba encrypted password file
smbpasswd    (8) - change a user's SMB password
```

If the output is blank, you first need to create a man page database with the following command:

```
# makewhatis
```

One alternative to the man page is the info manual. Unfortunately, custom info manuals aren't available for all commands. As you can see if you run the **info ls** command, the information available is formatted differently. But if there is no info manual available for a command, such as for the smbpasswd file, the command returns a view of the man page.

To see the full capabilities of an info manual, compare the output between the **man grub** and **info grub** commands. When you run **info grub**, use the cursor to highlight a menu item and press ENTER, or press N to go forward and P to go back. Fortunately, you don't need to know how to use the info manual in any additional detail for the Linux+ exam.

Exam Tip

Know how to create the database for the **whatis** command, and know the difference between info and man pages.

Package Documentation

There's a variety of documentation available for different Linux packages. While the variations are as many as the number of packages, there are common themes such as README files and dedicated /usr/share/doc directories.

Online Documentation

There's a wide variety of online documentation available for different Linux packages. Traditional Linux documentation is associated with HOWTOs on a variety of subjects, available online from the Linux Documentation Project at www.tldp.org. The developers behind many Linux services maintain their own documentation on their home pages.

The developers behind the selected distributions maintain their own documentation online at their respective websites. There are also mailing lists available for each distribution.

Web-based forums and IRC channels are also popular options. For the Linux+ exam, I personally like the ProProfs.com forums, available at www.proprofs.com. For more general Linux questions, I like the forums at www.linuxquestions.org. Active and helpful forums (and IRC channels) are available with many Linux user groups worldwide. One list of groups is maintained at www.linux.org/groups/.

Licensing

There are several major licenses associated with Linux software. Most are approved by the Open Source Initiative (OSI). The biggest name among these licenses is the GNU General Public License (GPL), as sponsored by Richard Stallman's Free Software Foundation (FSF). While licensing is beyond the scope of the Linux+ exam, it is an essential documentation skill for any Linux administrator.

Stallman developed the GPL to give GNU and Linux software the advantages that were once available with Unix. Three basic principles are associated with the GPL:

- All developers of GPL software must make a complete copy of the source code freely available. The code must include clear documentation.
- Any software added to GPL licensed software must also include clear documentation. If there is any interaction between the two software packages, the package as a whole must be distributed under the GPL.
- All GPL software comes without a warranty.

Legal interpretations of the actual license are subject to various copyright laws, which is beyond the scope of this book. The "viral" nature of the GPL leads some to refer to the license as a form of "copyleft."

The GPL has been recently revised. The latest release is known as GPL version 3 (GPLv3). As software and copyright law has developed into areas such as Digital Rights Management (DRM) and patents, GPLv3 is designed to address these concerns while retaining the basic principles of "copyleft."

Linus Torvalds has declared that Linux will not use GPLv3. However, the developers behind several components commonly included in Linux, such as Samba, have already declared that they will relicense their products under GPLv3.

CHECKPOINT

✔**Objective 10.01: Document a System Performance Baseline**   Four basic commands can help document system performance: **top** provides a current view of hardware usage and processes, **sar** supports a customizable system activity report, **vmstat** illustrates memory statistics, and **pstree** organizes running processes in a tree-style hierarchy.

✔**Objective 10.02: Create Installation, Configuration, and Security Management Procedures**   Documenting the current installation supports backup as well as replication for new clients, with desired configuration files. Security management procedures go beyond standard Linux tools.

✔**Objective 10.03: Document the Installed Configuration**   Understanding the installed configuration requires knowing how to find a list of installed packages and how source packages are compiled. It also requires a list of current hardware and consistent networking. Maintenance procedures help administrators keep systems running smoothly.

✔**Objective 10.04: Troubleshoot System and Application Errors with Logs**   When troubleshooting a Linux system, start with the system logs in the /var/log directory and dedicated application log files, normally in service-specific /var/log subdirectories.

✔**Objective 10.05: Access System Documentation**   Linux is well documented with man pages, info manuals, README files, and other pages on a local system. It's also well documented online with HOWTOs, service-specific websites, and more.

REVIEW QUESTIONS

Before leaving for the next chapter, take a few minutes to go through these questions. While doing so, take in both the content and the question format. Understanding what to expect on the exam can increase your chances for success.

1. Which of the following answers best describes what you see when running the **info cat** command?

    A. Exactly the same information as the output to the **man cat** command

    B. The manual for the cat page in the GNU Info reader

    C. A description of all man pages that include the **cat** command

    D. Information on the RPM package that contains the **cat** command

2. Which of the following commands provides more information about the Samba RPM package?

    A. rpm -i samba

    B. rpm -q samba

    C. rpm -V samba

    D. rpm -qi samba

3. Which of the following commands creates a searchable database of man pages?

    A. updatedb man

    B. whatis -d

    C. makewhatis

    D. whatis -r

4. Which of the following commands identifies processes with PIDs and users in a tree format?

    A. ps aux

    B. pstree -au

    C. ps axl

    D. pstree -pu

5. If you want to upgrade to the latest available kernel, where should you look first?

    A. The www.kernel.org repositories

    B. The update repositories associated with the current distribution

    C. The kernel update site at www.sourceforge.org

    D. The local /var/log/rpms directory

6. Which of the following commands searches the man page database for the term "cat" in a format similar to the locate command?

    A. whatis cat

    B. man cat

    C. search cat

    D. apropos cat

7. Which of the following commands identifies the release version of the currently running kernel?

   A. uname -r

   B. uname -k

   C. uname -v

   D. uname -p

8. If there are two man pages for the **man** command, which of the following commands would read the man page in the latter chapter? Assume *later* is the latter number; *earlier* is the earlier number.

   A. man *earlier* man

   B. man *later*

   C. man *later* man

   D. man *earlier*

9. Which of the following commands lists CPU usage and available memory, four times, once every 15 seconds?

   A. vmstat

   B. vmstat 4 15

   C. vmstat 15 4

   D. vmstat -n 4 15

10. Which of the following does not provide information about command documentation for the ls command?

   A. man ls

   B. info ls

   C. apropos ls

   D. ls -l

REVIEW ANSWERS

1. **B**   The **info** command opens the manual for the command that follows, in the GNU Info reader.

2. **D**   The **rpm -q** *packagename* command confirms the installed version number of a package. Additions to **rpm -q** provide more information: the answer, the **rpm -qi** *packagename* command, provides information about the package; **rpm -ql** *packagename* provides a list of files; **rpm -qc** *packagename* identifies configuration files; **rpm -qf** *filename* verifies the package associated with a file; and **rpm -qa** lists all installed packages.

3. **C**   The **makewhatis** command creates a searchable database from the installed man pages, which helps especially if there are multiple man pages available.

4. **D**   The **pstree** command lists processes in a tree format. The -p switch lists processes. The -u switch lists users.

5. **B**   The first place to look for a kernel update is the repository associated with the current distribution. Only if there is no update should you look to www.kernel.org for a later update.

6. **D**   The **apropos cat** command searches through the database of man pages, returning the titles of all pages with the "cat" string.

7. **A**   The **uname -r** command returns the version number of the currently loaded kernel. In contrast, the **uname -v** command shows the date the kernel was built; the **uname -m** command lists the associated architecture.

8. **C**   When citing a man page where multiple man pages are available, you need to include in the **man** command the number associated with the chapter, to be sure you get the right man page.

9. **C**   The **vmstat** command lists CPU usage and available memory. The first number specifies the interval between checks. The second number lists the number of checks.

10. **D**   The **ls -l** command is a regular command. The other commands provide documentation on the associated man pages.

PART

VI

Hardware Issues

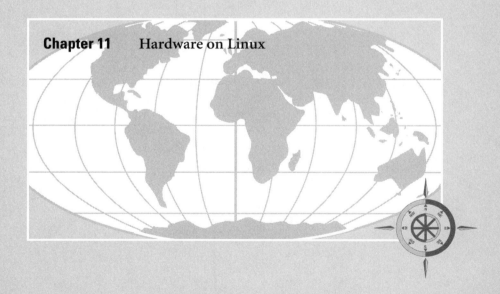

Chapter 11   Hardware on Linux

Hardware on Linux

	NEWBIE	SOME EXPERIENCE	VETERAN
ETA	40+ hours	8 hours	4 hours

Perhaps CompTIA's most successful exam is the A+ Hardware Exam. Building on that success has led to the inclusion of hardware questions in several other CompTIA exams, including Linux+. The first version of the CompTIA Linux+ exam objectives allocated 19 percent weight to hardware-related questions. The current Linux+ exam allocates 8 percent weight to these questions. In my opinion, a few of the hardware topics for the Linux+ exam have little relationship to the Linux operating system.

Fortunately, these questions are now limited to common hardware components such as connectors and channels. Many hardware components can be diagnosed using Linux tools such as the kernel ring buffer and the /proc directory. Hardware power management is related to Advanced Power Management (APM) and the Advanced Configuration and Power Interface (ACPI). Modern removable system hardware is focused on USB and IEEE 1394 devices. Coverage of mass storage devices is focused on drives: hard, floppy, tape, and CD/DVD.

Travel Advisory

Many acronyms in this chapter should already be familiar to qualified Linux+ exam candidates. Therefore, this chapter doesn't give the full name of some acronyms until the section in which they are discussed.

Objective 11.01

Describe Common Hardware Components

The hardware components available on a PC are constantly evolving. Those available today go beyond those available when the Linux+ objectives were released. Even then, a wide variety of connectors were available on PCs. They communicate through the motherboard to the operating system via a variety of hardware channels; they interface with the Linux kernel through modules. And if you're not sure whether a component is compatible with Linux, there are various Hardware Compatibility Lists (HCLs) available.

Connectors

A wide variety of connectors are available for PCs; those which may apply for the Linux+ exam are listed in Table 11.1. Many of these connectors are described in more detail in other sections in this chapter. By definition, all connectors listed are associated with external devices. The acronyms in Table 11.1 should be familiar, and in any case are explained in following sections.

TABLE 11.1	Standard PC Connection Ports
Connector	**Description**
Serial port	Connection to devices such as a modem or mouse
Parallel port	Connection to devices such as a printer, tape, or hard drive
VGA port	Associated with monitors; may come from AGP or PCI devices
PS/2	Typical connection to a keyboard and mouse
SCSI	Typically for older external hard drives
IEEE 1394	Connection to external hard drives and video devices
USB	Common standard connection for a variety of devices
PCMCIA	The slot in the side of a laptop; comes in various sizes

Other connectors include game ports, multimedia ports for speakers and microphones, and so on. There are also ports typically internal to a PC, such as for ISA, PCI, and AGP devices. On the other hand, newer devices such as card readers came into common use after the Linux+ objectives were released.

Basic Hardware Channels

While it's still important to know some basic hardware channels for the Linux+ exam, it's not necessary to know them in much detail. They are associated with connectors described in Table 11.1. Conflicts between channels such as interrupt requests (IRQ), input/output (I/O) addresses, and direct memory access (DMA) channels can prevent external hardware from communicating with the operating system.

In the next few years, PS/2, serial, and parallel ports may become obsolete as their functionality is supplanted by hardware connected to USB ports.

Interrupt Requests

An IRQ is how a device sends a request to a CPU for service. For example, when you type something, the keyboard sends an IRQ signal to the CPU for service. Older PCs have 16 IRQ ports available, 0 through 15. Lower numbers get higher priority. Conflicts were fairly common when the number of IRQ ports was so limited.

Modern PCs, developed after the Linux+ objectives were released, have an Advanced Programmable Interrupt Controller (APIC), which supports up to 256 IRQ ports. Configured IRQs on a Linux system are listed in /proc/interrupts.

Input/Output Addresses

Every device requires a few bytes of RAM in one or more I/O addresses. Information stored in these addresses is exchanged with other parts of the computer, and these addresses are typically shown in hexadecimal notation. Configured I/O address ranges are listed in /proc/ioports.

Local Lingo

Hexadecimal notation   A numeral system that is configured to base-16; in other words, it uses the following 16 digits: 0, 1, 2, 3, 4, 5, 6, 7, 8, 9, a, b, c, d, e, and f.

Serial and COM Ports

While a COM port (short for communication port) is a Microsoft concept, it is a recognized shorthand for serial ports. Such ports use I/O addresses and IRQs; those listed in Table 11.2 are the standard associated with these ports. Many older PCs have two serial ports, which come in 9- and 25-pin versions, associated with so-called DB-9 and DB-25 connectors.

While additional COM ports are frequently used today, they are beyond the scope of the Linux+ exam. COM ports are not limited to external devices; they are common on internal modems. Linux administrators can customize serial port IRQ and I/O settings with the **setserial** command.

Parallel (LPT) Ports

Older PCs, including most of those available when the Linux+ objectives were released, have one or two parallel ports. While they can be used to connect external hard drives and more, they are commonly known as printer ports. As such, they are also known as LPT ports, based on the original Line Print Terminal printer. They are normally associated with IRQ and I/O addresses, as shown in Table 11.3.

ISA Cards

Older internal PC cards are based on the Industry Standard Architecture (ISA) specification. Most PCs today don't even have an ISA slot. The selected Linux distributions include the **isadump** and **isaset** commands to examine and set, respectively, the I/O addresses associated with ISA registers. Just remember, as ISA cards are relatively rare, these commands may not be installed by default.

TABLE 11.2	Standard COM Ports			
COM Port	**Serial Interface**	**Device File**	**IRQ**	**I/O Address**
COM1	Serial Port 1	/dev/ttyS0	4	03f8
COM2	Serial Port 2	/dev/ttyS1	3	02f8
COM3	Serial Port 1	/dev/ttyS2	4	03e8
COM4	Serial Port 2	/dev/ttyS3	3	02e8

TABLE 11.3   Standard Printer Ports

Printer Port	Device File	IRQ	I/O Address
LPT1	/dev/lp0 or /dev/parport0	7	0378
LPT2	/dev/lp1 or /dev/parport1	5	0278

PCI Cards

PCI cards may be the most common type of internal card on current PCs. But most importantly, they are connected directly to the motherboard; different PCI standards support peak transfer rates of 133 MBps and 266 MBps. The different PCI standards are no longer important on the Linux+ exam.

PCI devices are described in detail in the output to the **lspci** command. As shown in Figure 11.1, PCMCIA cards, as shown by the CardBus controller, communicate through the PCI bus. (PCMCIA is short for the Personal Computer Memory Card Interface Association.) More information on each PCI device is available with the **lspci -v** command and even more information is available with the **lspci -vv** command.

Local Lingo

PCI (Peripheral Component Interconnect)   A bus for communications with a motherboard, or peripheral cards which connect to that bus. There are several variations on PCI standards, most prominently PCI Express. For the purpose of the Linux+ exam, a PCI card is just a PCI card, no matter the standard, as they communicate through the same PCI bus.

```
[root@enterprise5hp ~]# lspci
00:00.0 Host bridge: ATI Technologies Inc RS200/RS200M AGP Bridge [IGP 340M] (rev 02)
00:01.0 PCI bridge: ATI Technologies Inc PCI Bridge [IGP 340M]
00:02.0 USB Controller: ALi Corporation USB 1.1 Controller (rev 03)
00:06.0 Multimedia audio controller: ALi Corporation M5451 PCI AC-Link Controller Aud
io Device (rev 02)
00:07.0 ISA bridge: ALi Corporation M1533/M1535 PCI to ISA Bridge [Aladdin IV/V/V+]
00:08.0 Modem: ALi Corporation M5457 AC'97 Modem Controller
00:09.0 Network controller: Intel Corporation PRO/Wireless 2200BG Network Connection
(rev 05)
00:0a.0 CardBus bridge: O2 Micro, Inc. OZ601/6912/711E0 CardBus/SmartCardBus Controll
er
00:10.0 IDE interface: ALi Corporation M5229 IDE (rev c4)
00:11.0 Bridge: ALi Corporation M7101 Power Management Controller [PMU]
00:12.0 Ethernet controller: National Semiconductor Corporation DP83815 (MacPhyter) E
thernet Controller
01:05.0 VGA compatible controller: ATI Technologies Inc Radeon IGP 330M/340M/350M
[root@enterprise5hp ~]# 
```

FIGURE 11.1   The **lspci** command and PCI card information

Graphics Cards

There are two categories of graphics cards available. Accelerated Graphics Port (AGP) cards support 3-D acceleration, and originally had an advantage over PCI graphics cards. But now, PCI Express cards are becoming a more popular option. Graphics cards may also be embedded in the motherboard.

> **Travel Advisory**
>
> Drivers for some graphics cards are proprietary, and Linux drivers may not always be available from the card manufacturer. As it is difficult to "reverse engineer" hardware drivers, Linux connections to proprietary graphics cards are not always fully functional.

Module Management

Every hardware device needs a Linux driver. Many drivers are configured as loadable modules. The standard location for available modules is the /lib/modules/*a.b.c*/kernel/drivers directory, where *a.b.c* is the version number of the kernel, available as the output to the **uname -r** command. It's common to see the command embedded in the directory in back quotes, as described in the Chapter 3 section "Shell Command Management"; don't be surprised to see a command such as the following:

```
# ls /lib/modules/`uname -r`/kernel/drivers
```

Modules can be managed with commands such as **lsmod**, **insmod**, **rmmod**, and **modprobe**.

lsmod

Before installing a new driver, you should check to see if it is already installed with the **lsmod** command. Take a look at the following excerpt:

```
Module                   Size  Used by
lp                      23120  0
loop                    26640  10
parport_pc              38312  1
parport                 49292  2 lp,parport_pc
snd_via82xx             37544  1
snd_ac97_codec         114824  1 snd_via82xx
snd_seq_dummy           12548  0
snd_seq_oss             40704  0
snd_seq_midi_event      16640  1 snd_seq_oss
snd_seq                 63776  5
```

The Module column lists loaded modules. The Size column lists the amount of memory used by each driver, in bytes. The Used by column lists the number of programs currently using that driver. The final column, which has no title, could be called "Dependencies," as it lists other modules that depend on that driver. For example, the *lp* and *parport_pc* modules depend upon and can't be installed without the *parport* module.

insmod, rmmod, and modprobe

Closely related to **lsmod** are the **insmod** and **rmmod** commands. Just as **lsmod** lists loaded modules, **insmod** *module* inserts the noted module, assuming that module is available somewhere in the /lib/modules directory. Similarly, the **rmmod** *module* command removes the noted module.

As just described from the output to the **lsmod** command, some modules have dependencies. If you try to remove a single module with dependencies, **rmmod** refuses, with a message similar to the following:

```
# rmmod parport
ERROR: Module parport is in use by lp,parport_pc
```

So, to remove the module with dependencies, you would have to specify the module and its dependencies all at once:

```
# rmmod parport lp parport_pc
```

More efficient than **insmod** and **rmmod** is the **modprobe** command. It removes and installs modules with their dependencies—or at least tries to do so. When I try to remove the *parport* module with the **modprobe -r** (remove) command, I get the following message:

```
FATAL: Module parport is in use.
```

But it's sufficient to know that **insmod** *module* is functionally equivalent to **modprobe** *module*, and **rmmod** *module* is functionally equivalent to **modprobe** **-r** *module*.

Hardware Compatibility Lists

Hardware Compatibility Lists (HCLs) describe hardware that is known to work with Linux. The general Linux HCL, available at http://tldp.org/HOWTO/ Hardware-HOWTO/index.html, is just a starting point; it refers to other documents and websites. For example, more detail on compatible USB devices is available at www.linux-usb.org.

Most importantly, HCLs are maintained by the people behind each major distribution, and can be found on the distribution websites.

Objective 11.02 Diagnose Hardware Issues

There are a variety of hardware issues cited in the Linux+ objectives. To quote, objective 6.02 states: "Diagnose hardware issues using Linux tools (for example: /proc, disk utilities, **ifconfig**, /dev, live CD rescue disk, dmesg)."

To elaborate, the virtual files in the /proc directory provide highly detailed hardware information. Disk utilities can help address problems such as power failures. Commands such as **ifconfig** can help diagnose network hardware. Device files in the /dev directory support communication between Linux and hardware. Live CDs, used as rescue disks, can help diagnose problems when the Linux system is installed on a troubled hard drive. Finally, the **dmesg** command lists hardware-related kernel messages during the boot process.

Hardware Detected in /proc

The variety of hardware and channels loaded into the /proc directory can tell you a lot about what hardware is installed and detected on Linux. For example, information on the CPU is available in the /proc/cpuinfo file. Some important /proc files and directories are listed in Table 11.4.

Many subdirectories in /proc are numbers, specifically PID numbers, which provide in-depth information on each active process. Details are beyond the scope of the Linux+ exam.

Using Disk Utilities

After power is cut on many nonjournaling filesystems, the **fsck** command is used to check the integrity of the filesystem. If you ever suspect problems with a

TABLE 11.4   Key /proc Files and Directories

/proc File or Directory	Description
acpi/	ACPI settings
asound/	Sound hardware information
bus/	PCI and USB connected device information
cpuinfo	Detected CPUs
dma	Active DMA channels
ide/	Connected drive settings
interrupts	IRQs
iomem	I/O memory addresses
mounts	Mounted directories
net/	A variety of network settings, including IP Forwarding

hard drive, such as errors when reading a disk, the **fsck** and **badblocks** commands can help.

But if you ever need to run these commands on a partition, unmount it first with a command like **umount /dev/hda2**. Otherwise, you might see a variation on the following message:

```
/dev/hda2 is mounted.

WARNING!!!  Running e2fsck on a mounted filesystem may cause
SEVERE filesystem damage.

Do you really want to continue (y/n)? no

check aborted.
```

If you accidentally continue this process while a filesystem is mounted, **fsck** does things that make the data on that filesystem unreadable. Similar consequences can come from the use of the **badblocks** command. So if you ever need to run either of these commands on a partition, unmount it first!

But it's not possible to unmount a top-level root directory filesystem after booting.

One alternative that allows the use of the **fsck** or **badblocks** command on a top-level root directory is with a Live CD, which loads a complete version of Linux without mounting any local hard drive partitions.

Using a Live CD as a Rescue Disk

As there is no standard for rescue disks, or even Live CDs (or Live DVDs) for the selected distributions, detailed knowledge of rescue disks or Live CD/DVDs is not required for the Linux+ exam. However, you do need to know the basics on how a Live CD can be used to rescue a system. By definition, a Live CD loads a fully functional version of Linux. The basic steps are as follows:

1. Boot Linux from the Live CD. The computer should load a fully functional version of Linux from the CD.

2. Run required commands from the Live CD, such as **fsck** to fix partitions. Of course, there are as many variations as there are potential problems.

3. Exit from the Live CD and try the installed Linux system again.

Unless you need special tools available only on a Live CD, it's better to use a rescue disk or mode provided by the distribution. For example, a rescue disk is available from the first Red Hat/Fedora installation CD; typing **linux rescue** at the boot prompt initiates the rescue mode for that distribution.

Travel Advisory

It seems as if just about every modern distribution has a Live CD. I prefer the Knoppix Live DVD, as it has a wide variety of tools that can rescue and back up troubled hard drives.

Network Hardware

Network hardware is more than just variations on Ethernet cards. Any physical device that supports network communication is network hardware. Even the lowly telephone modem is also network hardware. Just as administrators can control an Ethernet card with a command like **ifconfig eth0**, administrators can control a modem with a command like **ifconfig ppp0**.

In fact, you can change the hardware channels associated with a card with the **ifconfig** command. On pre-APIC systems, which had only 16 IRQ channels, IRQ conflicts were common. The following command assigns IRQ 10 to the first Ethernet card:

```
# ifconfig eth0 irq 10
```

If the Ethernet card with a direct connection to an ISP has to be replaced, you may need to give it the hardware address of the old card, in hexadecimal notation. For example, the following command assigns the noted hardware address:

```
# ifconfig eth0 hw ether ab:01:cd:02:ef:03
```

Local Lingo

MAC Address   Network card hardware addresses are also known as MAC addresses. MAC is short for Media Access Control.

Some hardware has characteristics of both an Ethernet card and a telephone modem. One example is DSL, or Digital Subscriber Lines, which is most closely associated with high-speed Internet over telephone wires. Such connections are implemented with Point-to-Point Protocol (PPP) over Ethernet (PPPoE), which itself is also a TCP/IP network protocol.

Exam Tip

Recognize that PPPoE is the common network protocol for DSL connections to a Linux system.

Hardware Detection Commands

There are a variety of hardware detection commands available. Most are distribution specific, such as Red Hat's **system-config-*** utilities and SUSE's YaST. But there are a few generic commands available that show detected hardware, as listed and described in Table 11.5. Not all of these commands are available on all selected distributions, but because they're not distribution specific, they're fair game for the Linux+ exam.

As described earlier in the "Describe Common Hardware Components" section, the **lspci** command is especially useful for getting information on PCI hardware.

With one exception, the tools in Table 11.5 just list hardware already detected. The **alsaconf** command starts a generic tool, shown in Figure 11.2, that detects sound cards.

As Red Hat/Fedora uses its own configuration tool for sound cards, **alsaconf** is not available for that distribution. However, it also uses the **alsactl** command to store and restore sound card settings from the /etc/asound.state configuration file. You can do it yourself with the **alsactl store** and **alsactl restore** commands, respectively.

Exam Tip

The **alsaconf** command detects sound cards, and the **alsactl** command controls sound card configurations.

Reviewing Device Files

Device files represent the way Linux communicates with many hardware components. Every component is associated with some device file in the /dev/ directory. Typical device file examples are shown in Table 11.6.

TABLE 11.5   Hardware Detection Commands

Detection Command	Description
alsactl	Detects sound cards
lshal	Lists hardware detected through the Linux hardware abstraction layer (HAL)
lsmod	Lists loaded modules, including hardware modules
lspci	Lists detected PCI hardware
lspcmcia	Displays detected PC Card hardware, starting with the controller
lsusb	Shows USB busses and hardware

```
                    ALSA  CONFIGURATOR
                         v1.0.4

                   This script is a configurator for
            Advanced Linux Sound Architecture (ALSA) driver.

          If ALSA is already running, you should close all sound
          apps now and stop the sound driver.
          alsaconf will try to do this, but it's not 100% sure.



                            <Ok>
```

FIGURE 11.2 **alsaconf** detects sound cards.

If a hardware component is missing and an expected device file is not there, Linux may have trouble detecting that component. For example, if you have a telephone modem, it should have a /dev/modem device file soft linked to the actual port, such as /dev/ttyS0. If the modem is not detected, the /dev/modem device file probably does not exist or isn't properly linked to the actual port.

Reviewing dmesg Output

The **dmesg** command lists the kernel ring buffer. As a command, it prints out boot messages. Hardware detection is part of the boot process. The information is also available as a log file, in /var/log/dmesg. It is primarily focused on the hardware detection part of the boot process. As shown in Figure 11.3, the **dmesg** command displays a variety of hardware information, such as the RAM map, DMA information, and more.

TABLE 11.6 Example Device Files

Device File	Hardware
/dev/hda	IDE drive
/dev/sda	SCSI or SATA drive
/dev/audio	Sound card device
/dev/bus/usb/*	USB devices
/dev/cdrom	Soft link from a CD/DVD drive
/dev/modem	Soft link from a detected telephone modem
/dev/mouse	Soft link from a detected mouse; options include /dev/input/mice and /dev/psaux
/dev/parport1	First printer port
/dev/ttyS0	First COM port

```
Linux version 2.6.20-2925.9.fc7xen (kojibuilder@xenbuilder1.fedora.redhat.com) (
gcc version 4.1.2 20070502 (Red Hat 4.1.2-12)) #1 SMP Tue May 22 09:29:36 EDT 20
07
Command line: ro root=/dev/sdb2 rhgb quiet
BIOS-provided physical RAM map:
 Xen: 0000000000000000 - 00000000741d0000 (usable)
Entering add_active_range(0, 0, 475600) 0 entries of 256 used
end_pfn_map = 475600
Entering add_active_range(0, 0, 475600) 0 entries of 256 used
Zone PFN ranges:
  DMA             0 ->    475600
  DMA32      475600 ->    475600
  Normal     475600 ->    475600
early_node_map[1] active PFN ranges
    0:        0 ->    475600
On node 0 totalpages: 475600
  DMA zone: 6502 pages used for memmap
  DMA zone: 1099 pages reserved
  DMA zone: 467999 pages, LIFO batch:31
  DMA32 zone: 0 pages used for memmap
  Normal zone: 0 pages used for memmap
DMI 2.3 present.
ACPI: RSDP (v000 VIAK8M                        ) @ 0x00000000000f7720
:█
```

FIGURE 11.3   The **dmesg** command displays hardware information.

Other hardware items returned by the **dmesg** command include the power management setting (whether it be ACPI or APM), detected CPUs, monitor and graphics card, PS/2 controllers, RAM, PCI settings, parallel ports, USB ports, IEEE 1394 ports, hard and optical drives, network cards, and more.

If you're not sure if Linux has detected some local hardware component, use the **grep** command to filter the output. For example, to review detected CPUs, run the following command:

```
# dmesg | grep CPU
```

Excerpts from that output on my dual core system include

```
Initializing CPU#0
Initializing CPU#1
```

Kernel Hardware Boot Parameters

If there are problems with some hardware components, it's possible to disable them during the boot process. Doing so involves including the right parameter on the kernel command line. While the method for accessing the boot options varies, the boot parameter you add is the same. Several common boot parameters are listed in Table 11.7.

TABLE 11.7	Kernel Boot Parameters

Kernel Boot Parameter	Description
1	Boots into runlevel 1, also known as single-user mode; synonymous with **single**
mem=xyzM	Tells the kernel that the system has the noted amount of RAM
noacpi	Disables ACPI; synonymous with **acpi=off**
noapm	Disables APM; synonymous with **apm=off**
nosmp	Disables symmetric multiprocessing; commonly associated with problems with multiple CPUs and related kernels

Travel Advisory

Depending on distribution, if you're using the GRUB bootloader, kernel hardware boot parameters may be included in the boot menu Boot Options or Kernel Arguments. Distribution-specific methods aren't covered on the Linux+ exam.

 **Objective 11.03** # Understand Hardware Power Management

There are two basic standards for hardware power management: Advanced Power Management (APM) and the Advanced Configuration and Power Interface (ACPI). Current Linux distributions conform to the ACPI standard. Both standards were available when the current Linux+ objectives were released.

Working with Advanced Power Management

APM was not obsolete when the current Linux+ objectives were released. In Linux, APM was implemented with the **apmd** daemon, and was primarily used to monitor laptop batteries. When **apmd** is active, battery data is stored in the /proc/apm file and may be confirmed by the **apm** command, which leads to output similar to

```
AC on-line, battery status high: 90% (2:31)
```

APM was used when the Linux implementation of power management was less than complete. But various APM settings related to batteries and system responses such as suspend could be configured in the /etc/sysconfig/apm configuration file.

Managing the Advanced Configuration and Power Interface

Linux monitors a wide variety of data with ACPI, which can be reviewed in various /proc/acpi files and subdirectories. For example, if CPU throttling is active, associated settings (for the first CPU or CPU core) can be found in the /proc/acpi/processor/CPU0/throttling file. Temperatures are updated regularly in the /proc/acpi/thermal_zone/THRM/temperature file.

The way ACPI handles the power button is a bit tricky, because the selected Linux distributions now all use different configuration files, all in the /etc/acpi/events/ directory. When the Linux+ objectives were released, the ACPI settings were standardized in the sample.conf configuration file.

If you have trouble with ACPI, it can disabled during the boot process by adding the **acpi=off** directive to the kernel command line.

Exam Tip

Be aware that when the Linux+ objectives were released, ACPI actions related to the power button were governed by the now obsolete /etc/acpi/events/sample.conf configuration file.

Objective 11.04

Identify and Configure Removable System Hardware

There are three major categories of removable system hardware listed in the Linux+ objectives: PC Cards, USB devices, and IEEE 1394 devices. These are all fairly high-speed devices, and can even support connections to higher-speed networks.

Other removable system hardware includes parallel-port drives, which connect to the parallel port normally associated with older printers. As transfer speed to these drives is limited to 115 Kbps by the serial bus, parallel port drives are essentially obsolete.

PC Cards

The PC Card category encompasses 16- and 32-bit PCMCIA cards. Current Linux distributions all configure 32-bit PCMCIA cards, configuring the socket with the *cardbus* driver module. It includes adapter settings for 16-bit cards. Older versions of the PCMCIA socket used modules such as i82365 and especially yenta_socket.

PC Cards were once controlled with the **cardctl** utility, now superseded by the **pccardctl** utility. Common options identify inserted cards and, more importantly, can warn Linux that you're about to remove a card:

```
# cardctl eject
```

Modules associated with inserted cards are over and above those associated with the PCMCIA socket. More information on inserted cards may be available in the output to the **cardctl ident** (or **pccardctl ident**) command.

This section does not address the various PC Express Cards or smart card sockets associated with handheld devices such as Palm Pilots and cameras because they came into common use after the Linux+ objectives were released.

USB Devices

To some extent, USB ports have evolved into the universal port for external devices. To see what devices are detected on a local system, run the **lsusb** command. The following output shows a USB root hub as Device 001, a USB key as Device 002, and an external drive as Device 003:

```
Bus 001 Device 003: ID 0c0b:b001 Dura Micro, Inc. (Acomdata)
Bus 001 Device 002: ID 04e8:1623 Samsung Electronics Co., Ltd
Bus 001 Device 001: ID 0000:0000
```

USB 1.x devices can communicate at up to 12 MBps. USB 2.x devices can communicate at up to 480 MBps; they are also commonly used for networking as well as external hard drives. The **lspci** command can also provide more information. The relevant line indicates that this USB system conforms to the slower, 1.1 standard:

```
00:02.0 USB Controller: ALi Corporation USB 1.1 Controller (rev 03)
```

The USB standard suggests that with appropriate hubs, any computer can handle up to 127 devices connected through USB ports.

IEEE 1394 Devices

IEEE 1394 devices are designed for digital video connections. With the associated high-speed data transfer rate of up to 400 MBps, IEEE 1394 is also suitable and commonly used for connections to external hard drives.

IEEE 1394 storage devices connected to a Linux system require an sbp2 module, short for Serial Bus Protocol 2, which is an IEEE 1394 data transport protocol. Linux IEEE 1394 modules that can accommodate video systems include dv1394 and video1394.

When connected and detected by Linux, IEEE 1394 storage devices are set up as if they were SCSI devices, as shown in these lines from my /var/log/messages file:

```
Aug 31 14:22:36 localhost kernel: [17207454.816000] scsi2 : \
SCSI emulation for IEEE-1394 SBP-2 Devices
Aug 31 14:22:37 localhost kernel: [17207455.924000] ieee1394: \
sbp2: Logged into SBP-2 device
Aug 31 14:22:37 localhost kernel: [17207455.924000]       \
Vendor: WDC WD12  Model: 00BB-00DAA3       Rev:
```

> ### Local Lingo
> **IEEE 1394**   A standard of the Institute of Electrical and Electronics Engineers, more commonly known by the trade names FireWire (Apple) and iLink (Sony).

 # Identify and Configure Mass Storage Devices

Objective 11.05

Mass storage devices need to be identified by Linux, in appropriate device files, before they can be used. Hard drives (ATAPI, SCSI, and SATA), floppy drives, tape drives, flash memory devices, and CD/DVD (optical) drives are essentially the types listed in the Linux+ objectives. While there are more options for mass storage devices available, this book covers only those associated with the Linux+ exam.

Hard Drives

Three basic categories of hard drives are commonly installed on modern PCs. Traditional internal PC drives are known as IDE, ATAPI, or PATA drives. The latest PCs include hard drives built to the SATA standard. In contrast, drives commonly installed on servers are SCSI drives. These categories and acronyms are explained in the following subsections.

Traditional Internal PC Drives

Traditional internal PC drives are based on Integrated Drive Electronics (IDE), now known as the Advanced Technology Attachment (ATA) standard. On such

PCs, there are two IDE controllers, known as primary and secondary. Ribbon cables are connected to each controller. Older ribbon cables have 40 wires; higher-density cables with 80 wires were introduced with the Ultra DMA standard associated with 66 MBps transfer, UDMA/66, and have been continued with the current UDMA/133 standard.

Each ribbon can connect to one or two hard or CD/DVD drives. The drive attached to one connector is known as the master; the drive attached to the other connector is known as the slave. These drives are associated with Linux device files as described in Table 11.8.

Due to the introduction of SATA drives, described next, traditional internal PC drives are now known as Parallel ATA (PATA) drives. For more information on detected PATA drives on your system, try the **dmesg | grep hd** command. When I run it on my older laptop system, these are some of the messages I see, which show my hard and CD/DVD drives:

```
hda: IC25N060ATMR04-0, ATA DISK drive
hdc: QSI CD-RW/DVD-ROM SBW-241, ATAPI CD/DVD-ROM drive
```

Travel Advisory

Closely related acronyms for the same category of hard drive are Advanced Technology Attachment (ATA) and AT Attachment Packet Interface (ATAPI). With the advent of SATA hard drives, traditional internal PC hard drives are now commonly known as PATA, which is short for Parallel ATA drives.

SATA Drives

Serial ATA hard drives, known as SATA drives, are now in common use on modern laptop and desktop systems, but they post-date the release of the current Linux+ objectives. SATA device drive files are named like SCSI drive device files; in other words, the first SATA drive device file is /dev/sda, the second SATA drive device file is /dev/sdb, and so on. Except for device filenames and connectors, internal SATA drives are for our purposes identical to IDE and ATAPI drives.

TABLE 11.8	Traditional Drive Device Files	
Device File	**Controller**	**Connector**
/dev/hda	Primary	Master
/dev/hdb	Primary	Slave
/dev/hdc	Secondary	Master
/dev/hdd	Secondary	Slave

SCSI Drives

SCSI (Small Computer System Interface) drives are still common, especially on servers, under a wide variety of standards, in three categories: SCSI-1, SCSI-2, and SCSI-3. They can be controlled by an 8- or 16-bit bus, associated with 50- or 68-pin cables, respectively. All SCSI devices are controlled by a host adapter, connected in series. The last device in a SCSI series has a *terminator*, which identifies the end of a chain of devices.

The number of available SCSI devices is associated with the number on the bus; 16-bit devices are associated with 16 SCSI numbers, also known as Logical Unit Numbers (LUN). The number assigned to a device determines its priority. The highest-priority bus has a LUN of 7; the order of priority, from highest to lowest, is 7, 6, 5, 4, 3, 2, 1, 0, 15, 14, 13, 12, 11, 10, 9, 8.

The Linux device files associated with SCSI devices are based on their priority—the device with the first priority is associated with /dev/sda, the second with /dev/sdb, and so on.

External Hard Drives

Modern external hard drives are typically connected through either a USB or IEEE 1394 connection. Transfer speeds often exceed internal IDE/ATAPI/PATA hard drives. External hard drives with these connections are seen as SATA drives, with priorities after the internal drives. For example, my desktop system has two SATA hard drives, /dev/sda and /dev/sdb. When I connect an external drive for backups to the IEEE 1394 or USB port, that drive is designated as /dev/sdc.

Floppy Drives

Floppy drives, especially those that hold 1.44MB discs, were still in common use when the current Linux+ objectives were released. The first floppy drive on a Linux system is associated with the /dev/fd0 device file. When detected on my desktop, I see the following output to the **dmesg | grep fd0** command:

```
Floppy drive(s): fd0 is 1.44M
```

Tape Drives

Tape drives are frequently used for backups; specialized tape drives exist that can even transfer data at hundreds of terabytes (TB) per hour. Generally, when tape drives are detected on a Linux system, they are associated with device files such as /dev/st0. Common commands associated with tape drives include **tar**. Some of these commands are described in the Chapter 4 section "Back Up and Restore Data."

Flash Memory Devices

The most obvious example of a flash memory device is a USB key. Flash memory devices are "nonvolatile"; in other words, they do not depend on a power source to retain the information stored in their circuits. They also by and large do not include moving parts; standard hard drives with rotating discs are not flash memory devices.

Once connected to a Linux system, a flash memory device is seen as if it were any other storage device. The device files follow the SATA drive format; in other words, flash memory devices are associated with device filenames such as /dev/sda, /dev/sdb, and so on. Flash memory devices can be formatted and mounted just like any other hard drive. Just remember to apply the **umount** command to any mounted flash memory partitions before removing the device, or else data that you may have thought was written may be lost.

CD/DVD Drives

With respect to their device files, CD/DVD drives are essentially identical to internal hard drives. If a CD/DVD drive is connected to an ATAPI/PATA/IDE ribbon cable, it can be associated with the /dev/hda, /dev/hdb, /dev/hdc, or /dev/hdd device file. If it's connected to a SCSI or SATA cable, it can be associated with the /dev/sd$x$ device file, where x represents the priority of the device.

For CD/DVD PATA/IDE drives associated with the Linux 2.4 kernel, the SCSI emulation module, ide-scsi, is required to activate the drive as a writer. You may see this module in the boot loader configuration file with a directive such as the following in the GRUB configuration file, /boot/grub/grub.conf,

```
kernel /vmlinuz-2.4.22 ro root=/dev/hda2 hdc=ide-scsi
```

or the following directive in the LILO configuration file, /etc/lilo.conf:

```
append="hdc=ide-scsi"
```

CHECKPOINT

✔ **Objective 11.01: Describe Common Hardware Components** Required knowledge of PC hardware components goes beyond Linux, to the variety of connectors and hardware channels available. Most hardware communicates with Linux through kernel modules. Linux-compatible hardware is identified in Hardware Compatibility Lists (HCLs).

✔ **Objective 11.02: Diagnose Hardware Issues** Detected hardware and associated settings are often listed in /proc. Disk and network utilities, along with other commands, can help diagnose hardware issues. Detected hardware is listed in /var/log/dmesg.

✔**Objective 11.03: Understand Hardware Power Management** Two basic standards for hardware power management are Advanced Power Management (APM) and Advanced Configuration and Power Interface (ACPI).

✔**Objective 11.04: Identify and Configure Removable System Hardware** Removable system hardware can be installed and detached while a computer is running. Much of this hardware can be connected as PC Card, USB, and IEEE 1394 devices.

✔**Objective 11.05: Identify and Configure Mass Storage Devices** Linux works well with a variety of mass storage devices. Hard drives can be internal ATAPI/PATA, SATA, or SCSI. Other mass storage devices include floppy, tape, and CD/DVD drives.

REVIEW QUESTIONS

Before leaving for the next chapter, take a few minutes to go through these questions. While doing so, take in both the content and the question format. Understanding what to expect on the exam can increase your chances for success.

1. When booting a system with multiple CPUs, which of the following messages activates only one CPU when applied as a kernel message?
   A. onecpu
   B. nosmp
   C. noduo
   D. single

2. Which of the following commands gets information on the first IDE hard drive from the kernel ring buffer?
   A. kern | grep hda
   B. cat /var/log/messages | grep hda
   C. dmesg | grep hda
   D. dump /var/log/kern.log

3. On a system with a PATA or IDE hard drive, which of the following options provides information on whether DMA is enabled on that drive?
   A. /proc/ide/hda/settings
   B. /etc/ide/hda.conf
   C. /etc/ideinfo.conf
   D. hdparm -d1 /dev/hda

4. Which of the following hardware modules is associated with a PCMCIA card adapter?

   A. pccard

   B. yenta_socket

   C. cardctl

   D. pcmcia

5. Which of the following directories configures ACPI actions when users press the power button or close the lid on a laptop system?

   A. /etc/acpi

   B. /etc/acpi/events

   C. /proc/acpi/events

   D. /etc/sysconfig/acpi

6. Which of the following utilities can help configure the sound card on Linux?

   A. cardctl

   B. system-config-soundcard

   C. sndconfig

   D. alsactl

7. For systems with the Linux 2.4 kernel, which of the following modules is required to enable writing on a CD/DVD drive?

   A. scsi

   B. ide-scsi

   C. scsi-ide

   D. cdrw

8. Which of the following cable configurations is associated with the ATA/133 standard?

   A. 40 pins and 40 wires

   B. 40 pins and 80 wires

   C. 80 pins and 40 wires

   D. 80 pins and 80 wires

9. Which of the following hardware components is not normally associated with a DMA channel?

   A. Floppy drive

   B. Keyboard

   C. PATA hard drive

   D. Sound card

10. Which of the following directories has kernel-related ACPI settings that are loaded during run time?

   A. /etc/acpi/actions
   B. /etc/acpi/events
   C. /proc/acpi
   D. /proc/apm

REVIEW ANSWERS

1. **B**   The **nosmp** message, when applied to the kernel to the boot process, activates only one CPU.

2. **C**   The kernel ring buffer lists messages during the boot process, recorded in the /var/log/dmesg file, and can be listed with the **dmesg** command.

3. **A**   Settings associated with the hard drive, including whether DMA is enabled, are listed in /proc/ide/hda/settings. They can be changed with the **hdparm** command.

4. **B**   The yenta_socket module is one available Linux PCMCIA controller driver, which is a prerequisite for other PCMCIA cards. Other possible PCMCIA controller drivers include i82365 and cardbus.

5. **B**   Configuration options associated with ACPI settings are located in the /etc/acpi/events directory.

6. **D**   The **alsactl** utility is the generic utility that can help control the sound card configuration. The system-config-soundcard and sndconfig tools are only available for certain Red Hat releases.

7. **B**   The ide-scsi module is required on systems with Linux kernel 2.4 to enable writing on a CD/DVD drive.

8. **B**   The ATA 133 standard connects drives with a 40-pin, 80-wire ribbon cable. The 40 extra wires are all ground wires, necessary to enable higher transfer rates.

9. **B**   A DMA channel can be enabled for a floppy drive, a PATA hard drive, and a sound card. DMA channels are not normally associated with keyboards (though specialty keyboards which require direct memory access are certainly available).

10. **C**   The /proc/ directory includes kernel-related settings that are loaded when Linux boots, aka during "run time." Those settings related to ACPI are loaded in the /proc/acpi directory.

Appendixes

About the CD-ROM

Mike Meyers' Certification Passport CD-ROM Instructions

The CD-ROM included with this book comes complete with MasterExam and the electronic version of the book. With the Wine (Wine Is Not an Emulator) software, it's even possible to install MasterExam on the selected Linux distributions. Of course, the software is also easy to install on any Windows 98/NT/2000/XP/Vista computer.

> **Travel Advisory**
>
> While this appendix provides tips on how to make MasterExam function on Linux, there is no guarantee or warranty associated with said functionality. In fact, some of the fonts associated with MasterExam aren't recognized in some default Linux configurations, and could appear blank. No support will be provided for any such installation.

To register for a second, bonus MasterExam, simply click the Online Training link on the Main Page and follow the directions to the free online registration.

System Requirements

Full software installation requires 20MB of hard disk space and either Linux with a 2.6 kernel and Wine software or Windows 98 or higher and Internet Explorer 5.0 or above. If you need to install and compile the Wine software from source code, you may need 1GB of hard disk space or more. The electronic book requires Adobe Acrobat Reader or an equivalent Linux reader such as GPdf or KPDF.

Installing and Running Wine

Binary RPMs for three of the selected distributions are available from the Wine team at www.winehq.org/site/download. They're also available from the installation media on many Linux distributions, including openSUSE 10.2 and Mandriva 2007 Free. Basic instructions for installing RPMs are available in the Chapter 2 section "Perform Post-Installation Package Management."

If you're running a distribution for which a Wine RPM is not available, it's possible to download and install Wine from the source code. As there was no Wine RPM available on Turbolinux Celica, I demonstrate how to download and compile Wine from source code using that distribution with the following steps:

1. Download the tarball; the source cited at www.winehq.org is http://ibiblio.org/pub/linux/system/emulators/wine/.

2. The tarballs at the noted source are in tar.bz2 format, so they need to be unpacked with the **tar xjvf** command. For example, when I downloaded the wine-0.9.45.tar.bz2 package, I unpacked it with the following command (the **v** adds verbose output, which is useful for diagnosing errors). Substitute the version number of the downloaded wine tarball in this and the steps that follow.

   ```
   # tar xjvf wine-0.9.45.tar.bz2
   ```

3. This extracts the source code in the wine-0.9.45/ subdirectory. Navigate to that subdirectory with the following command:

   ```
   # cd wine-0.9.45
   ```

4. The instructions are available in the README file in this directory. The current instructions for this version suggest compiling by running the following command as a regular (not root) user. Be aware, this process required nearly 2GB of space when I installed it.

   ```
   $ tools/wineinstall
   ```

   You may see messages about other packages that need to be installed. This could easily raise the amount of space required to well over 2GB. The process takes some time. At some point, you'll be prompted for the root password.

5. When complete, continue on to the next set of instructions, which show how to install the LearnKey software in Linux using Wine.

Now that you have Wine installed, you can install and run MasterExam on a Linux system.

One alternative that uses Wine in a more user-friendly fashion is CrossOver Office, available from www.codeweavers.com.

Installing and Running MasterExam

On Linux, once Wine is installed, you should be able to install MasterExam using the following steps:

1. Open a GUI; MasterExam is a GUI-based tool.

2. Mount the CD; on some distributions, it's mounted automatically in the GNOME or KDE desktop environments, as confirmed in the output to the **mount** command. If you don't already see it mounted on a device such as /dev/cdrom, mount it with the following command as an administrative root user (some variations may be possible depending on the device associated with the CD/DVD drive and available directories):

   ```
   # mount /dev/cdrom /mnt
   ```

3. Open a console as a regular user, and run the following command (assuming the CD is mounted on the /mnt directory):

   ```
   $ wine /mnt/LaunchTraining.exe
   ```

4. Click the MasterExam link and follow the prompts.

On Microsoft Windows, if your computer CD-ROM drive is configured to AutoRun, the CD-ROM automatically starts when you insert the disc. From the opening screen, you may install MasterExam by clicking the MasterExam buttons. This begins the installation process and creates a program group named LearnKey. To run MasterExam, choose Start | Programs | LearnKey. If the AutoRun feature did not launch your CD, browse to the CD and click the LaunchTraining.exe icon. Then click the MasterExam link and follow the prompts.

Once MasterExam is installed, run the **/mnt/LaunchTraining.exe** command as the root user in Linux; or choose Start | Programs | LearnKey in Microsoft operating systems, and click the MasterExam link to access the exam.

If it isn't already expanded, click the plus sign next to Linux+ Certification Passport to show the Quiz and MasterExam options. If you select Quiz, you're prompted to choose the number of questions. If you select MasterExam, you're presented with a more realistic exam with the specified 98 questions and 90-minute time limit.

Due to font issues, the Quiz and MasterExam options may be blank in some Linux distributions. The Report button provides a historical record of exams taken, with associated scores. The Options button provides custom settings, which may also be blank in some Linux distributions. If that situation applies to you, review Figure A.1, from a Mandriva Linux 2007 Free installation.

In addition, some of the buttons in the exam may be obscured, as shown in Figure A.2, which illustrates the exam in Turbolinux. From left to right, the buttons are Prev (for Previous), Next, Jump To, Hint, Reference, Report, and Main.

Depending on the configuration, not all of the buttons will be visible. As you can see in Figure A.3, the buttons appear just fine in SUSE Linux.

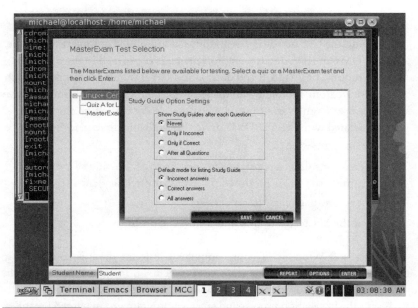

FIGURE A.1   MasterExam Test Selection in Mandriva Linux

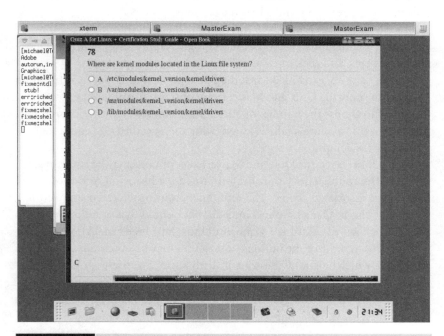

FIGURE A.2   MasterExam in Turbolinux

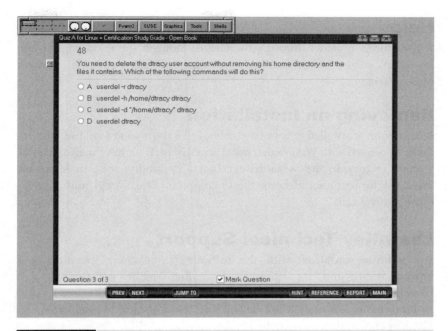

┌─────────────────┐
│ **FIGURE A.3** │   MasterExam in SUSE Linux
└─────────────────┘

MasterExam

MasterExam provides you with a simulation of the actual exam. The number of questions, the type of questions, and the time allowed are intended to be an accurate representation of the exam environment. You have the option to take an open-book exam, which includes hints, references, and answers; a closed-book exam; or the timed MasterExam simulation. When you launch MasterExam, a digital clock display appears in the upper-left corner of your screen. The clock continues to count down to zero unless you choose to end the exam before the time expires.

┌──┐
│ **Exam Tip** │
├──┤
│ Throughout the book, I've formatted commands, directives, and daemon names in │
│ bold. Unfortunately the MasterExam software supports only one font, and does │
│ not support bold or italic. So when you use MasterExam, you'll have to be extra │
│ careful when reading questions such as "Why is less more capable than more?" │
│ It refers to the additional features associated with the **less** command, relative to │
│ the **more** command, but there's no way to know from the font. Consider │
│ it an additional challenge; if you can recognize the command from the │
│ context without the benefit of bolding, you may be more ready than │
│ you think. │
└──┘

Help

A help file is provided through the Help button on the main page in the lower-left corner. Individual help features are also available through MasterExam.

Removing an Installation

MasterExam is installed to your hard drive. In Linux, if you've followed the defaults associated with Wine-based installation, MasterExam is installed in your home directory, in the .wine/drive_c/LearnKey subdirectory. In Microsoft Windows, for best results, choose Start | Programs | LearnKey | Uninstall to remove MasterExam.

LearnKey Technical Support

For technical problems with the software (installation, operation, and uninstallation) and for questions regarding online registration, visit www.learnkey.com or e-mail techsupport@learnkey.com.

Please note: LearnKey technical support does not include installations on Linux operating systems described in this appendix.

Content Support

For questions regarding the technical content of the electronic book or MasterExam, visit www.mhprofessional.com or e-mail customer.service@mcgraw-hill.com. For customers outside the 50 United States, e-mail international_cs@mcgraw-hill.com.

Career Flight Path

CompTIA Linux+ Certification generally serves as the base of origin for any number of career flight paths. Most people in the Linux community believe that CompTIA Linux+ Certification is the entry-level certification for Linux. That is consistent with CompTIA's literature, which suggests that Linux+ Certification requires 6 to 12 months of Linux experience. From CompTIA's Linux+ Certification, you have a number of certification options, depending on whether you want to focus more on a specific distribution or become a generalist in Linux administration. Take a look at these three programs in particular:

- Red Hat certifications
- Novell (SUSE) certifications
- Linux Professional Institute certifications

While there are other Linux certifications available, including SAIR (www.linuxcertification.org) and Brainbench (www.brainbench.com), they do not have the recognition, and therefore the cachet among hiring managers, of the other three.

Red Hat Certifications

There are several Red Hat certifications available. All of them use practical problems; in other words, expect to configure services and troubleshoot issues on a real Linux computer during the Red Hat exams. The available Red Hat exams, as of this writing, are listed here approximately in order of difficulty. For the latest information on Red Hat certifications and associated training programs, see www.redhat.com/training/.

Red Hat Certified Technician (RHCT)

The Red Hat Certified Technician (RHCT) exam, per the Red Hat site, "tests your abilities to set up and configure a Workstation and to eliminate common errors." It includes two sections: Troubleshooting and System Maintenance, and

Installation and Configuration. In the first section, RHCT candidates are presented with several problems, all of which must be solved. In the second section, RHCT candidates are told to install Red Hat Enterprise Linux, and configure it to certain criteria. As every topic on the RHCT exam is included on the RHCE exam, you can use RHCE training materials such as *RHCE Red Hat Certified Engineer Study Guide, Fifth Edition*, also published by McGraw-Hill and written by this author, to study for the RHCT exam. Red Hat also has its own prep course for the RHCT exam, RH133, available from the aforementioned Red Hat website.

Red Hat Certified Engineer (RHCE)

The Red Hat Certified Engineer (RHCE) exam includes every requirement on the RHCT exam. Per the Red Hat site, it also "tests configuration, security, and service troubleshooting." It includes the same two sections seen on the RHCT: Troubleshooting and System Maintenance, and Installation and Configuration. RHCE candidates must meet all RHCT requirements for those problems, and solve several more advanced problems befitting of an engineer certified on Linux. Naturally, you can use appropriate training materials such as *RHCE Red Hat Certified Engineer Study Guide, Fifth Edition*, also published by McGraw-Hill and written by this author. Red Hat also has its own prep course for the RHCT exam, RH300, available from the aforementioned Red Hat website. The course lasts four days, with the full-day exam given on the fifth day.

Red Hat Certified Security Specialist (RHCSS)

Before qualifying as a Red Hat Certified Security Specialist (RHCSS), you must already have a current RHCE. You then need to pass the following three practical exams:

- Red Hat Enterprise Security: Network Services (EX333)
- Red Hat Enterprise Directory Services and Authentication (EX423)
- Red Hat Enterprise SELinux Policy Administration (EX429)

These exams are associated with the Red Hat courses RHS333, RH423, and RHS429, respectively. Similarly to RH300, each of these courses lasts four days, with a full-day exam given on the fifth day.

Red Hat Certified Datacenter Specialist (RHCDS)

Red Hat just introduced the Red Hat Certified Datacenter Specialist (RHCDS) certification in late 2007. As described on the Red Hat website, it certifies that candidates have the "skills and knowledge necessary to build reliable, available, scalable, and manageable solutions in mission-critical datacenter environments." In a couple of ways, it's similar to the RHCSS. It requires the passing of three exams over and above the RHCE, including one of the same exams as that required for the RHCSS (EX423):

- Red Hat Enterprise Deployment, Virtualization, and Systems Management (EX401)
- Red Hat Enterprise Directory Services and Authentication (EX423)
- Red Hat Enterprise Clustering and Storage Management (EX436)

These exams are associated with the Red Hat courses RH401, RH423, and RH436, respectively. Similarly to RH300, each of these courses lasts four days, with a full-day exam given on the fifth day.

Red Hat Certified Architect (RHCA)
The Red Hat Certified Architect (RHCA) exam, as listed on the Red Hat website, shows that qualified candidates have proven skills required to design and manage a complete infrastructure for large, complex environments. It also has the RHCE as a prerequisite, and requires passing the following exams:

- Red Hat Enterprise Security: Network Services (EX333)
- Red Hat Enterprise Deployment, Virtualization, and System Management (EX401)
- Red Hat Enterprise Directory Services and Authentication (EX423)
- Red Hat Enterprise Clustering and Storage Management (EX436)
- Red Hat System Monitoring and Performance Tuning (EX442)

These exams are associated with the Red Hat courses RHS333, RH401, RH423, RH436, and RH442, respectively. You may note there is some overlap between the exam requirements for the RHCA, RHCDS, and RHCSS certifications.

Novell/SUSE Certifications
There are two major SUSE-based Linux certifications available: the Novell Certified Linux Professional (CLP) and the Novell Certified Linux Engineer (CLE). Exam versions are tied to releases of the SUSE Linux Enterprise distribution; currently there are exams available for SUSE Linux Enterprise Server versions 9 and 10.

Local Lingo
SUSE is a German acronym; it used to be SuSE until the company behind that distribution was purchased by Novell.

Novell Certified Linux Professional (CLP)

The Novell Certified Linux Professional (CLP) certification is described on the Novell training website at www.novell.com/training/certinfo/clp/. Per the description, it "validates to your current and potential employers that you have what it takes to begin your successful career as a Linux administrator." Based on SUSE Linux Enterprise Server 10, Novell offers the following three courses to prepare for the associated exams:

- SUSE Linux Enterprise Server 10 Fundamentals (3071)
- SUSE Linux Enterprise Server 10 Administration (3072)
- SUSE Linux Enterprise Server 10 Advanced Administration (3073)

Functionally similar (in my personal opinion) to the RHCT, the CLP exam is a practical exam, testing real-world skills on an actual Linux system.

Novell Certified Linux Engineer (CLE)

The Novell Certified Linux Engineer (CLE) certification is described on the Novell training website at www.novell.com/training/certinfo/cle/. Per the description, it "proves engineer-level skills for managers or architects of enterprise networks." Novell offers two courses to prepare for the associated exams:

- SUSE Linux Enterprise Server 10 Networking Services (3074)
- SUSE Linux Enterprise Server 10 Security (3075)

Functionally similar (in my personal opinion) to the RHCE, the CLE exam is a practical exam, testing real-world skills on an actual Linux system.

Linux Professional Institute (LPI)

The Linux Professional Institute (LPI) has three levels of certifications, which for the most part are distribution neutral. In other words, if you take the LPI exams, expect to see problems associated with both the RPM distributions associated with Linux+ and Debian-based distributions. The actual program is known as the Linux Professional Institute Certification (LPIC) program. Certifications are available at three levels: LPIC-1, LPIC-2, and LPIC-3. There is also an allied Ubuntu Certified Professional (UCP) exam. The basic requirements are listed at www.lpi.org/en/lpi/english/certification/the_lpic_program.

The LPI exams are more than just multiple choice exams. When I took the LPI exams, I encountered a number of fill in the blank questions, which tested my knowledge of commands and configuration directives beyond even what I saw on the RHCE exam.

LPI Level 1

Candidates need to pass two exams, LPI 101 and LPI 102, to gain the LPIC-1 certification credential, known as the Junior Level Linux Professional. As listed at the aforementioned website, the requirements suggest that a qualified LPIC-1 professional can work at the Linux command line, perform easy maintenance tasks, and install and configure a workstation.

To qualify as an Ubuntu Certified Professional (UCP), a candidate needs to pass both LPI 101 and LPI 102 exams as well as the LPI 199 exam, dedicated to Ubuntu Linux. For more information, see www.ubuntu.com/training/certificationcourses/professional.

LPI Level 2

Candidates for the LPIC-2 credential first need to pass the LPIC-1 exams. There are two additional exams associated with LPI Level 2, LPI 201 and LPI 202. Certification to this level, per the LPI website, qualifies the candidate as an Advanced Level Linux Professional who can administer a small to medium-sized site and plan, implement, maintain, keep consistent, secure, and troubleshoot a small mixed (MS, Linux) network.

Qualifications not tested include supervisory skills, as well as skills required to advise management on automating the network and purchasing new equipment.

LPI Level 3

Candidates for the LPIC-3 credential need to also pass the LPIC-1 and LPIC-2 exams. There are two additional exams associated with LPI Level 3. One is a Core exam (LPI 301), taken by LPIC-3 candidates. As of this writing, there is only one other exam available, LPI 302 Specialty (Mixed Environment). Several additional, optional exams are in the works, so it is best to refer to the aforementioned LPI website for the latest information. A candidate who qualifies for the LPIC-3 certification is considered to be a Senior Level Linux Professional.

Installing CentOS-5, Step by Step

This appendix is straightforward. It illustrates the steps required to install CentOS-5, which can be used to study for the Linux+ exam. CentOS-5 is a "rebuild" of Red Hat Enterprise Linux 5, which means it's built from essentially the same source code. The difference is that CentOS-5 does not use Red Hat trademarks.

As Red Hat is the most popular of the selected distributions, and possibly the most useful for future employment, it's useful to learn this distribution. Because CentOS is built from the same Red Hat source code, it provides the same experience with the Red Hat distribution without the cost associated with a subscription. Many enterprises (in my understanding, primarily small and medium-sized businesses) use CentOS and hire Linux professionals (like yourself?) to administer those systems.

Download CentOS-5

Before downloading CentOS, review the website at www.centos.org. The CentOS team strongly encourages downloading from a list of public mirrors, available at www.centos.org/modules/tinycontent/index.php?id=13. Doing so reduces costs for this community-based distribution, and besides, downloads from geographically closer mirror sites are usually faster. Available peer-to-peer download options such as BitTorrent and Jigdo are beyond the scope of this book.

Downloads of various Linux distributions, including CentOS, are based on large files with .iso extensions. These files can be burned to CD/DVDs using standard Linux or even Microsoft burning applications. Alternatively, if you're running VMware (as I am), you can use the ISO file directly in the virtual machine. For example, I've downloaded the CentOS-5.0-i386-bin-DVD.iso file and opened it directly from my VMware virtual machine, as shown in the Use ISO Image text box in Figure C.1.

Install CentOS-5

I assume you already know how to boot your system directly from a CD/DVD, which can be configured from the BIOS menu, or often from a menu available when booting modern PCs by pressing a key such as ESC or F12.

Travel Advisory

Even if free space is available on the local system, don't use this installation method (or any installation method) without a reliable backup.

Once you've loaded the CD or DVD (or configured the ISO file on a VMware virtual machine), and booted from that media, you'll see a boot screen. One op-

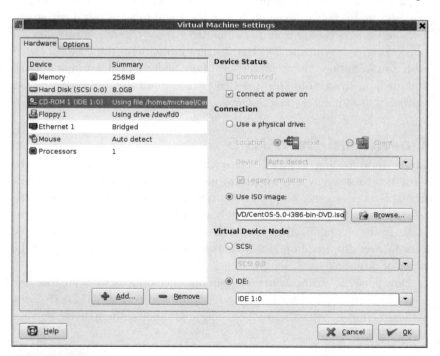

FIGURE C.1   VMware can handle ISO files.

tion is to press ENTER and type **text** for text mode installation, which is compatible with the broadest range of hardware. If you do nothing, the default GUI
installation starts automatically after 60 seconds.

Travel Advisory

Some hardware requires installation in text mode. For example, I had
to install Red Hat Enterprise Linux 5 on my wide-screen laptop
in text mode. The associated steps are similar to those described
in this appendix.

The installation options described here are generally the simplest available,
which is all that's required for the Linux+ exam. To become a real Linux expert,
we encourage you to explore all of the options. If you're dual booting with another operating system such as Microsoft Windows, you may need to create
space and an empty partition; we do not explain that process in this book.

Travel Advisory

If you have a genuine copy of Red Hat Enterprise Linux 5, the
required steps are almost identical to those shown here (though,
due to different colors and icons, many screenshots appear quite
different).

Once the default installation starts, take the following steps:

1. The first thing you see after the default installation starts is the following
   screen that allows you to check the integrity of the CD or DVD disc.
   You can switch between options by pressing the TAB key. I recommend
   that you highlight OK and press the SPACEBAR to allow the check.

2. Choose Test to start the check.

3. When the test is complete, you should see a "The media check PASSED" message. If you do, click OK. Otherwise, you may need to redownload and re-create the CD/DVD, and start over.

4. If there is another CD/DVD, repeat Steps 2 and 3; otherwise, select Continue.

5. You should see a CentOS 5 screen. Click Next to continue.

6. Note the variety of languages available for installation. Select a language and click Next to proceed.

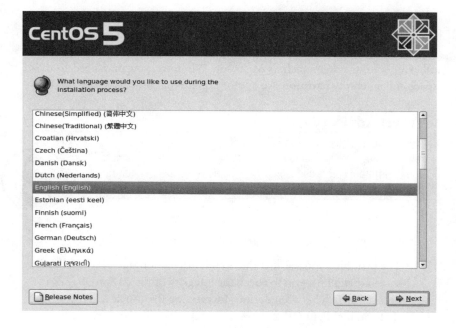

7. Select a keyboard, and click Next to continue.

8. If the hard drive is blank, you'll see a note to the effect that the partition table is unreadable, and suggesting that the drive will be initialized. Click OK if the drive is blank; otherwise click No, which starts a search for existing installations.

9. For the screen shown next, I assume you can select Remove All
    Partitions On Selected Drives And Create Default Layout in the top
    drop-down text box. Also select the Review And Modify Partitioning
    Layout check box, and click Next to proceed.

    If you don't select the Review And Modify Partitioning Layout check
    box, a default partition and a bootloader configuration are selected; in
    that case, skip to Step 13.

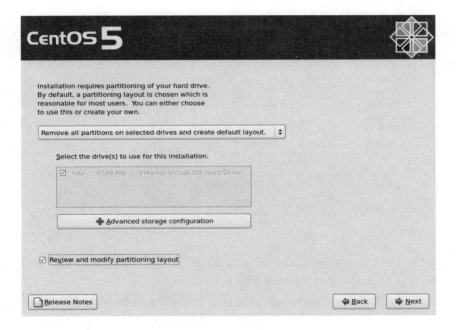

10. When prompted, accept the warning to remove partitions (and
    associated data) by clicking Yes.

11. Review the partition layout—as configured in the Red Hat–developed
    tool known as Disk Druid. Note that there are separate areas for the
    /boot directory, swap space, and the top-level root directory. Unless

you have a reason to do otherwise, leave the configuration as is, and click Next to proceed.

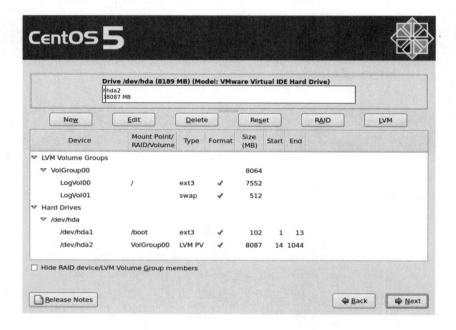

12. Note the options associated with the GRUB bootloader, make any desired changes, and click Next to continue.

13. Look at how you can configure local network settings. Note the options associated with DHCP configuration for IPv4 and IPv6 addressing, manual hostname assignment, and so-called Miscellaneous Settings associated with a network gateway and DNS addresses, which might also be assigned by a DHCP server. Make any desired changes and click Next to move forward.

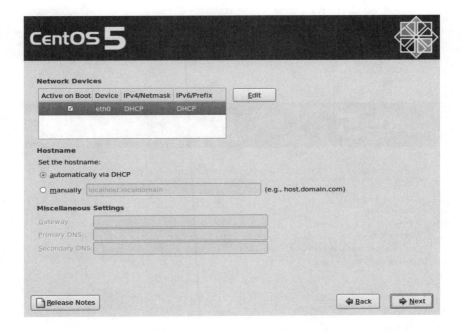

14. Note the Time Zone screen, and select the one associated with your geographic location. The System Clock Uses UTC option should be checked unless there's another operating system such as Microsoft Windows on the same system in a dual boot configuration. Click Next to continue.

15. Type in the same root password in the two cited text boxes to confirm it's the password that you intend to use, and click Next to proceed.

16. Review the available options for generic groups of software packages. The options shown here happen to differ from those associated with Red Hat Enterprise Linux 5, but those differences aren't significant for the Linux+ exam. If you want to review and select detailed packages,

select Customize Now. For these instructions, select Customize Later and click Next to continue. The installation program takes a bit of time to check dependencies for any additional packages that might need installation.

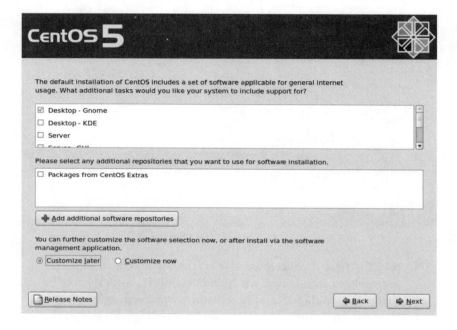

17. When ready to start the actual installation process, click Next.

18. After the installation process is complete (which can take more than a few minutes, especially if you're installing from multiple CDs), you get a final screen where you can click Reboot to finish the process and start Linux for the first time.

CentOS-5 (and related distributions such as Red Hat) don't include some configuration steps commonly performed during the installation process, such as the creation of regular user accounts.

Testing Linux with VMware

When studying for a certification exam, it's helpful to have a virtual machine. You can test commands and more on that machine without affecting actual production systems. With enough RAM and hard drive memory, you can even set up virtual machines for each of the selected Linux distributions. To that end, this appendix describes how to configure VMware Server as a virtual machine, ready for installation of one of the selected distributions.

VMware Server is freely downloadable for noncommercial use, and installing it on Microsoft Windows and various Linux distributions is a straightforward process. The interface is easily customizable with a variety of hardware components.

In contrast, Xen (as of this writing) can be run only on Linux. It is the default virtualization tool associated with the latest Red Hat and SUSE distributions. This may change, due to agreements between XenSource and Microsoft. But for now, Xen requires a specialized kernel and, in some cases, a so-called "paravirtualized" kernel, which is available for at least Red Hat and SUSE distributions. As this is well beyond the experience associated with Linux+ exam candidates, I do not describe how to create a Xen-based virtual machine here. For more information, see the downloads available for *RHCE Red Hat Certified Engineer Study Guide, Fifth Edition*, at www.mhprofessional.com.

Local Lingo

Paravirtualization A virtualization technique that is effectively simpler than the full virtualization often associated with VMware. It does not require emulation of all regular PC hardware.

While there are several VMware products available, I recommend the use of VMware Server, because it is freely available, supports hardware customization, allows practice with various Linux installation programs, and includes "snapshots," which allow you to restore a working configuration in case you forget the changes you've made.

Before installing VMware Server, make sure there's sufficient RAM and hard drive space on the local system. RAM is required not only for the operating system on the virtual machine, but also to continue to run the local host operating system. Hard drive space is required for the large files used to simulate virtual machine hard drive files. In my experience, 4GB is sufficient for the selected distributions.

Travel Advisory

I have a multiboot system on my laptop, with Ubuntu Linux, Red Hat Enterprise Linux, and Microsoft Windows XP. I store my VMware Virtual Machine files on a VFAT partition, accessible to both Linux and Microsoft operating systems. I can run the same virtual machines from any of the operating systems on my laptop.

The steps described in this appendix are basic, and may not answer all of your questions. For more information, VMware has a knowledge base and community discussion forum available at www.vmware.com/support/.

Acquiring VMware Server

1. You can get VMware Server from www.vmware.com. With free registration, VMware provides needed serial numbers, which enable full functionality. Follow these steps (as of this writing) to register and download VMware Server: Navigate to the Download VMware Server page at www.vmware.com/download/server/. Click the "register for your free serial number(s)" link, fill in the required information, and click Submit.

2. Print out the serial number(s) automatically generated from the website.

3. Return to the Download VMware Server page, click the Download Now button for the latest version of VMware Server, accept the license agreement (assuming you're willing), and then download the package as an EXE file for Microsoft Windows, as an RPM for the selected

distributions, or as a "tarball" in tar.gz format for other Linux distributions.

I'll describe how I've installed VMware Server on my Microsoft Windows and Ubuntu Dapper Drake (6.06) systems. For your information, when writing this book, I installed Red Hat Enterprise Linux 5, openSUSE 10.2, Mandriva 2007, and Turbolinux Celica on individual VMware Server virtual machines on an Ubuntu Dapper Drake system.

Whether you install the RPM or unpack the tarball, you'll get a directory with the installation files you need. Then you'll be able to install using the same vmware-install.pl script. If you're installing VMware Server on Microsoft Windows, read the section that follows. If you're installing VMware Server on Ubuntu Dapper Drake, skip to the corresponding section.

Installing VMware Server on Microsoft Windows

As CompTIA expects candidates for the Linux+ exam to have 6 to 12 months of experience, many candidates may still be using Microsoft Windows, at least part time. It may be the only operating system available to many candidates at work or home. In this section, I demonstrate the installation of VMware Server on Microsoft Windows XP Media Center, with Service Pack 2. I have not tested the installation of VMware Server on any other Microsoft operating system, so the steps may vary.

To install VMware Server on Microsoft Windows, take the following steps:

1. Navigate to the directory where the VMware Server executable was downloaded and run that VMware Server file.

2. The executable should, after a bit of time, start the Installation Wizard. Click Next, read and accept the license agreement (assuming you really do want to install VMware Server), and click Next again.

3. Unless you're strapped for disk space, select Complete for a complete installation of all VMware Server and Client components, and click Next.

4. If you see a warning about the VMware Management Interface being supported only on Server operating systems, just make a note of it and click OK (which is the only choice available).

5. Accept the default location for VMware Server installation, or change it if a different location is preferred. If you've installed different VMware products, you may want to install VMware Server in a different directory. Otherwise, click Next.

6. Click Install to begin the installation. The process may take a few minutes. Click Finish when prompted.

7. Now you should be able to open the installed VMware. Click Start | All Programs | VMware | VMware Server | VMware Server Console.

8. To continue, start with Step 2 of "Preparing VMware for Linux Installation," later in the appendix. The steps will be the same.

Installing VMware Server on Ubuntu Dapper Drake

This section shows how to install VMware Server on an Ubuntu Dapper Drake system, but if you'd rather install VMware Server on one of the selected distributions, first apply the **rpm -i** command to the downloaded RPM file, with a command like **rpm -i VMware-server-1.03-44356.i386.rpm**, and then start with Step 3. This section assumes that you've installed the latest kernel and source code or kernel development packages with kernel modules. It also assumes that you've installed the GNU C Compiler package for your distribution. Otherwise, there are hints in these steps. You should know how to open another virtual console to run other commands as needed.

To install VMware Server on my Ubuntu Dapper Drake system, I took the following steps:

1. I downloaded the tarball. For this example, I've downloaded the file, VMware-server-1.03-44356.tar.gz, to the /tmp directory.

2. While not covered elsewhere in this book, the way to unpack an archive from a tarball with the .tar.gz extension is with the **tar xzvf** command, which extracts (**x**), unzips (**z**), verbosely (**v**) in case of errors, from the filename which follows:

   ```
   # tar xzvf /tmp/VMware-server-1.03-44356.tar.gz
   ```

3. This should add the **vmware-config.pl** script to the /usr/bin directory. You need the administrative (root) password to run the script from a regular account with the following command:

   ```
   $ sudo vmware-config.pl
   ```

4. Read and accept the end user license agreement. VMware then stops any related running processes, with messages similar to

   ```
   Making sure services for VMware Server are stopped.

   Stopping VMware services:
       Virtual machine monitor                    [  OK  ]
   ```

5. In the next step, VMware runs GTK+ libraries. You can then choose an icons directory; the default is usually good enough, as it is a standard for most Linux distributions:

```
Configuring fallback GTK+ 2.4 libraries.

In which directory do you want to install the mime type icons?
[/usr/share/icons]
```

6. In the step which follows, I recommend that you accept the defaults for the applications directory for desktop entries, and pixmaps icons. However, if you see the following message, you don't have the GCC compiler installed:

```
None of the pre-built vmmon modules for VMware Server is
suitable for your running kernel.  Do you want this program
to try to build the vmmon module for your system (you need
to have a C compiler installed on your system)? [yes]
```

Install the gcc package, associated with the gcc RPM or Debian-based gcc-*.deb package (for Ubuntu); otherwise, the following steps won't work. You can do so in a different terminal before continuing. With a network connection (and a separate command-line console), the command for current Red Hat/Fedora distributions would be **yum install gcc**; the corresponding command for Ubuntu would be **apt-get install gcc**.

7. If and when the gcc package is installed, you'll see the following message:

```
Using compiler "/usr/bin/gcc". Use environment variable
CC to override.
```

8. You may also need kernel source code, normally installed in the /usr/src/linux directory. If there's nothing in this directory on your system, you may see the following message:

```
What is the location of the directory of C header files
that match your running kernel? [/usr/src/linux/include]
```

If you need to install the source code, it's often easiest to install a package such as kernel-devel (for Red Hat/Fedora) or linux-headers (for Ubuntu). Assuming an active network connection, this is possible in a second terminal using a command like **yum install kernel-devel** or **apt-get install linux-headers**. You may need to specify the same version number as the running kernel. If it works, when you continue the VMware Server installation process, you should see a message similar to the following (the version numbers will vary):

```
What is the location of the directory of C header files that match
your running kernel? [/lib/modules/2.6.18-8.1.8.el5/build/include]
```

9. Watch for mismatches in version numbers. The installation may not work if you use kernel code with a different version from the kernel currently running on your system.

10. As the installation proceeds, you should generally accept defaults for networking, a network bridge, and more. Some of the steps may appear to "hang" for a minute or two as the script configures useful subnets.

11. If everything goes well, the following message eventually appears:

```
The module loads perfectly in the running kernel.
```

12. While the default port for remote connections to a VMware Server is 902, it may already be in use. If so, the installation script suggests an alternative. If you're just using a VMware Server locally, the port number does not matter.

13. When the following message appears, it may help to set the directory for the virtual machine to a subdirectory of your home directory, or perhaps a VFAT partition if you want the virtual machine to be accessible from both Linux and Microsoft Windows:

```
In which directory do you want to keep your virtual machine files?
[/var/lib/vmware/Virtual Machines]
```

14. When you see a prompt for a serial number, enter the registration code described earlier in the "Acquiring VMware Server" section. Review the following message, which readies VMware for use:

```
Starting VMware services:
 Virtual machine monitor                          [ OK ]
 Virtual ethernet                                 [ OK ]
 Bridged networking on /dev/vmnet0                [ OK ]
 Host-only networking on /dev/vmnet1 (background) [ OK ]
 Host-only networking on /dev/vmnet8 (background) [ OK ]
 NAT service on /dev/vmnet8                        [ OK ]

The configuration of VMware Server 1.0.3 build-44356
for Linux for this running kernel completed successfully.
```

If you run into problems during the script, press CTRL-C. While this stops the script, it allows you to fix problems such as missing packages. Once fixed, you can restart the process again with the **vmware-config.pl** command.

Preparing VMware for Linux Installation

In this section, I assume you have downloaded and burned the installation CD/DVD for at least one of the selected distributions. As it is possible (and in my opinion, fairly easy for anyone considering taking the Linux+ exam) to burn downloaded installation CD/DVD files even on Microsoft systems, I shall not explain that process here. The following steps work on VMware Server installed on a Linux system. The steps and the look and feel of the VMware Server windows are significantly different when run on a Microsoft host. With that in mind, follow these steps to prepare VMware for Linux installation:

1. Start VMware in a GUI. In Linux, one standard method is to run the **vmware** command in a command-line console inside the GUI. When the Connect To Host window appears, click Connect to move to the main VMware Server Console window, shown next.

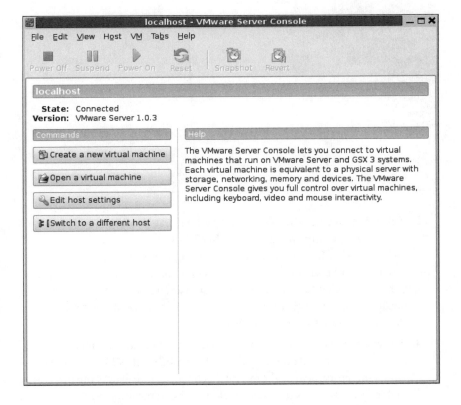

2. To prepare for Linux installation, click Create A New Virtual Machine. This starts the New Virtual Machine Wizard. Click Next, select the Custom configuration, and then click Next to see the operating system

options shown here. (The steps are different if a Typical configuration is selected.)

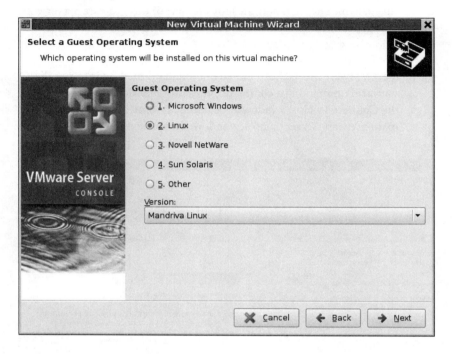

3. Select Linux. Click the Version drop-down text box arrow and review the variety of Linux distributions that VMware Server can handle. Select the distribution that you're planning to install. If the latest version is not available, the previous version should work. For example, when I installed Red Hat Enterprise Linux 5, that option was not available; selecting Red Hat Enterprise Linux 4 worked fine for me. Make your selection and click Next.

4. Select a name for your system, and a directory for the virtual machine files. I often override the defaults with a name such as Mandriva2007 and a directory such as /home/michael/VM/Mandriva. As the directory will contain the files for the virtual machine, typically several gigabytes large, make sure the directory is in a partition that can handle such files. After making needed changes, click Next.

5. For systems with multiple processors (or a multicore CPU), VMware prompts you to set the number of processors allocated to the virtual machine. Select a number and click Next.

6. As follows, VMware supports different access rights for the virtual machine. Unless you want to share it, just accept the default to make it private and click Next.

7. Set the RAM for the virtual machine; just make sure not to take away too much from the host system. Click Next to see the networking options.

8. Unless there is no networking on the host operating system, retain the default, Use Bridged Networking. The guest Linux system can then connect to the network (even through a Microsoft host) as a separate computer. Click Next to continue.

9. The step that follows illustrates VMware's support for IDE (PATA) and two different SCSI Adapters. Make a selection between SCSI Adapters and click Next.

10. Select Create A New Virtual Disk and click Next.

11. Read the Select A Disk Type window. Most users will want to select a SCSI Virtual Disk Type, which most closely simulates a Linux server. Click Next to see the Disk Size options shown here:

12. In my experience, a 4GB disk size is sufficient for a test system. Your experience may vary depending on the packages you want to install with the selected distribution. And it's best to select Allocate All Disk Space Now, especially if you're running VMware Server on Microsoft Windows. Fragmentation is a serious problem with VMware Server disk files, especially on compressed NTFS filesystems. Click Next when you've finished changing settings.

13. Assign a name to the disk file. If you've set it to be split into 2GB files, there will be multiple files with names such as Mandriva-f001.vdmk and Mandriva-f002.vdmk. Click Finish.

14. Assuming an installation from a CD/DVD, click Power On This Virtual Machine, and let it boot from that drive. Click inside the virtual machine window, and you should be able to proceed with a normal Linux installation.

VMware Snapshots

One of the main reasons I use VMware Server is the ease with which I can take "snapshots." In other words, when I've configured a Linux system on a VMware virtual machine to my satisfaction, I take a snapshot (which is available as a button command in the top menu bar). I then make changes to test the system to some new configuration. If I make a mistake, I can restore the system from the snapshot by clicking the Revert button.

Glossary

? A wildcard that represents one alphanumeric character.

. (dot) Represents the current directory.

.. (double dot) Represents the parent of the current directory.

/etc The directory with basic configuration files.

/etc/fstab The configuration file that lists partitions or volumes to be mounted during and after the boot process.

/etc/group The file that lists all groups; may include passwords.

/etc/hosts The configuration file that associates computer names and IP addresses.

/etc/hosts.allow The configuration file that lists TCP services, along with IP addresses and users allowed to access them. Read before /etc/hosts.deny.

/etc/hosts.deny The configuration file that lists TCP services, along with IP addresses and users *not* allowed to access them.

/etc/inittab The configuration file that specifies the default runlevel, virtual consoles, and more.

/etc/passwd The configuration file that lists all local users. If no user passwords exist in this file, see /etc/shadow.

/etc/printcap The configuration file for printers; used for sharing.

/etc/sudoers   The configuration file that grants administrative permissions to specific users.

/etc/syslog.conf   The configuration file that specifies the location of various log files.

/etc/XF86Config   The main configuration file for the X Window based on the XFree86 server.

/etc/xorg.conf   The main configuration file for the X Window based on the X.Org server.

<   A redirection arrow; the content from the term to the right of the arrow is redirected as standard input to the left of the arrow. Commonly used to input several terms or a list of data from a file to a program.

>>   A double redirection arrow; standard output from the term to the left of the arrow is redirected to the file to the right of the arrow, at the end of the file. If the file exists, the contents are *not* overwritten.

>   A redirection arrow; standard output from the term to the left of the arrow is redirected to the file to the right of the arrow. If the file exists, it is overwritten.

~ (tilde)   A symbol representing the home directory of the current user.

A+   The CompTIA exam on hardware and operating system technologies. The Linux+ hardware objectives are based in part on the A+ exam.

Advanced Configuration and Power Interface (ACPI)   The modern system for power management; configuration is specified in the /proc directory.

Advanced Power Management (APM)   The legacy system for power management; succeeded by ACPI.

AGP (Accelerated Graphics Port)   A specialized PCI port customized for data transfer to a graphics card; being superseded by PCI Express graphics cards.

algorithm   A set of instructions for solving a task; encryption methods are algorithms.

alias   A Linux command used to designate a word equivalent to a Linux command.

ALSA (Advanced Linux Sound Architecture) The driver system for sound cards; replaces the Open Sound System (OSS).

alsactl The command that controls the ALSA sound-card driver.

alsamixer The sound-card mixer for the ALSA driver.

Apache The Linux Web server; the associated daemon is **httpd** and the configuration file is httpd.conf or apache2.conf.

AppArmor Security software alternative to SELinux.

apropos A command that searches the whatis database of man pages.

ARP (Address Resolution Protocol) A protocol used with the command of the same name; associates a MAC address with an IP address.

ATAPI (ATA Packet Interface) A standard for hard drives and CD/DVD drives. *See also* PATA and IDE.

AutoYaST Tool developed for SUSE; supports automated Linux installation.

awk A database manipulation command; known by its developers as a programming language.

bash (Bourne Again Shell) The default Linux command-line user interface.

BIOS (Basic Input/Output System) The first program that runs when you start a computer. It initializes hardware and starts the boot process.

bunzip2 A command that uncompresses files associated with the .bz2 extension.

CardBus A PCMCIA card slot that supports 16- and 32-bit PC Cards.

cardctl A command that controls PC Cards; succeeded by **pccardctl**.

chage A command that controls password aging.

chgrp A command that controls group ownership.

chmod A command that changes file/directory permissions.

chown   A command that controls user ownership.

CIFS (Common Internet File System)   Microsoft's name for the updated Server Message Block (SMB) protocol; associated with Microsoft networking.

Classless Internet Domain Routing (CIDR)   A shorthand for subnet or network masks. For example, a network mask of 255.255.255.0 can be read as the number of bits associated with that mask, /24. A network mask of 255.255.0.0 is associated with a CIDR mask of /16. Other examples: 255.255.254.0 corresponds to /23, and 255.255.255.128 corresponds to /25.

clone   In computing, a program or command that is functionally identical to another, developed independently and based on different source code.

codec (compressor/decompressor)   A software routine that compresses and decompresses.

cpio   A command that copies files to and from archives.

Crack   A password decryption program.

cron   A Linux service that executes commands organized in a regular schedule.

CUPS (Common Unix Printing System)   The latest default Linux print service; successor to LPD.

database server   A system configured with database services and software.

dd   A command that copies the contents of a file, directory, or partition.

Debian   A Linux distribution run entirely by volunteers.

dhclient   A command-line client for DHCP.

DHCP (Dynamic Host Configuration Protocol)   A protocol that supports automated IP address settings for a client.

dhcpcd   A command-line client for DHCP.

diff   A command that compares files line by line, and notes the differences.

digiKam   Photo management software associated with KDE.

distribution An integrated collection of software packages, which can be installed as a complete operating system.

dmesg A command that reads the "kernel ring buffer," the messages associated with the Linux boot process.

DNS (Domain Name System) A system that translates domain names such as McGraw-Hill.com and hostnames such as Enterprise5 to IP addresses such as 205.142.52.242.

domain A group of computers administered as a single unit.

domain controller A system that stores the Microsoft-style user and server account information for its domain in a database, which can also be configured with Samba on Linux.

e2fsck A command that checks the integrity of ext2 and ext3 filesystems.

ELILO (Extended Firmware Interface LILO) The LILO boot manager designed for 64-bit Itanium systems. *See also* LILO.

Ethernet A standard LAN technology. Standard Ethernet has a maximum data transmission speed of 10 Mbps. Fast Ethernet has a maximum data transmission speed of 100 Mbps. Gigabit Ethernet has a maximum data transmission speed of 1000 Mbps.

Evolution An e-mail client, also known as a Mail User Agent (MUA).

ExpressCard A serial PC Card successor to CardBus PC Cards.

ext2 The Linux second extended filesystem; does not include a journal.

ext3 The Linux third extended filesystem; includes a journal.

extended partition A partition designed to contain multiple logical partitions; the way to configure more than four partitions on a hard drive. A primary partition can be reassigned as an extended partition.

FHS (Filesystem Hierarchy Standard) The standardized way to store files on different directories in Linux.

File server A system designated as a central repository for files on a LAN.

filesystem   A format associated with partitions; examples include ext2, ext3, and ntfs.

find   A command that can identify files in different directories, using filters such as UIDs.

firewall   A system that regulates traffic between networks such as a LAN and the Internet.

floppy disk   An older removable storage media.

floppy drive   A hardware slot that can accommodate removable floppy disks.

Free Software Foundation (FSF)   The group behind the GNU components of Linux. Because of their work, the people behind the FSF believe that Linux is more properly known as GNU/Linux.

fsck   A command associated with checking filesystems; a front-end to filesystem-specific commands such as **ext2**, **ext3**, and **vfat**.

FTP (File Transfer Protocol)   A protocol used to transfer files between two computers in a TCP/IP network.

fully qualified domain name (FQDN)   A name that uniquely identifies a computer; consists of a hostname and domain name. For example, if the hostname is linux and the domain name is mommabears.com, the FQDN is linux.mommabears.com.

gateway   The name given to a computer or device, such as a router, that transfers messages between networks.

gateway IP address   The IP address on a LAN that also connects to a router or computer with a forwardable connection to another network such as the Internet.

GID (group ID)   The number in /etc/group associated with a specific group such as users.

GNOME (GNU Object Model Environment)   Most commonly associated with the GNOME desktop environment.

GNOME Office   An office suite associated with the GNOME desktop environment.

GNU   GNU really does stand for "GNU's Not Unix." Recursive acronyms like GNU are sort of Linux's jab at the normal way of doing things. GNU is the name of the project that developed clones for most of the components of Unix except the kernel. GNU software is a major part of Linux.

GNU/Linux   The term used by FSF adherents to refer to the Linux operating system.

grep   A command that searches through a file based on a text term.

groupmod   A command that modifies characteristics associated with a group.

grpconv   A command that converts /etc/group to /etc/gshadow while configuring the Shadow Password Suite.

grpunconv   A command that restores information from /etc/gshadow to /etc/group while deactivating the Shadow Password Suite.

GRUB (GRand Unified Bootloader)   A bootloader common on current Linux distributions; successor to LILO.

gunzip   A command that uncompresses a zip archive, normally with a .zip extension.

HAL (hardware abstraction layer)   A part of the operating system that readily accesses hardware information.

hard link   Two files that are created with the ln command and point to the same location on a hard drive. If one file is deleted, access is still possible through the other file.

Hardware Compatibility List (HCL)   A list of hardware components that work seamlessly with one or more Linux distributions.

hdparm   A command that can collect and set hard drive parameters.

head   A command that by default lists the first ten lines of a text file.

hex (hexadecimal)   A numbering system based on 16 hexadecimal numbers, known as 0, 1, 2, 3, 4, 5, 6, 7, 8, 9, a, b, c, d, e, and f.

hostname   A name given to a computer; on a network, each computer should have a unique hostname. *See* fully qualified domain name (FQDN).

HTTP (Hypertext Transfer Protocol)   The standard TCP/IP protocol associated with the World Wide Web.

HTTPS (HTTP, Secure)   An encrypted form of HTTP; formerly used with Secure Sockets Layer (SSL), and now used with Transport Layer Security (TLS). *See also* HTTP.

I/O (input/output)   Input/output addresses. Dedicated locations in RAM for peripherals to store information while waiting for service from a CPU.

IDE (Integrated Drive Electronics)   A specification for hard drives and CD drives, now known as PATA drives. *See also* PATA.

IEEE (Institute of Electrical and Electronics Engineers)   Association of engineers that also sets standards such as IEEE 1394.

IEEE 1394   The IEEE standard that governs communication with video devices and some external hard drives. Also known by its trade names, FireWire and iLink.

ifconfig   A command that lists and customizes network card configuration.

ImageMagick   Software that composes and edits bitmap images.

IMAP (Internet Message Access Protocol)   A protocol for incoming e-mail; uses TCP/IP port 143. The current version is IMAP4.

init   A command that sets the current runlevel.

input device   A device that sends information from human input to a computer, such as a keyboard or mouse.

Internet Super Server   The xinetd service that regulates connections to multiple network services configured in /etc/xinetd.conf and files in the /etc/xinetd.d directory.

Intrusion Detection System (IDS)   Applications that detect unwanted connections; examples include Tripwire and Snort.

IP forwarding   A term associated with firewalls; the rules by which messages sent through a gateway or router are forwarded between cards connected to different networks.

IP masquerading   A term associated with IP addressing; the rules by which the IP address displayed to outside networks is different from that associated with the actual client.

IPP (Internet Printing Protocol)   A print protocol, using port 631, associated with CUPS.

iptables   A command associated with Linux firewalls.

IPv4 (IP version 4)   The standard method of IP addressing used since the development of TCP/IP in the 1970s. An IPv4 address has 32 bits.

IPv6 (IP version 6)   The method of IP addressing being incorporated into Linux today. An IPv6 address has 128 bits.

IRQ (interrupt request)   A request for CPU time from a component such as a keyboard or mouse. Older PCs were limited to 16 IRQ channels; current PCs have 256 IRQ channels.

ISA (Industry Standard Architecture)   An older standard for internal PC peripherals.

ISO 9660   The standard filesystem format for CD/DVD drives.

jfs   A 64-bit filesystem available for Linux that supports journaling. Short for Journaled File System.

Kaffeine   A media player for Linux, normally installed on the K Desktop Environment.

KDE (K Desktop Environment)   Also known as the KDE Desktop Environment. One alternative GUI for the Linux desktop.

kernel   The part of the operating system that translates commands between programs and hardware.

Kickstart   The Red Hat utility associated with automated Linux installations.

kill   A command that can stop running processes.

KOffice   The KDE-based office suite.

KVM (Kernel-based Virtual Machine)   An infrastructure and specialized kernel that supports virtual machines on Linux.

LILO (LInux LOader)   A bootloader common on older Linux distributions; has been supplanted by GRUB in most cases.

Linux Professional Institute (LPI)   The group behind the LPI exams, one option for more advanced exams after Linux+.

Linux+   The certification exam developed by the Computing Technology Industry Association (CompTIA) for the Linux operating system. It is intended to qualify Linux professionals with 6 to 12 months of experience.

ln   A command that creates a link from an existing file.

localhost   An alias for the loopback address of 127.0.0.1, referring to the current machine.

locate   A command that searches through a database of existing files.

log priorities   Log messages in Linux are organized in levels of severity; in order from lowest to highest, log priorities are **debug, info, notice, warn, err, crit, alert**, and **emerg**.

logical partition   A division of an extended partition; can be configured with files or swap space, just like any primary partition.

logical volume (LV)   A construct based on chunks of a physical volume.

logical volume management (LVM)   Supports a filesystem on part or all of multiple partitions.

loopback address   The 127.0.0.1 IP address reserved for the local system; can be used to verify proper installation of network software.

LPD (Line Printer Daemon)   One print server formerly popular for Linux and Unix systems; superseded by CUPS.

lpq   A command that checks current print jobs in the queue.

lprm   A command that removes current print jobs from the queue.

LPT port   The Microsoft designation for a parallel port; associated with device files like /dev/parport0.

lsof   A command that lists files open by processes such as server services.

LUN (Logical Unit Numbers)   A numbering system that specifies the priority associated with different SCSI devices.

lvcreate   A command that creates a new logical volume from the space of an existing volume group.

lvextend   A command that extends the space available to a logical volume.

lvreduce   A command that reduces the size of a logical volume.

MAC (Media Access Control) address   A hardware address assigned to a network card.

mail   A Linux command-line based e-mail manager.

Mail Transfer Agent (MTA)   Any e-mail server, such as sendmail or Postfix.

Mail User Agent (MUA)   Any e-mail client.

make   A command commonly used to compile source code.

Makefile   A file used to set rules for compiling source code.

makewhatis   A command that creates a database of man pages for the **whatis** command.

man   A command used to cite an available manual for specified commands or a configuration file.

Mandrake   One Linux distribution specified in the Linux+ objectives; supplanted by Mandriva.

Mandriva   A Linux distribution based on the merger of the Mandrake and Connectiva distributions.

master boot record (MBR)   The first area read on a hard drive; it locates boot information on appropriate partitions.

MD5 (Message Digest 5)   A cryptographic hash function with a 128-bit value, commonly used to check the integrity of files.

md5sum   A command that computes the MD5 message digest, commonly used for verifying the integrity of downloads. Similar to **sha1sum**.

mkfs   A command that formats a specified partition device.

mkswap   A command that formats a specified partition for swap space.

modem   Short for *mod*ulator-*de*modulator, named for the actions required to translate the 1s and 0s of computer communication to the sine waves of sound transmitted through regular telephones.

mount   A command that activates a filesystem by linking the partition or volume with a directory.

mount point   A directory from which the contents of a configured filesystem can be read.

MPlayer   A common GUI application for playing multimedia files.

mutt   A mail reader based on the command line.

MySQL   A database management system based on the Structured Query Language (SQL).

named   The name of the DNS service daemon based on the Berkeley Internet Name Domain (BIND) software.

netmask   *See* network mask.

netstat   A command that lists current open network ports and statistics.

Network Information Service (NIS)   A central database for users and passwords on a Unix/Linux network.

network mask   An IP address that helps define a range of IP addresses on a single LAN. Also known as a *subnet mask* or *netmask*.

NFS (Network File System)   The standard file sharing protocol for Linux/ Unix systems.

NTLDR   A Microsoft bootloader for Windows NT/2000/XP; succeeded by Vista's Bootmgr.

open source   The release technique that supports freely redistributable software and associated source code.

Open Source Initiative (OSI)   A group started by Eric Raymond to defend free software; the OSI has a license similar to the GPL.

OpenOffice.org   Perhaps the most popular open source office suite available today; even available for Microsoft Windows.

openSUSE   The community version of SUSE as released by Novell.

OSS (Open Sound System)   The legacy driver system for sound cards.

parallel port   A connection for peripherals, based on the DB-25 connector, most commonly used for a printer.

partition   A logical part of a hard drive.

PATA (Parallel Advanced Technology Attachment)   Formerly known as IDE or ATAPI, the older standard for internal connections to hard drives and CD/ DVD drives.

patch   A unit of code, or program, that can be added to a command, program, or application to repair or upgrade its capabilities.

PATH   A Linux variable that specifies directories where Linux automatically looks for a command.

PC Card   Credit card–sized peripherals for various slots associated with laptop systems. Developed by the PCMCIA. Available in 16-bit (yenta_socket), 32-bit (cardbus), and ExpressCard formats.

pccardctl   A command that controls PC Cards; successor to **cardctl**.

PCI (Peripheral Component Interconnect)   A standard for the most common internal PC peripherals. Inclusive of similar formats such as PCI Express and mini-PCI.

PCMCIA (Personal Computer Memory Card International Association)   The group of manufacturers behind the PC Card standards.

physical volume (PV)   A partition designated for use in logical volumes.

PID (Process Identifier)   A number associated with each running process on a Linux system.

ping   A command that checks a network connection.

pipe   A Linux command construct that uses the | character, where the standard output from one command is directed as standard input to a second command.

Pluggable Authentication Modules (PAM)   A scheme that integrates different authentication schemes.

POP (Post Office Protocol)   A protocol for receiving e-mail; common option for Internet service providers. The current version is POP3.

PortSentry   One option for Intrusion Detection Systems (IDS).

Postfix   A server for outgoing e-mail; one option to sendmail.

PostgreSQL   A database management system based on the Structured Query Language (SQL). Alternative to MySQL.

Power-On Self-Test (POST)   A series of hardware tests performed by a computer when powered on.

PPP (Point-to-Point Protocol)   A protocol that supports connections primarily through telephone modems. Also used in high-speed DSL connections. *See* PPPoE.

PPPoE (PPP over Ethernet)   A protocol that supports PPP connections on a higher-speed DSL network, using Ethernet networking.

Preboot eXecution Environment (PXE)   The method for booting with a network card; commonly used for automated installations and diskless workstations.

primary partition   A partition that can include a master boot record (MBR). Each hard disk can be configured with up to four primary partitions.

proxy server   A service that caches Internet data for local access. The standard Linux proxy server is known as Squid, which can also track where clients navigate through their browsers.

ps   A command that lists active processes; for example, **ps aux** lists all active processes by all users.

pstree   A command that lists all active processes in tree format, enabling tracking of processes that start others.

pump   A DHCP command-line client; alternative to **dhcpcd** and **dhclient**.

pvcreate   A command that creates a physical volume.

pvremove   A command that removes a configured physical volume from availability for logical volume management (LVM).

pwconv   A command that converts passwords to the Shadow Password Suite; moves passwords from /etc/passwd to the more secure /etc/shadow.

pwunconv   Opposite of **pwconv**.

quota   A method to regulate users and/or groups by number of inodes (files) or disk space. Also a command that lists current quota status.

RADIUS modem server   A server that receives connections and login requests via telephone modem.

RAID (Redundant Array of Independent Disks)   A storage method for increasing speed or providing redundancy using multiple disks or partitions. Also known as Redundant Array of Inexpensive Disks.

RAID 0   An array that uses two or more partitions or hard drives. Reads and writes are performed in parallel. Does not include redundancy; if any partition or drive in the array is damaged, all data in the array is lost. Also known as a striped set.

RAID 1   An array that uses two or more partitions or hard drives. Also known as disk mirroring, as the same data is written to both drives.

RAID 10   A combination of RAID 1 and RAID 0; two RAID 0 arrays are mirrored. In contrast, RAID 01 would be a striped set of two disk mirrors.

RAID 4   An array that requires three or more partitions or disks; parity information is saved on one disk. If either of the other disks is damaged, data can be rebuilt from the parity information.

RAID 5   An array that requires three or more partitions or disks; parity information is spread out on all three disks. If any one of the disks is damaged, data can be rebuilt from the parity information on the surviving disks.

RAID 6   An array that requires four or more partitions or disks; two sets of parity information are spread out on all four disks. If one or two of the disks are damaged, data can be rebuilt from the surviving parity information.

RAWWRITE.exe   An MS-DOS command that can be used to create a Linux boot disk.

Red Hat   Currently the company with the largest share of the enterprise Linux market. One of the selected distributions for the Linux+ exam.

Red Hat Certified Engineer (RHCE)   Perhaps the elite certification available for Linux system administrators. Also the subject of a book by this author (*RHCE Red Hat Certified Engineer Study Guide*, published by McGraw-Hill).

Red Hat Certified Technician (RHCT)   Another elite certification for moderately experienced Linux administrators. Often considered a stepping stone to the RHCE. As the RHCT exam is a complete subset of the RHCE exam, candidates can also use the *RHCE Red Hat Certified Engineer Study Guide* to prepare for the RHCT exam.

reiserfs   A filesystem alternative to ext2 and ext3; includes journaling.

remote logging   Configures log messages sent to other systems; requires directives such as **@log.server** in the system logging configuration file, syslog.conf or syslog-ng.conf.

rlogin   A command that supports remote logins.

root   There are five definitions for root. 1. The root user is the default Linux administrative user. 2. The top-level root directory, signified by the forward slash (/), is the highest-level directory on a Linux system. 3. The /root directory, which is the home directory of the root user, is a subdirectory of the top-level root directory (/). 4. The **root** directive in a GRUB configuration file, when coupled with a hard disk partition location such as (hd0,1) specifies the partition with the /boot directory. 5. The **root** directive in a GRUB configuration file, when coupled with a partition or logical volume device, specifies the mount point for the top-level root directory.

route   A command that lists current routing information; it can also be used to add a route. For example, **route add net 10.11.12.0 netmask 255.255.255.0 gw 192.168.0.1** adds a route to the 10.11.12.0/255.255.255.0 network via the gateway system at 192.168.0.1.

RPC (Remote Procedure Call)   A system that supports access to other programs; frequently used by NIS and NFS.

RPM (Red Hat Package Manager)   A system for package management, first developed by Red Hat and used by many Linux distributions, including all of those associated with the Linux+ exam.

rsh   A command that supports remote logins. Similar to **ssh**.

rsync   A command that synchronizes data on different directories; can be used to synchronize and back up systems to remote servers.

runlevel   A construct where a group of services are started and stopped. There are seven standard Linux runlevels, 0, 1, 2, 3, 4, 5, and 6.

Samba   A server service for connections to Microsoft-based networks.

SANE (Scanner Access Now Easy)   Provides a standard interface between Linux and scanners.

sar   A command associated with system activity information.

SATA (Serial ATA)   Successor to PATA; used for connections to hard drives and CD/DVD drives. SATA drives appear like SCSI device files, such as /dev/sda.

SCSI (Small Computer System Interface)   A type of connector for disk drives and other peripherals.

SCSI number   The designator given to a SCSI device. Depending on whether it's attached to an 8-bit or 16-bit SCSI bus, there are 8 or 16 SCSI numbers available. They have a priority depending on the number: 7, 6, 5, 4, 3, 2, 1, 0, 15, 14, 13, 12, 11, 10, 9, 8. Also known as a Logical Unit Number (LUN).

SD (Secure Digital)   A newer format for media cards.

Security-Enhanced Linux (SELinux)   A system for security policies based on mandatory access controls. Developed by the U.S. National Security Agency.

sed   A command, short for "stream editor," that transforms text, normally within a file.

sendmail   A server for outgoing e-mail; provides an alternative to Postfix. (sendmail is all lowercase; there is a commercial version known as Sendmail.)

serial device   Any hardware device that uses a serial port, such as /dev/ttyS0 or /dev/ttyS1 (known in the Microsoft world as COM1 or COM2).

service   In Linux, a server such as Apache, DNS, DHCP, or sendmail. Service scripts are typically located in the /etc/init.d/ directory.

sftp   A command that connects to remote FTP services securely, using encryption.

SGID (Super Group ID)   A specialized permission, allowing all users the same executable permission as the group owner of the file or directory.

SHA1   A Secure Hash Algorithm, used as a cryptographic hash function. Used for SSL and TLS connections.

sha1sum   A command that computes the SHA1 message digest, commonly used for verifying the integrity of downloads. Similar to **md5sum**.

Shadow Password Suite   The set of files and commands associated with encrypted passwords in Linux, including **pwconv**, **pwunconv**, **grpconv**, **grpunconv**, /etc/shadow, and /etc/gshadow.

shadow passwords   Encrypted passwords, stored in /etc/shadow and /etc/gshadow; more secure because access to these files is limited to the root user.

shell script   A group of shell commands collected into an executable file. The first line in a shell script is a "shebang" (#!), followed by the selected shell, such as /bin/sh.

showmount   A command that lists available directories shared from an NFS server.

shutdown A command that shuts down or reboots Linux.

single-user mode A runlevel at which only the root user can run programs in Linux. Commonly associated with runlevel 1; can be started with the **init 1** or **telinit 1** command.

SMB (Server Message Block) The protocol associated with file sharing on Microsoft networks; Linux can use Samba to connect to such networks. *See also* CIFS.

smbclient A command that connects to remote servers on a Microsoft network.

smbpasswd A command that can set user passwords on a Microsoft network.

smbtree A command that browses available shares on a Microsoft network.

smbusers A file on Samba Linux servers that serves as a database of Linux and Microsoft usernames.

SMTP (Simple Mail Transfer Protocol) The protocol associated with outgoing e-mail.

Snort An Intrusion Detection System.

soft link A link between files; a soft-linked file does not include a copy of the original file.

source code The directives and instructions behind commands and applications, in an uncompiled programming language.

SQL (Structured Query Language) A computer language for database management.

Squid A service used for caching Web data locally, speeding access to common sites from within a network. Can also be used to log the sites that clients visit on outside networks such as the Internet.

SSH (Secure Shell) The service associated with secure remote logins.

ssh The command that connects to an SSH server.

ssh_keygen   The command that generates a public/private key pair; public keys from clients should be stored in appropriate authorized_keys or authorized_keys2 files.

SSL (Secure Sockets Layer)   Protocol for secure Web communications; succeeded by TLS.

sticky bit   A permission that allows files in a directory to be controlled only by their owner (or root).

su   A command that opens another account; if an account is not specified, the root account is assumed.

subnet mask   *See* network mask.

sudo   A command associated with asserting root privileges based on the configuration defined in /etc/sudoers.

SUID   The Set User ID bit; grants other users the same executable permissions as the owner of the file.

SUSE   One of the selected distributions for the Linux+ exam; now owned by Novell.

swap partition   A volume on the hard disk that is set up for overflow from RAM. The standard size is twice the size of RAM.

sync   A command that makes sure any data in cache is actually written to disk.

syslog   The service that logs data from various services, based on /etc/syslog.conf.

tail   A command that reads the last lines of a file; ten lines is the default.

tar   A command that archives and unarchives a group of files; can accommodate compression.

tarball   Colloquial term used to refer to an archive created with the **tar** command.

TCP Wrappers   A system where network services that communicate with TCP are regulated in /etc/hosts.allow and /etc/hosts.deny.

tcpdump   A command that reads all traffic on a network; normally interpreted by tools such as Ethereal and Wireshark.

TCP/IP (Transmission Control Protocol/Internet Protocol)   A suite of protocols for networking that is most commonly associated with the Internet.

Telnet   The clear-text remote access service.

terminator   A device that is installed at the end of a chain of SCSI devices.

testparm   A command that checks the syntax of a Samba configuration file.

The GIMP   Common name for The GNU Image Manipulation Program.

Thunderbird   A Mail User Agent (MUA), functionally similar to mail, mutt, Evolution, and Outlook.

TLS (Transport Layer Security)   The protocol that encrypts communication to modern websites; successor to SSL.

top   A command that displays currently running tasks; can be used to determine which process is taking up the most CPU and RAM.

Totem   An application primarily used for viewing video files.

traceroute   A command that requests messages from every router on a path between source and destination. Useful for diagnosing network problems.

Tripwire   An Intrusion Detection System.

tune2fs   A command used to add journaling to an ext2 formatted filesystem; can also be used to change the mount count for periodic filesystem checks.

Turbolinux   One of the selected distributions for the Linux+ exam.

Ubuntu   A popular Linux distribution that uses a Debian-based packaging system, and is therefore not well suited for studying for the Linux+ exam.

UID (user ID)   The number associated with each user account.

umask   A command that sets up default permissions.

umount   A command that unmounts a previously mounted partition.

Unix   The operating system developed in the late 1960s and early 1970s by and for programmers at Bell Labs, and the functional ancestor to Linux.

USB (universal serial bus)   A standard type of peripheral connection.

useradd   A command that automates the creation of Linux users.

userdel   A command that deletes local Linux user accounts; it does not delete that user's home directory without the -r switch.

usermod   A command that modifies user account settings such as group membership and password life.

utmpdump   A command that lists logins from /var/log/wtmp in readable format.

vfat   The Linux designation for current Microsoft FAT16 and FAT32 formatted filesystems.

vgcreate   A command that creates a volume group from two or more available physical volumes.

vgextend   A command that extends an existing volume group with a newly available physical volume.

vgreduce   A command that removes a physical volume from an existing volume group.

vi   The basic Linux text editor.

video card   An expansion card that works with the CPU to produce the images that are displayed on your computer's display.

virtual console   A command line where you can log into and control Linux. As Linux is a multiterminal operating system, you can log into Linux, even with the same user ID, several times.

virtual hosts   An Apache concept that supports multiple websites on a single Web server.

virtual machine   A software implementation of a computer. In this book, virtual machine commonly refers to a hardware virtual machine, in which software components emulate every physical part of a computer, from the CPU to RAM to USB ports.

virtual terminal Every terminal or console where a user can log into Linux, whether it be local or remote.

vmstat A command that reports virtual memory statistics.

VMware A third-party virtual machine company commonly used on, and to test, Linux systems.

volume A partition or logical volume (LV), designated for mounting as a filesystem.

volume group (VG) A construct based on a configured portion of one or more logical volumes (LVs).

w A command that shows logged-in users.

whereis A command that locates the full path to a command and its manual (man) page.

who A command that shows currently logged-in users.

wildcard A character such as * or ? used to represent other characters. The * represents zero or more alphanumeric characters; each individual ? represents a single alphanumeric character.

winmodem A telephone modem that uses Microsoft Windows driver libraries to control some hardware modem functions.

X Window The Linux graphical user interface. Desktops such as KDE and GNOME exist atop the X Window System.

X.Org The organization that distributes the X Window software common on today's Linux distributions; successor to XFree86.

Xen The virtual machine software native to Linux; requires a specialized kernel.

xf86config A text-based GUI configuration tool.

XFree86 The organization that distributed the X Window software common on Linux distributions when the current Linux+ objectives were released.

xfs Two definitions: an abbreviation for the X Font Server, and the xfs filesystem.

ypbind   The service daemon for NIS clients.

ypserv   The service daemon for the NIS server.

Zeroconf   Short for Zero Configuration Networking; known in the Microsoft world as Automatic Private IP Addressing (APIPA). It's associated with the 169.254.0.0/255.255.255.0 Class B network.

Index